Modern Theatre

Realism and Naturalism to the Present

Oscar G. Brockett

University of Texas at Austin

ALLYN AND BACON, INC.
Boston London Sydney Toronto

Portions of this book first appeared in *History of the Theatre, Fourth Edition*, by Oscar G. Brockett, copyright ©
1982, 1977, 1974, 1968 by Allyn and Bacon, Inc.

Library of Congress Cataloging in Publication Data

Brockett, Oscar Gross, (date)
  Modern theatre

  Bibliography: p.
  Includes index.
  1. Theater—History—20th Century. 2. Theater—
History—19th century. I. Title.
PN2189.B65   809.2'912   82-1781
ISBN 0-205-07760-9   AACR2

  Managing Editor: Robert M. Roen
  Designer: Valerie Fraser Ruud

Printed in the United States of America.

10 9 8 7 6 5 4 3 2 1   86 85 84 83 82

Contents

Preface

In this book I have attempted to trace the development of the European and American theatre from the 1870s, when the modern theatre is usually said to have begun, through 1980, when my manuscript was completed. The four chapters that make up this book are the final four chapters of my *History of the Theatre, Fourth Edition*, 1982. These chapters on the modern era are being published as a separate volume to meet the needs of students and teachers who wish to devote their study entirely to trends and practices during the past century. This is typically the period of greatest interest to those working in or studying the theatre of today. To these chapters I have added an Introduction, in which I seek to provide such background as may be needed by the reader. Those who feel the need for a fuller introduction should turn to the more comprehensive, parent work, which traces the history of the theatre from its beginnings to the present.

The theatre is an extremely complex institution, since it encompasses playwriting, directing, acting, costume, makeup, scenery, lighting, properties, the-atre architecture, machinery, special effects, management, audiences, and criticism. In this book I have touched on all of these areas, although the emphasis I give to each varies. My objective is to provide a chronological narrative of the theatre's development rather than an exhaustive treatment of any one aspect. Furthermore, since the theatre cannot be divorced from the many forces that have shaped it, I have tried to suggest why it took the particular paths it did.

Although the study of history aims at recapturing the past, historical study is seldom purely factual. The evidence, whether slight or copious, always needs interpretation. Thus, I encourage readers to consult various accounts before accepting any as definitive.

A book of this type obviously depends heavily on the work of many scholars. I have included bibliographies, arranged according to chapter, as both an indication of the principal sources I have used and a guide to further reading. Since the theatre can at times be best understood through a study of visual materials, I have also supplied many illustrations in each chapter, both to clarify the text and to give a flavor of the time periods. As a further aid to understanding, I urge the readers of this book to study as many playscripts as possible.

I acknowledge the assistance of many persons in the preparation of this book. In addition to the published works of established scholars, I am also indebted to countless students in classes and seminars who have contributed to my knowledge. My indebtedness to individuals, publishers, libraries, and col-lections for permission to reprint materials is acknowledged in the credits that accompany illustrations and source materials.

I would also like to acknowledge the assistance of Richard Mennen, Robert Findlay, Ben Mordecai, and Russell Vandenbroucke. I owe a special debt of gratitude to Mark Pape for valuable help and advice on various problems. For their editorial assistance, I wish to acknowledge my indebtedness to Robert Roen, Valerie Ruud, and Paula Carroll of Allyn and Bacon, Inc.

Introduction

What we now call the "modern" theatre had its beginnings a little more than 100 years ago in two movements, Realism and Naturalism. These movements were outgrowths of socioeconomic, political, and artistic forces that had been accelerating since 1800. Among these forces, two of the most important were industrialization and urbanization, both products of the industrial revolution. Industrialization was made possible by such inventions as the steam engine, power loom, steamship, and locomotive, for they supplied the means needed to mass produce goods and to transport raw materials and finished products efficiently. As the potentials of these new means were exploited, factories were built and individual craftspeople soon found it impossible to compete with the low-cost industrial products. Driven out of business, they had to go to work in the factories and, since there were no public transportation systems, they had to live near their work. Thus, the trend toward urbanization began. With urbanization came slums and wretched living conditions that cried out for social legislation. Unfortunately, the governments of European countries lived in the fear that revolutions like the one that took place in France in the 1790s would recur, and they viewed any demand for reform as a threat. Consequently they did little to better living conditions, and the desperation of workers found outlet in a series of rebellions between 1830 and 1850. By the mid-nineteenth century it had become evident that Europe had to deal with its socioeconomic problems.

Among the proposals for handling the situation, the one that seemed most appealing was the application of scientific method to social problems. This suggestion was set forth persuasively by Auguste Comte (1798–1857) in his *Positive Philosophy* (1830–42) and *Positive Polity* (1851–54). Comte championed a new "science of society" (i.e., sociology) that would analyze social problems scientifically to discover their causes and provide means for controlling their effects. Interest in the work of Comte and others gradually led many to believe that all major problems could be solved through the scientific approach and that an era of truth, justice, and prosperity could be created. Out of this faith in science there emerged in the 1850s a movement called Realism.

The advocates of Realism, which first became evident in France, agreed on a few major tenets: art must depict the real, physical world truthfully; truth can be attained only through direct observation; only contemporary life and manners can be observed directly; and the observer must strive to be impersonal and objective. It was also in France that playwrights first sought to put these new ideas into practice. The most important of these dramatists were Alexandre Dumas *fils* (1824–95) and Emile Augier (1820–1889), who wrote numerous plays about contemporary social problems (e.g., the rights of illegitimate children; the power of the press and clergy; conflicts among the aristocracy, newly rich merchants, and manufacturers; divorce; kept women). They set their plays in familiar surroundings and made characters dress and talk like their real-life counterparts. Although these plays created a great deal of discussion, they offended few theatregoers because they upheld the sanctity of marriage and the home and of traditional morality in general. Furthermore, the plays were entertaining because they used the techniques of the "well-made" play that had been popularized by Eugene Scribe (1791–1861): careful exposition and preparation, cause-to-effect arrangement of incidents, scenes built to a climax, withheld information, startling reversals, suspense, and clear-cut resolutions.

In England, a similar type of drama was written between 1865 and 1870 by Thomas William Robertson (1829–71), whose stories of contemporary life were set in highly particularized locales, every detail of which was meticulously described in the script. Many important points were made primarily through pantomime and stage business, which recreated such everyday domestic events as making, serving, and drinking tea. These plays were given carefully mounted productions in the theatre run by Marie Bancroft (1839–1921) and Squire Bancroft (1841–

1926). The Robertson-Bancroft collaboration helped to create a taste for Realism in England.

Realism was not to triumph in dramatic writing, however, until Henrik Ibsen began to write his prose plays in the late 1870s. Rather, through most of the nineteenth century the impact of trends toward realism movement was felt primarily through the visual aspects of performance. In certain respects, realism had been evident since the Renaissance, when the picture-frame stage was invented; thereafter settings most typically sought to depict place convincingly, although until the late eighteenth century sets were generalized—that is, they represented a type of place (a garden, a prison, a palace)—and were used over and over again in numerous productions. Settings were composed of two-dimensional painted wings and drops. In addition, only those pieces of furniture or props demanded by the action were brought on stage. In other words, although a set might be painted to look like a room, it was not outfitted with the furniture and accessories that would be found in a real room.

In the late eighteenth century, interest in depicting specific times and places in settings and costumes began to appear, and it accelerated as the nineteenth century progressed. Increasingly, plays from the past were staged with sets and costumes that depicted precisely the architecture and dress of the period in which the action was set. In the 1850s, Charles Kean (1811–68), provided his audiences at the Princess' Theatre in London with lists of the sources he had consulted to make sure that all the details of a production were accurate. In Germany, Friedrich Haase (1827–1911) showed a similar devotion to antiquarianism. This ideal was also much in evidence at the Burgtheater in Vienna, perhaps the major German-language theatre of the nineteenth century.

Other producers sought to bring this same care for detail to plays about contemporary domestic subjects. In the 1830s, Mme Vestris (1797–1856) introduced into England the box set, with its three solid walls and ceiling, and she outfitted it with all the furniture, rugs, and bric-a-brac that would have been found in similar rooms in real life. In the 1860s, the Bancrofts adopted a similar method for staging Robertson's plays. Thereafter the box set, complete with furniture and accessories, became standard in most theatres.

During the nineteenth century the use of such three-dimensional elements as steps, platforms, and columns also increased. These pieces could not be shifted easily or quickly, for since the Renaissance the stage had been designed to use wing-and-drop settings and the floor had been raked upward toward the rear to enhance the perspective painting which most settings made use of. However, as use of three-dimensional elements increased, the traditional stage began to seem inflexible. In 1869, Edwin Booth (1833–93), one of the greatest actors of the nineteenth century, did away altogether with grooves and the raked stage in the theatre he had built for his company in New York. In 1881, when Henry Irving (1838–1905), one of England's greatest actor-managers, remodeled his Lyceum Theatre, he removed the grooves and flattened the floor. Thereafter, the trend everywhere was toward the flat, ungrooved floor on which scenery could be placed wherever one desired.

This new stage architecture created new problems in the efficient shifting of heavy, three-dimensional pieces and box settings. Irving employed a veritable army of stagehands to change his sets, and in many theatres the waits between scenes became very long as sets were being changed. New technology to assist in scene-shifting was sought. Booth's theatre of 1869 was equipped with several small hydraulically operated elevator traps that permitted heavy pieces of scenery or furniture to be raised or lowered through the stage floor. In 1879, Steele Mackaye (1842–94), one of the United States' most prolific inventors and playwrights, installed two elevator stages, one above the other, in his Madison Square Theatre in New York. These elevators permitted complete set changes in forty seconds. After 1890

experimentation with stage architecture would accelerate.

As theatrical productions became more complex during the nineteenth century, the need grew for centralized control over all aspects of production. Such control was slow to develop, however, for theatrical personnel traditionally enjoyed considerable independence. Examples of centralized control, though scattered and sporadic, can be found from 1800 onward. Johann Wolfgang von Goethe (1749–1832), working at Weimar between 1798 and 1815, was able to achieve almost total control over productions and created a unified style known as Weimar Classicism. Ludwig Tieck (1773–1853), working in Berlin in the 1840s, staged a few productions over which he had absolute authority. He also managed to counteract the trend toward Realism by recreating a version of the Shakespearean stage. Victorien Sardou (1831–1908), one of France's most popular and prolific playwrights, and Adolphe Montigny (1805–80) are often credited with establishing the art of directing in France. In England, the Bancrofts gave Robertson full authority in the staging of his own plays, and Irving controlled every element of his productions at the Lyceum Theatre between 1871 and 1902. Similarly, in the United States Augustin Daly (1836–99) was the undisputed master in his theatres.

By the late nineteenth century, then, several persons had demonstrated the superior results that could be achieved through centralized authority. However, certain practices of the time prevented full realization of the possibilities. Among these inhibitors, perhaps the most important was the star system, under which major actors, because of their popularity and box office appeal, thought it their right to avoid ensemble effects that would make them blend into the company as a whole. Furthermore, stars altered their costumes as they saw fit to make them more attractive. Another tradition that worked against unity was the almost universal practice of recruiting supernumeraries off the streets. Usually a different group appeared each night. This impromptu handling of crowd scenes clashed harshly with the polish of the stars' major scenes. In addition, each act of a play often was designed by a different designer and costumes often came from a variety of sources, interfering still further with stage unity.

Equally important, realistic staging was applied most often to scripts that were not realistic themselves. The plays of Shakespeare and other writers of poetic drama were often burdened by an overabundance of visual detail, and the action was often interrupted and obscured by the waits required for scene changes. Nor could the melodramas, the most char-acteristic plays of the nineteenth century, be made realistic by the addition of visual detail. Although such pictorial realism added picturesque touches to the plays, such touches were not essential to the dramatic action.

By the 1870s, the need for change was evident, and it was soon to come. The theories of Wagner and the Naturalists, the directorial practices of Saxe-Meiningen and Antoine, and the plays of Ibsen, Zola, and others were to coalesce in the years between 1875 and 1900 to create what we now call the modern theatre.

The Beginnings of the Modern Theatre, 1875–1915

For the most part, the theatre during the late nineteenth century was merely a logical outgrowth of what had gone before. But after 1875 several writers and directors made a marked break with the past and initiated the "modern" theatre. Nevertheless, in the beginning the changes were essentially intensifications of trends already underway. Richard Wagner supplied a theoretical foundation for a "master art work" created by a single artistic consciousness, and Saxe-Meiningen demonstrated the value of the all-powerful director who can weld all the elements of production into a unified whole. In playwriting, Ibsen was the first to realize fully the goals set forth by the realists and to make the public aware that a new era in the theatre had begun.

Wagner and Saxe-Meiningen

Richard Wagner (1813–1883) was brought up in a theatrical family (his stepfather and four of his brothers and sisters were employed in the theatre). His first opera, *Die Feen*, was written in 1831,

but he did not achieve critical success until 1842 with *Rienzi*, which also brought him an appointment as conductor at the Dresden opera house. Banished for his part in the revolution of 1848, he spent twelve years in exile, during which he formulated those theories that were to influence the course of the modern theatre.

Wagner rejected the contemporary trend toward realism, arguing that the dramatist should be a myth-maker rather than a recorder of domestic affairs. To him, true drama was concerned with the ideal world, which is left behind as soon as spoken dialogue is admitted. He suggested that drama should be "dipped in the magic fountain of music" to combine the greatness of Shakespeare and Beethoven. He also argued that music, through melody and tempo, permits greater control over performance than is possible in spoken drama, in which interpretation is subject to the performers' personal whims. Thus, for Wagner the effectiveness of music-drama depended upon performance as well as upon composition, and he argued that the author-composer should supervise every aspect of production in order to synthesize all the parts into a *Gesamtkunstwerk*, or "master art work." From these ideas were to stem much of modern theory about the need for a strong director and unified production.

In addition to his theories, Wagner's practice also exerted considerable influence, especially on theatre architecture. To house his idealized music-drama, Wagner created a new kind of theatre. The structure that he eventually built is said to have been suggested as early as 1841 by Schinkel. The first concrete plans were made in 1864 by Gottfried Semper, who had worked with Tieck on his reconstruction of the Fortune theatre, and were later reworked by several persons, including the architects Wilhelm Neumann and Otto Brückwald and the machinist Karl Brandt. Originally planned for Munich, the opera house was built in Bayreuth.

Begun in 1872 and opened in 1876, the new opera house was soon famous throughout the world and was to inspire many reforms in architectural design. Since Wagner wished to create a "classless" theatre, he abandoned the box, pit, and gallery arrangement. The main part of the auditorium had thirty stepped rows of seats; there were no side boxes or center aisle, and each row led directly to a side exit. At the rear of the auditorium was a single large box surmounted by a small gallery. The total seating capacity was 1,745. To insure good sight lines, the auditorium was shaped like a fan, measuring about 50 feet across at the proscenium and 115 feet at the rear of the auditorium. Since all seats were said to be equally good, a uniform price was charged. The orchestra pit was hidden from view, much of it extending underneath the apron of the stage. This feature helped to create a "mystic chasm" between the real world of the auditorium and the "ideal" world of the stage, an effect reenforced by darkening the auditorium during performances and by framing the stage with a double proscenium arch.

The arrangement of the auditorium was the theatre's greatest innovation, since the stage was essentially conservative in design. The stage floor was raked upward toward the back, and the chariot-and-

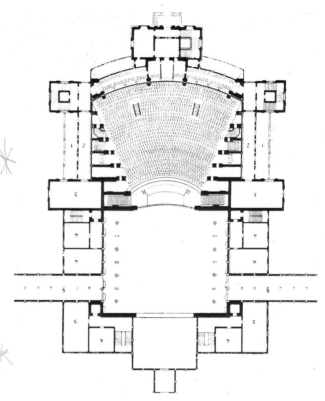

Figure 1.1   Plan of Wagner's theatre at Bayreuth. From Sachs, *Modern Opera Houses and Theatres* (1896–1898).

pole system of scene shifting was retained. The principal innovation was a system of steam vents to create realistic effects of fog and mist and a "steam curtain" to mask scene changes. The proscenium opening, about 40 feet wide, gave onto a stage 80 feet deep by 93 feet wide. About 100 feet of overhead space and 32 feet of below-stage space were provided. The building also included ample workshops, storage, dressing rooms, and rehearsal space.

Although Wagner's theories later inspired several nonillusionistic approaches, his own productions aimed at complete illusion. He forbade the musicians to tune their instruments in the orchestra pit and allowed no applause during performances or curtain calls at the end. He sought precise historical accuracy in scenery and costumes and employed such devices as moving panoramas. His taste for minute detail may be seen in *Siegfried*, for example, in which he used a dragon with realistic scales and movable eyes and mouth. To Wagner, the ideal was to be reached through total illusion. Thus, Wagner's theatrical practice was grounded solidly in the nineteenth-century tradition. Nevertheless, his conceptions of the master artwork, the director, the unified production, and theatre architecture were to inspire many pioneers of the "modern" theatre.

While Wagner's opera house was being constructed, another potent force, the Meiningen Players, came to the fore. Although plays had been performed in the Duchy of Meiningen since the late eighteenth century, a permanent court theatre was not opened until 1831, and the productions there remained commonplace until Georg II (1826–1914) succeeded to the throne in 1866. Georg II, Duke of Saxe-Meiningen, had received extensive art training, had been at the Prussian court in Berlin when Tieck worked there, and had seen Charles Kean's Shakespearean productions in London, Friedrick Haase's in Coburg-Gotha, and the superior ensemble of the Burgtheater. Thus, his intense interest in the theatre was well developed before a Prussian invasion of Meiningen forced his father to abdicate in his favor.

Upon succeeding to the throne in 1866, Georg II immediately began to change the repertory of the court theatre and to take a personal interest in its affairs. In managing the troupe, the duke at first depended heavily on Friedrich von Bodenstedt (1819–1892), and after 1871 on Ludwig Chronegk (1837–1891). Trained as a singing comedian, Chronegk had been employed at Meiningen in 1866 as a comic actor. His appointment as director came as a surprise to the company, for there seemed little in his background to justify it. Nevertheless, the fame of the troupe probably owes as much to Chronegk as to Saxe-Meiningen, since not only was he an indefatigable worker, but he also conceived and arranged

the tours which made the company famous. A third major influence was Ellen Franz (1839–1923), an actress who in 1873 became the duke's third wife. After this time she assumed responsibility for proposing the repertory, adapting the texts, and supervising stage speech. Thus, it is difficult to assign credit for the company's accomplishments, although it is now typical to allot sole responsibility to the duke.

From 1866 until 1874 the company played entirely in Meiningen, and when it appeared in Berlin in 1874 it took the astonished spectators completely by surprise. After its initial success, the company began a long series of tours. Between 1874 and 1890, it played in thirty-eight cities in nine countries, including Russia, Sweden, Austria, Denmark, Belgium, Holland, and England, giving about 2,600 performances of forty-one plays. By 1890, when it gave up touring,

Figure 1.2   The auditorium and stage of the Bayreuth Festival Theatre. On stage can be seen a setting for *Parsifal* designed by Max Brückner. From *Le Théâtre* (1899).

Figure 1.3   Anthony's oration over the body of Caesar in Saxe-Meiningen's production of *Julius Caesar* as performed at Drury Lane, London, 1881. From *The Illustrated London News* (1881). Courtesy Theatre Museum, Victoria and Albert Museum.

the Meiningen commanded the greatest respect of any company in the world.

The accomplishments of the Meiningen Players were due to its methods rather than to its aims. The duke, like most producers of his day, sought to create the illusion of reality with accurate spectacle and life-like acting. His repertory, composed primarily of works by Shakespeare, Schiller, Grillparzer, and nineteenth-century romantic playwrights, was not unlike that of other producers except in its inclusion of more plays of high merit. Although Ibsen's *Ghosts* was presented for a few performances, the other contemporary plays in the repertory were mostly poetic, romantic works.

The Meiningen Players also resembled other groups of the time in emphasizing pictorial illusion, in which it excelled all previous standards because of its great accuracy. The duke divided each century into thirds and further distinguished among national differences within each time period. As a result, his productions attained unprecedented authenticity. Accuracy was further insured by the duke's refusal to permit actors to tamper with their costumes. In most theatres of the time, the stars either supplied their own garments or altered as they saw fit those provided by the theatre. Actresses often wore crinoline petticoats under dresses of all periods. Furthermore, the duke insisted upon authentic materials in place of the usual cheap substitutes. He used heavy upholstery fabrics, many imported from France and Italy and some made to his specifications; he introduced genuine chain mail, armor, swords, axes, halberds, and other instruments. In Roman plays the actors wore togas of enormous length. Authentic period furniture was always used. The success of the Meiningen Players led to the establishment of theatrical supply houses which manufactured furniture, properties, costume materials, and armor to meet the new demand from other troupes.

Saxe-Meiningen designed all of the costumes, scenery, and properties used by his troupe. The settings were usually painted by the Brückner brothers of Coburg, who also designed Wagner's and Haase's settings. Strong colors were used in scenery for the first time, reversing the former practice of having actors play against pastel scenery. This innovation probably accounts for the adverse comments by critics on the "garishness" of the Meiningen settings. The duke

Figure 1.4 Saxe-Meiningen's sketch for Act II of Julius Winding's *Pope Sixtus* V. Courtesy Theatermuseum, Munich.

was opposed to sky borders and used foliage, beams, banners, or other devices as overhead masking. He avoided symmetrical balance, for he thought this unnatural, and was careful to keep each detail in correct proportion and to blend painted and three-dimensional elements convincingly. He was also one of the first artists consistently to treat the stage floor as part of the design, breaking it up with fallen trees, rocks, hillocks, steps, and platforms.

While its use of scenery and costumes was probably superior to that of other troupes, the company's principal sources of power were totality of effect and, especially, ensemble acting. The duke maintained as complete authority over his actors as over the scenic investiture. Because he could not afford major performers, his company was composed either of beginners or of older actors who had not attained outstanding success. Although guest actors sometimes performed with the troupe, they had to conform to the company's rules against stars. Perhaps to discourage any tendency toward the "star complex," Saxe-Meiningen required all actors not cast in leading roles to appear as supernumeraries. This, in turn, made possible the effective crowd scenes for which the company was noted. Saxe-Meiningen used no supernumeraries who were not permanent members of the troupe. While this limited the number of persons available for crowd scenes, the effect of large masses was achieved by settings kept sufficiently small to force many of the actors into the wings (thus suggesting that great numbers were out of sight offstage) and by diagonal and contrasting movements to create effects of confusion and agitation. In rehearsing crowd scenes, the duke divided his actors into small groups, each under the charge of an experienced performer who aided in training those under him. Furthermore, each member of a mob was given individualizing characteristics and specific lines; then all were carefully coordinated. The results obtained in this manner, contrasting sharply with the usual mob scenes, were considered revolutionary.

Fortunately, the duke could depend upon long rehearsal periods. Since Meiningen had a population of only 8,000, the theatre was open only twice a week for six months of the year. This schedule and the duke's authority made it possible to rehearse in a way quite different from that in use elsewhere. Each work was rehearsed from the first with full settings, furniture, and properties. Costumes were not always available from the beginning, but were always used for some time prior to the premiere. Actors were required to "act" from the first day rather than merely "walking through" the part as was typical in many theatres. Rehearsals, held in the evening after the duke's state duties were completed, often lasted five or six hours and continued until the play was judged ready for performance, even if this required several months. Because he did not work against a deadline, the duke conceived many details as he went along, and rehearsals were frequently delayed while furniture was rearranged or new plans made.

The impact of the Meiningen Players came from the complete illusion attained in every aspect of the production. Thus, the company stands as the culmination of trends that had begun in the Renaissance. More important, it stands at the beginning of the new movement toward unified production, in which each element is carefully selected because of its contribution to the total effect; the actor had given way

to the director as the dominant artist in the theatre. Saxe-Meiningen's example influenced such men as Antoine and Stanislavsky, who were to figure significantly in the formation of the modern theatre. By the time the Meiningen Players discontinued touring in 1890, the theatre was already entering the new era which they had helped to inaugurate. By that time the public had also become aware of a new direction in playwriting, primarily through the work of Ibsen.

Ibsen

Henrik Ibsen (1828–1906), after publishing his first play in 1850, was appointed resident dramatist and stage manager at the newly created Norwegian National Theatre in Bergen in 1851. By 1857 he had assisted in staging 145 plays, and had written seven of his own. From 1857 until 1862, he worked at the Norwegian Theatre in Christiania (now Oslo). After 1864, he lived abroad except for brief intervals.

Between 1850 and 1899, Ibsen wrote twenty-five plays. Most of the early works are romantic verse-dramas about the Scandinavian past. These include *Lady Inger of Ostraat* (1855), *The Vikings at Helgeland* (1858), and *The Pretenders* (1864). The most important early works, however, are *Brand* (1866) and *Peer Gynt* (1867). *Brand*, a dramatic poem, depicts an uncompromising idealist who sacrifices everything, including his family, to his vision. It established Ibsen's reputation, and the financial security which it brought made it possible for him to work as he pleased. *Peer Gynt* contrasts sharply with *Brand*, for its protagonist is a man who avoids issues by skirting them. A skillful blending of fantasy and reality, *Peer Gynt* was interpreted by many as a satire on the Norwegian character.

In the 1870s Ibsen made a sharp break with his past. He now declared his intention of abandoning verse because it was unsuited to creating an illusion of reality. The future direction of his work first became apparent with *Pillars of Society* (1877), but it

Figure 1.5   Eleanora Duse (at left) in Ibsen's *Rosmersholm* at the Norwegian National Theatre, Oslo, 1906. From *Bühne und Welt* (1906).

was with *A Doll's House* (1879), *Ghosts* (1881), and *An Enemy of the People* (1882) that Ibsen established his reputation as a radical thinker and controversial dramatist. Above all, it was *A Doll's House* and *Ghosts* that shocked conservative readers and served as a rallying point for supporters of a drama of ideas. In *A Doll's House* Nora, upon realizing that she has always been treated as a doll, chooses to leave her husband in order to become a person in her own right. In *Ghosts* Mrs. Alving, conforming to traditional morality, has remained with a depraved husband only to have her only son go mad, presumably from inherited syphilis. Thus, both plays questioned the inviolability of marriage, while the allusion to venereal disease in *Ghosts* made it such a storm center throughout the world that it was forbidden production in most countries.

Ibsen soon turned in new directions. In *The Wild Duck* (1884), *Rosmersholm* (1886), *The Master Builder* (1892), *John Gabriel Borkman* (1896), and *When We Dead Awaken* (1899) he made increasing use of symbolism and of subjects more concerned with personal relationships than with social problems. In actuality, the basic theme of Ibsen's plays remained relatively constant: the struggle for integrity, the conflict between duty to oneself and duty to others. Mrs. Alving of *Ghosts* discovers too late that she had destroyed her life by overvaluing duty to others, whereas in many of the late plays the protagonists, while pursuing some private vision, destroy the happiness of others and finally their own.

Much of Ibsen's work contributed to the development of realism. In the prose dramas he refined Scribe's "well-made play" formula and made it more fitting to the realistic style. Ibsen discarded asides, soliloquies, and other nonrealistic devices, and was careful to motivate all exposition. Most often a character who has just arrived elicits information in a manner that appears completely natural by asking questions about happenings during his absence. All scenes are causally related and lead logically to the denouement. Dialogue, settings, costumes, and business are selected for their ability to reveal character and milieu, and are clearly described in stage directions. Each character is conceived as a personality whose behavior is attributable to hereditary or environmental causes. Internal psychological motivations are given even greater emphasis than external visual detail. In these ways, Ibsen provided a model for writers of the realistic school.

Ibsen's late plays were to influence nonrealistic drama as extensively as the earlier prose plays did realistic works. In them, ordinary objects (such as the duck in *The Wild Duck*) are imbued with significance beyond their literal meaning and enlarge the implications of the dramatic action. Furthermore, many of the works border on fantasy. In *Rosmersholm* a phantom white horse is significant, and in *When We Dead Awaken* the mountain heights exert an irresistible pull. This sense of mysterious forces at work in human destiny was to be a major theme of idealist drama.

Whether realistic or idealistic, almost all dramatists after Ibsen were influenced by his conviction that drama should be a source of insights, a creator of discussion, a conveyor of ideas, something more than mere entertainment. He gave playwrights a new vision of their role. Almost everywhere Ibsen's plays came to epitomize the break with the past and to be a rallying point for producers seeking new paths.

Zola and the French Naturalists

Even as Ibsen was writing his prose plays, the French naturalists, working quite independently, were also demanding a new drama. The naturalists considered heredity and environment to be the major determinants of man's fate. This doctrine was grounded (at least in part) in Charles Darwin's *The Origin of Species* (1859). (Recently it has been charged that Darwin stole his major ideas from Alfred Russell Wallace, one of his associates.) Darwin set forth two main theses: (1) all forms of life have developed gradually from a common ancestry; and (2) the evolution of species is explained by the "survival of the fittest." These theories have several important implications. First, they make heredity and environment the causes of everything man is or does. Second, since behavior is determined by factors largely beyond his control, no individual can truly be held responsible for what he does. If blame is to be assigned, it must go to a society that has allowed undesirable hereditary and environmental factors to exist. Third, Darwin's theories strengthened the idea of progress, since if man has evolved from an atom of being to the complex creature he now is, improvement appears to be inevitable. Nevertheless, it was argued, progress can be hastened by the consistent application of scientific method. Fourth, man is reduced to the status of a natural object. Before

the nineteenth century man had been set apart from the rest of creation as superior to it. Now he lost his privileged status and became merely another object for study and control.

Naturalism also attracted many adherents because of contemporary political and economic conditions. The Franco-Prussian War of 1870–1871 was a severe blow to French pride, for not only was France defeated, but it lost Alsace and Lorraine to Germany. The war also brought an end to Napoleon III's empire. In Paris a commune was established, but this was soon overthrown and France once more became a republic. The war and its aftermath served to emphasize that the working man enjoyed few privileges, and during the last quarter of the nineteenth century socialism began to gain support throughout Europe as many came to believe that only this form of social organization could insure equality to all. Such pressures motivated several European governments to adopt constitutions at last; by 1900 every major country in Europe except Russia had some degree of constitutional government. This interest in the lot of the working classes and the rights of the common man was to provide the main focus of the naturalist movement. As means of dealing with contemporary problems, science and technology were considered the major tools, and the naturalists argued that all problems could be solved if only the scientific method were applied systematically.

Naturalism as a conscious movement first appeared in France in the 1870s. Its primary spokesman was Emile Zola (1840–1902), an admirer of Comte and an advocate of the scientific method as the key to all truth and progress. Believing that literature must either become scientific or perish, Zola argued that drama should illustrate the "inevitable laws of heredity and environment" or record "case studies." He wished the dramatist, in his search for truth, to observe, record, and "experiment" with the same detachment as the scientist. Zola compared the writer with the doctor, who seeks the causes of a disease so that it may be cured; he does not gloss over infection, but brings it out into the open where it can be exam-

Figure 1.6 Ménessier's adaptation of Zola's novel, *The Earth*, as directed by Antoine at the Théâtre Antoine, 1902. Note the many naturalistic details, including the chickens in the foreground. From *Le Théâtre* (1902).

ined. Similarly, the dramatist should seek out social ills and reveal them so they may be corrected.

Zola's first major statement of the naturalist doctrine came in 1873 in the preface to his dramatization of his novel *Thérèse Raquin*; he expanded his views in *Naturalism in the Theatre* (1881) and *The Experimental Novel* (1881). Some of Zola's followers were even more radical than he in their demands for theatrical reform, arguing that a play should merely be a "slice of life" transferred to the stage. Thus, in their zeal to approximate scientific truth, they often obliterated virtually all distinction between art and life.

Naturalism, like many movements before it, was handicapped by a lack of good plays embodying its principles. Although a few plays, such as *Henriette Maréchal* (1863) by Edmond and Jules Goncourt and *L'Arlesienne* (1872) by Alphonse Daudet, were pro-duced, they made little impact. Even Zola's *Thérèse Raquin* failed to live up to the critical precepts except in the setting, for rather than a slice of life it was more nearly a melodrama about murder and retribution.

Ironically, it was Henri Becque (1837–1899) who most nearly captured the naturalist ideal in France, even though he and Zola were equally contemptuous of each other. Becque's *The Vultures* (1882) shows the fleecing of a family of women by their supposed friends following the death of the father; there are no sympathetic characters, the ending is pessimistic and ironical, and there are no obvious climaxes, merely a slow progression toward the cynical outcome. *La Parisienne* (1885) depicts a wife who considers her infidelity an asset to her husband's advancement in business. In these plays Becque raised French naturalism to its highest point.

That *The Vultures* was presented by the Comédie Française, a bastion of conservatism, would on the surface suggest that by the 1880s naturalism had been fully accepted in Paris. But Becque's play was ineffectually produced because he refused to comply with the company's request for revisions that would have brought the work more nearly into conformity with contemporary tastes. Because virtually all naturalist dramas that received a hearing failed to raise any serious questions about traditional values, the complacency of neither the public nor theatrical workers was seriously challenged. Something more was needed if significant change was to come. This new element was to be added by Antoine at the Théâtre Libre, where after 1887 naturalistic staging and writing were united for the first time.

Antoine and the Théâtre Libre

André Antoine (1858–1943) seemed a most unpromising source of revolution in 1887, for he was merely a clerk in a gas company, and his theatrical experience was limited to supernumerary acting with

Parisian professional companies and occasional appearances with an amateur group. When Antoine sought to produce a program of new plays, including a dramatization of Zola's *Jacques Damour*, his amateur circle refused its sanction and Antoine set off on his own. In search of a name for his company, he adopted Théâtre Libre (or "Free Theatre"). The success of his first program won him the endorsement of Zola and other influential figures. His second program was attended by major theatrical critics, who wrote lengthy reviews. Before the end of 1887, Antoine was famous. He gave up his clerk's job and thereafter until 1914 devoted himself to theatrical production.

Organized on a subscription basis, the Théâtre Libre was open only to members and therefore was exempt from censorship. As a result, many of the plays available to Antoine were those that had been refused licenses, and most were naturalistic. Much of the notoriety of the Théâtre Libre stemmed from its *comédies rosses* (plays in which the usual principles of morality are reversed), many so extreme that they repelled even Antoine's tolerant audience. It was largely because of these works that naturalism gained a reputation for depravity, but the publicity they attracted also gradually paved the way for greater freedom in established and conservative theatres.

In 1888 Antoine also began to produce one foreign work each year. After Tolstoy's *The Power of Darkness*, he went on to Ibsen's *Ghosts* and *The Wild Duck*. In this way, controversial foreign as well as domestic plays were given their first Parisian performances.

In addition to serving as a showcase for new dramas, the Théâtre Libre also became the proving ground for production techniques. Although Antoine had used a realistic approach from the beginning, he intensified his search for authenticity after witnessing the Meiningen Players and Irving's company in 1888. He now sought to reproduce environment in every detail. In *The Butchers* (1888), for example, he hung real carcasses of beef on the stage.

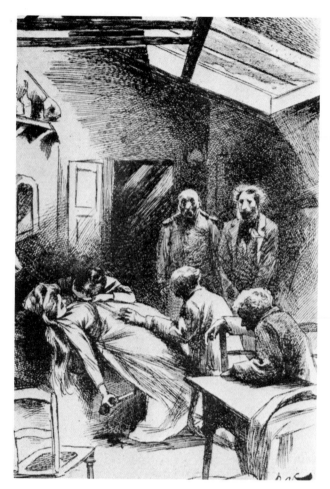

Figure 1.7 Final scene from Antoine's production of Ibsen's *The Wild Duck* at the Théâtre Libre. From a contemporary lithograph.

The "fourth wall" was observed consistently; in designing settings, he arranged rooms as in real life and only later decided which wall should be removed. Often furniture was placed along the curtain line, and actors were directed to behave as though there were no audience. Through his belief in the importance of environment, Antoine helped to establish the principle that each play requires its own setting quite distinct from that of any other work. After witnessing the Meiningen company, Antoine also gave special attention to ensemble acting. Although most of his performers were amateurs, he coached them carefully and autocratically. He discouraged conventionalized movement and declamatory speech, seeking natural behavior instead.

Antoine's success worked against him, for as soon as a playwright or actor established his worth, he was employed by a major company. Furthermore, Antoine's high standards of production kept him constantly in debt. Even at the height of its popularity, the Théâtre Libre gave no production for more than three performances. By 1893, the company began to weaken and in 1894 Antoine left it. By then he had presented sixty-two programs composed of 184 plays. In addition to playing in Paris, he had toured in Belgium, Holland, Germany, Italy, and England. His fame was worldwide, and the example he had set was to be followed in several other countries.

Antoine did not stay away from the Parisian theatre long. In 1897 he opened his Théâtre Antoine, run as a fully professional theatre, and in 1906 he was appointed director of the state-subsidized Odéon, which he completely modernized. Although he practiced it less assiduously, realism still dominated his work. Probably his most famous productions of this era were of French classical dramas, in which he attempted to recreate the theatrical conventions of the seventeenth century. Costumed actors served as onstage audience, chandeliers were hung over the stage, and candle footlights were conspicuous. Through this approach, he helped to establish a realism based upon past theatrical conventions rather than upon architecture and dress, as had been usual with other producers. Antoine also directed several outstanding productions of Shakespeare's plays. Near the end of his tenure at the Odéon, he staged a few works in which stylization (based on visual sources) was clearly evident, but he resigned his post before this new trend was fully explored. By 1914 he had presented a total of 364 works. No one else had

influenced the French theatre of the period so profoundly as had Antoine.

After 1890, most of the major new French dramatists were realists and many of these were given their first hearing by Antoine. Among these the most important were Porto-Riche, Curel, and Brieux. Georges Porto-Riche (1849–1930) was noted for subtle characterizations which emphasized internal conflicts. Probably his best play is *Infatuated* (1891) in which a husband tries to rid himself of his wife by arousing her interest in another man, only to discover that he cannot give her up. François de Curel (1854–1928) had his first play produced by Antoine in 1892. He made few concessions to popular taste, and his disregard for ordinary principles of dramatic construction often obscured his intentions. His concern for internal psychological conflicts, however, did much to forward realistic subject matter. Among his best works are *The Fossils* (1892), depicting a decaying aristocracy, and *The Lion's Feast* (1898), in which the protagonist attempts to improve the lives of workingmen. Eugène Brieux (1858–1932) was said by George Bernard Shaw to be the most important dramatist in Europe after the death of Ibsen. Given his first production by Antoine in 1892, Brieux went on to write *The Red Robe* (1900), showing the difficulty of obtaining justice from judges concerned primarily with promotion, *Damaged Goods* (1902), concerning syphilis and its transmission to a child, and *Maternity* (1903), in which a blistering attack is launched on a society that does not permit legal birth control. As Brieux's plays reveal, subjects that had been unacceptable to the general public when Ibsen began his work were to be seen in commercial theatres by 1900.

The Freie Bühne and German Realism

The pattern that emerged in France was repeated in Germany. The first step toward theatrical reform came in 1883, when the Deutsches Theater was opened in Berlin by Adolf L'Arronge (1838–1908) and Ludwig Barnay (1842–(1924), with a company headed by Josef Kainz (1858–1910), who had worked in the Meiningen troupe, and Agnes Sorma (1865–1927), later to be Germany's leading actress. Here a repertory of old and new plays was produced in the manner of the Meiningen Players. In 1888 Barnay left the Deutsches Theater to found the Berliner Theater, and in the same year Oskar Blumenthal (1852–1917) founded the Lessing Theater. Thus, by 1890 Berlin had several private companies of excellent quality. Nevertheless, their choice of plays was severely restricted by censorship.

Meanwhile, a group calling itself "Youngest Germany" had begun to advocate a new art based upon an objective observation of reality, while another calling itself *Durch* (or "Through") went even further than Zola in its demands for a naturalistic drama. Both groups found inspiration in Ibsen's plays, sixteen of which had been translated into German by 1890.

As in France, however, the new movement lacked focus until an "independent" theatre was formed. Taking its inspiration from the Théâtre Libre, the Freie Bühne (or "Free Stage") was organized in Berlin in 1889. Unlike Antoine's company, however, the German group was a democratic organization with officers and a governing council. Otto Brahm (1856–1912), a dramatic critic, was elected president and became its guiding spirit. In order to secure the services of professional actors, the Freie Bühne gave its performances on Sunday afternoons since its actors and most of its personnel were regularly employed by established theatres, especially the Deutsches, Berliner and Lessing. Each production usually involved different actors, over whom Brahm had little control. Thus, the Freie Bühne exerted little influence on theatrical production. Its major contribution was made by giving a hearing to plays forbidden by the censor. The opening production of *Ghosts* was followed with plays by Hauptmann, the Goncourts, Zola, Becque, Tolstoy, Anzengruber, and Strindberg. After the season of 1890–1891, regular performances were discontinued, although occasionally programs were arranged when a worthy play was forbidden a license. The Freie Bühne came to an end in 1894, when Brahm was named director of the Deutsches Theater.

The only truly important German dramatist introduced by the Freie Bühne was Gerhart Hauptmann (1862–1946). The furor that greeted his *Before Sunrise* (1889), the story of a Silesian family that sinks into viciousness after the discovery of coal on their land, established Hauptmann as a major new playwright. During the next fifty years he wrote about thirty plays. Of the early works, the best is *The Weavers* (1892), remarkable for its group-protagonist of workers engaged in an abortive revolt. Like Ibsen, Hauptmann went on to write plays in a more symbolic vein, notably *The Assumption of Hannele* (1893) and *The Sunken Bell* (1896). After 1912, his plays became increasingly nonrealistic. Before his death, Hauptmann lost much of his prestige because of his passive acceptance of Hitler's regime. All of Hauptmann's work shows great compassion for human suffering, but his protagonists, who are victims of circumstances beyond their control, are more pitiable than heroic.

The Freie Bühne stimulated the formation of several other stage societies in Germany. Although none achieved the fame of the original group, they helped to pave the way for a new drama. Perhaps of equal importance, a "people's" theatre was organized by socialist groups (the ban on which was lifted in 1890) interested in raising the cultural standards of the working classes. Using the Freie Bühne as a model, the Freie Volksbühne was organized in Berlin in 1890 to produce plays at Sunday matinees, for which season tickets were distributed by lot at a nominal price. Beginning with 1,150 members, the organization included 12,000 by 1908. In 1892 the Neue Freie Volksbühne, founded by the former director of the original group, began a similar program. By 1905, it was offering its subscribers a choice among productions at several major theatres. Before World War I the two groups had amalgamated, and their membership of 70,000 was soon to open one of the most modern theatres in Germany with its own permanent company. The workers' theatre movement flourished throughout Germany and Austria. To it must go considerable credit for creating the broad-based theatregoing public which has continued in Germany.

Before 1900, the new realistic drama was being accepted almost everywhere. At the Burgtheater in Vienna a wide selection of recent works was presented between 1890 and 1898, when Max Burckhardt (1854–1912) was director of the theatre. His successor, Paul Schlenther (1854–1916), a friend and admirer of Hauptmann, continued his policies. A somewhat similar pattern was followed elsewhere, for as public interest in the new plays grew the repertory expanded to include them.

In addition to Hauptmann, other important new dramatists include Sudermann and Schnitzler. Hermann Sudermann (1857–1928) was even more instrumental than Hauptmann in making realism acceptable to the public, for he tended to retain the well-made play techniques and to conform more nearly to accepted morality while writing about "advanced" subjects. His most popular play, *Magda* (1893), concerning a singer whose bohemian life brings her into conflict with her father, became a favorite vehicle of actresses. Sudermann continued to write until well into the twentieth century. The most important Austrian dramatist of this period was Arthur Schnitzler (1862–1931), a recorder of the melancholic world-weariness that characterized the turn of the century, and of the shallow sexual attitudes that accompanied it. The most famous of his works is *Anatol* (1893), a series of short plays, each of which records a different love intrigue. Even in the midst of happiness, Anatol knows that his momentary pleasure will dissolve into jealousy and boredom. A similar, though more shocking work to audiences, is *Reigen* (1900, variously translated as *Hands Around*, *La Ronde*, and *Round Dance*), with its ten characters who engage in a series of love affairs. Schnitzler, a friend of Sigmund Freud, was much concerned with the centrality of sexual behavior, but was also convinced that love cannot be built upon pure ego satisfaction. While he seldom strayed from this theme, Schnitzler occasionally wrote on other subjects, as in *Professor Bernhardi* (1912), a play about anti-Semitism.

The Independent Theatre and Realism in England

After the death of Robertson in 1871, the English theatre was given over largely to works in the tradition of Boucicault and Sardou or to lavish productions of the classics. A new direction was not evident until the 1890s, when Jones and Pinero appeared. These writers hold a place in English drama comparable to that of Dumas *fils* and Augier in French theatre, for both were sufficiently new to be slightly scandalizing, yet both were conventional enough to be acceptable to the censor and the theatregoing public.

Henry Arthur Jones (1851–1929) began his playwriting career with a successful melodrama, *The Silver King* (1882), and did not turn to more serious drama until after 1890 with *The Dancing Girl* (1891), *The Liars* (1897), and *Mrs. Dane's Defence* (1900). His most unusual play, *Michael and His Lost Angel* (1896), treats a love affair between a minister and one of his parishioners. Although Jones had high ideals for drama, he was not an original thinker. He aroused suspense and titillation without giving any significant new insights.

Arthur Wing Pinero (1855–1934) began his career in 1874 as an actor and turned to writing in 1877. His first major success came with a farce, *The Magistrate* (1885), a form in which he excelled. Although Pinero never professed interest in a "drama of ideas," it was his *The Second Mrs. Tanqueray* (1893), the story of a "woman with a past," that brought the first change in public attitudes, for when it proved a popular hit, producers began to look more favorably upon "Ibsenesque" drama. Pinero continued to write for an-

Figure 1.8   Scene from Act I of the original production of Pinero's *The Second Mrs. Tanqueray*, with Mrs. Patrick Campbell and George Alexander. From *The Graphic* (1893).

other thirty years, turning out such successful plays as *The Notorious Mrs. Ebbsmith* (1895), *Iris* (1901), and *Mid-Channel* (1909), but his popularity declined steadily after 1910.

While Jones and Pinero paved the way for public acceptance, the development of a more significant drama owes most to Ibsen. By 1880, William Archer and others had begun to translate Ibsen's plays and by 1890 all those then written were available in English. In 1889 Janet Achurch (1864–1916) presented *A Doll's House*, the first unadapted version of a play by Ibsen seen in England. Miss Achurch was to be one of the new drama's most ardent champions, appearing in many plays by Ibsen, Shaw, and others. Her production of *A Doll's House* reminded critics of

how far behind the continent English drama had fallen and supplied one of the motivations for founding the Independent Theatre.

Modeled on the Théâtre Libre and the Freie Bühne, the Independent Theatre was headed by J. T. Grein (1862–1935), a Dutch-born critic who had lived in London for many years. Like its predecessors on the continent, the Independent Theatre was organized on a subscription basis to avoid censorship, and like the Freie Bühne, it gave its productions on Sundays in order to gain the cooperation of theatre managers and actors. The opening play in 1891, *Ghosts*, prompted more than 500 articles, most of them vituperative. The second program, Zola's *Thérèse Raquin*, created almost as great a storm. This publicity began to make the general public aware of the new drama for the first time.

Between 1891 and 1897, the Independent Theatre presented twenty-six plays, mostly translations. It did little in the way of mounting the plays. Thus, like the Freie Bühne, it served primarily as a rejuvenator of drama rather than as an influence upon production. Grein had hoped to produce new English plays, for he was convinced that the low state of English drama was attributable to the conservatism of producers. He soon found, however, that no significant plays were available. His disappointment prompted George Bernard Shaw to complete *Widower's Houses*, the production of which in 1892 launched Shaw's career as a dramatist.

George Bernard Shaw (1856–1950), previously a novelist and critic, wrote regularly for the theatre from 1892 until his death. Unlike most of the new writers, who tended to be gloomy and intensely serious as a reaction against the shallowness of their predecessors, Shaw wrote primarily in the comic form. This choice may be explained in part by Shaw's interest in persuasion, which was best served by having characters arrive at perceptions that remove the barriers to a happy resolution. Shaw also delighted in using paradoxes to make both characters and audiences reassess their values. Thus, *Arms and the Man* (1894) punctures romantic notions about love and war, while *Major Barbara* (1905) upholds a munitions manufacturer as a greater humanitarian than an officer in the Salvation Army, because the Salvation Army prolongs an inequitable system by caring for victims whereas the manufacturer provides his workers with the means whereby to better themselves. Many of Shaw's plays, notably *The Doctor's Dilemma* (1906) and *Getting Married* (1908), are essentially extended discussions of specific problems. Other works, such as *Man and Superman* (1901) and *Back to Methuselah* (1919–1921), show Shaw's interest in "creative evolution" and the "life force," which he believed were striving to create a "superman" by working through superior individuals. In still other plays, like *Caesar and Cleopatra* (1899) and *Saint Joan* (1923), Shaw sought to correct popular misconceptions of historical figures and events. Perhaps his least characteristic work is *Heartbreak House* (1914–1919), a parable about the failures of Europe at the time of World War I. Shaw labeled it a play in the Chekhovian manner, perhaps to indicate its difference from his other works.

Figure 1.9 Shaw's *Caesar and Cleopatra* at the Savoy Theatre, London, 1907, under the management of Vedrenne and Barker. Forbes Robertson as Caesar, Gertrude Elliott as Cleopatra. From *Play Pictorial*, Vol. 10 (1907).

Although Shaw is related to the realistic movement through his concern for ideas and social problems, he differed markedly from most of the writers of this school. While acknowledging the importance of heredity and environment, Shaw always implies that man has freedom of choice. Furthermore, although his characters often speak in dialect, they are always articulate and seldom follow closely the patterns of everyday speech. Shaw was not objective, for he chose his characters and invented his stories to illustrate a point of view. His comic method eventually won a wide audience for the drama of ideas.

Shaw was not immediately successful, however, for at first his unconventional ideas and paradoxical situations only puzzled or irritated audiences. His reputation was built slowly through the efforts of organizations that succeeded the Independent Theatre. The first of these was the Incorporated Stage Society, founded in 1899 to present modern plays. At first its programs were given on Sunday afternoons but, as its membership grew from the original 300 to 1,500 by 1914, it added Monday matinees as well. By the time the group disbanded in 1939 it had presented about 200 works, many of which would otherwise not have been seen. It served as an experimental theatre which kept the English theatrical world abreast of the latest movements both at home and abroad.

The most significant company in this period was that at the Court Theatre, where between 1904 and 1907 Harley Granville Barker (1877–1946) and John Vedrenne (1863–1930) gave the new drama its first full hearing in a public theatre. Barker had begun his career as an actor in 1891, had worked with several organizations, including the Incorporated Stage Society, and had established himself as a dramatist before being invited to assist Vedrenne with a production of *Two Gentlemen of Verona*. This beginning soon developed into a permanent arrangement, under which one play was offered each evening for several weeks while another little-known or seldom-performed work was given at matinees. If the matinees engendered enough enthusiasm, the play was

Figure 1.10   Shaw's *Mrs. Warren's Profession* in its original English production, a private performance by the Incorporated Stage Society in 1902. Granville Barker is seen at the left. Courtesy Enthoven Collection, Victoria and Albert Museum.

moved to evening performances. Even successes, however, were not played consecutively for more than a few weeks. Between 1904 and 1907, the Court presented thirty-two plays by seventeen different authors, including Euripides, Hauptmann, Ibsen, Galsworthy, and Yeats. The mainstay of the theatre, however, was Shaw, eleven of whose plays were presented in productions directed by Shaw himself. These productions established Shaw's popularity with the British public.

The Court made other important contributions. It was noted for ensemble acting by a company that included some of the best actors of the period: Lillah McCarthy, Edith Wynne Matthison, Louis Calvert, Lewis Casson, and Godfrey Tearle. There were no stars. Since Barker believed that it is the director's primary task to give a thoughtful interpretation of the playwright's script, he sought to find in each work the style suited to it. Nevertheless, the dominant style of the Court productions was a subtle realism which avoided bravura. Simplicity and suggestion were the keynotes of both the acting and scenery. In 1907 Barker and Vedrenne moved to the much larger Savoy Theatre, but closed after one season because of lack of attendance and trouble with the censor. When Charles Frohman established a repertory company at the Duke of York's Theatre in 1910, he employed Barker to head it. After presenting seventeen plays in seventeen weeks and incurring a sizable deficit, Barker resigned.

In spite of these failures, the Barker-Vedrenne experiments engendered several imitators, especially in the provinces, where repertory companies began to be opened once more. The first important company was established by Miss A. E. F. Horniman (1860–1937) in 1907 in Manchester. Until it was discontinued in 1921 this was to be one of the best theatres in England, offering a wide variety of English and continental plays. Its encouragement of local writers gave rise to the "Lancashire School," of which Stanley Houghton (1881–1913), author of *Hindle Wakes* (1912), and Harold Brighouse (1883–1958), author of *Hobson's Choice* (1916), were the most important. Other vigorous repertory companies were founded at Liverpool in 1911 and at Birmingham in 1913. The Birmingham Repertory Company, under the direction of Barry Jackson (1879–1961), was to be especially influential after the First World War.

In addition to Shaw, a number of other dramatists in the realistic vein appeared after 1900. John Galsworthy (1867–1933), already one of England's most successful novelists, turned to playwriting in 1906 with *The Silver Box*, in which the justice meted out to a poor and a rich man for the same crime is contrasted. His later plays, *Strife* (1909), *Justice* (1910), and *Loyalties* (1922), were in the same vein. All are objective treatments of social problems and demonstrate Galsworthy's considerable gift for creating dramatic dialogue and clearcut conflicts. Harley Granville Barker won fame as a dramatist with such plays as *The Marrying of Ann Leete* (1902), *The Voysey Inheritance* (1905), *Waste* (1907), and *Madras House* (1910). Similar to Shaw in his interests, Barker lacked Shaw's sense of the comic, and his discussions now seem cold and deficient in intensity. St. John Hankin (1869–1909) was the most gloomy dramatist of the period. In such works as *The Return of the Prodigal* (1905) and *The Last of the DeMullins* (1908), he attacked abuses but offered no alternatives to the conditions depicted.

The Continuing Tradition in England, 1900–1914

Despite these "modern" trends, pictorial realism continued to be the principal goal in England until World War I. Furthermore, most of the major figures of the London stage between 1900 and 1914 had been trained in the Bancroft-Irving tradition, and they made few innovations. Of the actor-managers, the most important were John Hare, Forbes-Robertson, Martin-Harvey, and Tree.

John Hare (1844–1921) had won a considerable following before he left the Bancrofts in 1875 to manage the Court Theatre. Then, he managed St. James' Theatre from 1879 to 1888, when he moved to the Garrick. He retired in 1911. Hare was considered one of London's most versatile actors and most careful managers.

Johnston Forbes-Robertson (1853–1937) differed from most of the major actors of his day in being an excellent speaker of verse, an art which he had learned from Samuel Phelps. On the stage from 1874 until 1913, Forbes-Robertson acted with Phelps, the Bancrofts, and Irving. He also served as leading man to Helena Modjeska (1844–1909), the Polish actress who appeared with great success in England and the United States between 1877 and 1905, and to Mary Anderson (1859–1940), an American actress who won fame in England between 1883 and 1889 for her Shakespearean performances. Occasionally Forbes-Robertson undertook management, but his reputation rested primarily upon his acting. Some critics (including Shaw, who wrote *Caesar and Cleopatra* for him) consider him the finest Hamlet of all time.

John Martin-Harvey (1863–1944) made his debut in 1881 and after 1882 played for Irving, whom he succeeded as manager of the Lyceum Theatre. In his first independent production, an adaptation of Dickens's *A Tale of Two Cities*, he won such popularity that he was condemned to play the role of Sidney Carton through most of his remaining career. He gained new fame in 1912 for his performance in Reinhardt's London production of *Oedipus Rex*. Until about 1910, Martin-Harvey continued Irving's practices, but gradually accepted modern trends and after World War I abandoned pictorial realism altogether. More than any other producer, he successfully bridged the Victorian and the modern stage.

The most famous actor-manager between 1900 and 1914 was Herbert Beerbohm Tree (1853–1917). On the stage from 1878, he assumed the management of the Haymarket in 1887. From the profits made there on melodramas and light contemporary plays he built Her Majesty's Theatre in 1897. Although he had had little previous experience with Shakespearean drama, Tree's new theatre was to be the principal home of Shakespeare in London between 1900 and 1914. Tree continued, and even extended, the trend toward actualistic detail. His *A Midsummer Night's Dream* in 1900 featured live rabbits and a carpet of grass with flowers that could be plucked; although the scene changes added forty-five minutes to the playing time, the production's literal realism attracted more than 220,000 spectators, perhaps the largest number ever to witness any Shakespearean play in London. Beginning in 1905, Tree

Figure 1.11   Beerbohm Tree's production of Shakespeare's *A Midsummer Night's Dream* at Her Majesty's Theatre, London, 1900. Oberon stands in front of the tree center; Titania is at left surrounded by fairies. Courtesy Enthoven Collection, Victoria and Albert Museum.

annually held a festival of Shakespeare's plays in which many other companies took part.

Although not a very good actor, Tree often starred in his own productions. On the other hand, he employed the best performers available, and he worked on every production with unbounded enthusiasm. As the repertory system declined, Tree became concerned about the lack of effective training for young actors, and in 1904 he established the acting school which was to become the Royal Academy of Dramatic Art, still the most prestigious in England.

Following the outbreak of the war in 1914, Tree gave up his theatre. Before the hostilities ended, he

was dead. With him died much of English tradition, for after the war the actor-manager system, the dominant type of organization since 1700, was largely abandoned, and pictorial realism, long the standard of perfection, had come to seem old-fashioned.

The Moscow Art Theatre and Realism in Russia

Russia also had to await the "independent theatre" movement before needed reforms were to come. Although such Russian dramatists as Turgenev, Ostrovsky, and Pisemsky had already inaugurated a realistic school of writing, theatrical production still preserved conventions inherited from the eighteenth century, and the visit of the Meiningen Players in 1885 and 1890 had revealed to many Russian producers how far behind they were. Little significant progress was made, however, until the formation of the Moscow Art Theatre by Konstantin Stanislavsky (1863–1938) and Vladimir Nemirovich-Danchenko (1858–1943) in 1898.

The Moscow Art Theatre differed from the other independent theatres in being a fully professional organization from the beginning and in emphasizing theatrical production rather than neglected plays. Its first program, Alexei Tolstoy's *Tsar Feodor Ivanovich*, created a sensation because of its painstaking recreation of the Russia of 1600, its ensemble acting, and its absence of stars. Public interest waned, however, until the production of Chekhov's *The Sea Gull* established the originality of both the author and the company.

Anton Chekhov (1860–1904) began his dramatic career with vaudeville sketches and short plays in the comic-pathetic vein and then went on to long plays. When *The Sea Gull* (1896) was performed at the Alexandrinsky Theatre in St. Petersburg, it was a failure because the actors did not understand their roles and had not learned their lines. As a result, Chekhov was determined to give up playwriting. After reluctantly permitting the Moscow Art Theatre to perform *The Sea Gull*, he went on to provide it with three other plays: *Uncle Vanya* (1899), *The Three Sisters* (1901), and *The Cherry Orchard* (1904). Chekhov's reputation rests primarily upon these four plays.

Each of Chekhov's four major plays is set in rural Russia and depicts the monotonous and frustrating life of the landowning class. All of the characters aspire to a better life, but none knows how, or has the initiative, to achieve his goals. The plays are built upon infinite details, the connection among which is not always obvious. Yet gradually a unifying mood, clearly delineated characters, and a complete and simple action emerge. The absence of startling climaxes, strong suspense, and clear purpose has caused many readers to misunderstand the plays, which require detailed study and attention to nuance if the pattern behind the surface is to become clear.

Figure 1.12   Act I of Chekhov's *The Sea Gull* at the Moscow Art Theatre, 1898. Setting by V. A. Simov. From *Moscow Art Theatre, 1898–1917* (Moscow, 1955).

The methods of the Moscow Art Theatre were well adapted to the demands of Chekhov's plays. Stanislavsky always undertook a long study of each play before rehearsals began. He insisted upon careful attention to detail from each actor, and he sought to recreate the milieu only after visiting the site of the play's action, or after extensive research.

Despite its success with *The Sea Gull*, the Moscow Art Theatre ended its first season in debt and was saved only by the generosity of patrons. With the new support, it was able in 1902 to build its own theatre, with workshops and such up-to-date equipment as a revolving stage. It increased its acting company from 39 to one hundred members. Thereafter, it staged from three to five new plays each year, while keeping successful works in the repertory. The influence of the Moscow Art Theatre was soon felt throughout Russia, and by 1906 it was sufficiently well known abroad that it undertook a foreign tour.

Stanislavsky is now remembered above all for his attempts to perfect a method of acting. He became fully aware of the need in 1906 and made the first outline of his ideas in 1909, but he did not begin to publish his ideas until *My Life in Art* (1924) and *An Actor Prepares* (1936). The entire plan was not available outside of Russia until the appearance of *Building a Character* (1949) and *Creating a Role* (1961). Because of this piecemeal publication, the ambiguities in the theory, and the many changes made by Stanislavsky as he refined his approach, many conflicting interpretations of "the Stanislavsky system" have arisen.

Although no summary is entirely acceptable to all of Stanislavsky's admirers and critics, the system includes the following principles. (1) The actor's body and voice should be thoroughly trained so they may respond efficiently to all demands. (2) The actor should be schooled in stage techniques, since he must be able to project his characterization to an audience without any sense of contrivance. (3) The actor should be a skilled observer of reality, out of which he builds his role. (4) The actor should seek an inner justification for everything he does on stage. In doing so, he depends in part upon "the magic 'if'" (that is, the actor says, "If I were this person faced with this situation, I would . . .") and "emotion memory" (a process by which the actor relates the unfamiliar dramatic situation to some analogous emotional situation in his own life, although Stanislavsky was eventually to downgrade the importance of emotion memory). (5) If the actor is not merely to play himself, he must undertake a thorough analysis of the script and work within the "given circumstances" found there. He must define his character's motivations in each scene, in the play as a whole, and his relationship to each of the other roles. The character's primary "objective" becomes the "through line" of the role, around which everything else revolves. (6) On stage, the actor must focus his attention upon the action as it unfolds moment by moment. Such concentration will lead to the "illusion of the first time" and will guide the actor in subordinating his ego to the artistic demands of the production. (7) An actor must continue to strive to perfect understanding and proficiency.

Various aspects of this method have been emphasized by different interpreters. Taken as a whole, it is an attempt to analyze each phase of the actor's work and to make it as efficient as possible. Stanislavsky was never fully satisfied with his system and he continued to refine it up to the time of his death. He also cautioned others against adopting it without making changes required by different artistic needs and cultural backgrounds.

Although the Moscow Art Theatre had no stars, a number of outstanding actors came to the fore. In addition to Stanislavsky, these included Moskvin, Kachalov, and Knipper. Ivan Moskvin (1874–1946), a small man, was best suited to self-effacing characters such as Epikhodov in *The Cherry Orchard*. His was the art of understatement in which a few subtle touches brought out the emotional values of a scene. Vassily Kachalov (1875–1948), a tall, handsome man with a beautiful voice, was at his best in the roles of romantic heroes, rebels, or intellectuals. Olga Knipper (1870–1959), Chekhov's wife, played a wide variety of roles, but was best known as Madame Ranevskaya of *The Cherry Orchard*.

In addition to Chekhov, the Moscow Art Theatre also encouraged Maxim Gorky (1868–1936), already famous as a writer of realistic stories. *The Lower Depths* (1902), set in a flophouse and featuring a collection of characters defeated by life, became one of the troupe's greatest successes. Other plays by Gorky include *Summer Folk* (1904) and *Enemies* (1907). Gorky was much involved in the political struggles of the day, including the Revolution of 1905, which though largely unsuccessful won a small measure of representational government. Gorky's activities caused him to be exiled, but his reputation as a champion of the proletariat would later give him enormous influence among the Soviets.

The Revival of Idealism in France

The realistic and naturalistic outlook did not go unchallenged. Although the intellectual climate between 1850 and 1900 was largely anti-idealistic, the sweeping claims made for science at this time brought several protests. The most significant of these came from the symbolists, who launched their counterattack in 1885 in a "manifesto." Taking its inspiration from the works of Edgar Allan Poe, Baudelaire's poems and criticism, Dostoevsky's novels, and Wagner's music and theory, symbolism attracted representatives from all the arts. To the symbolists, subjectivity, spirituality, and mysterious internal and external forces represented a higher form of truth than that to be derived from the mere observance of outward appearance. This deeper significance, they argued, cannot be represented directly but can only be evoked through symbols, legends, myths, and moods. The principal spokesman for the movement was Stephane Mallarmé (1842–1898), whose views of drama—as an evocation of the mystery of existence through poetic and allusive language, performed with only the most essential and atmospherically ap-

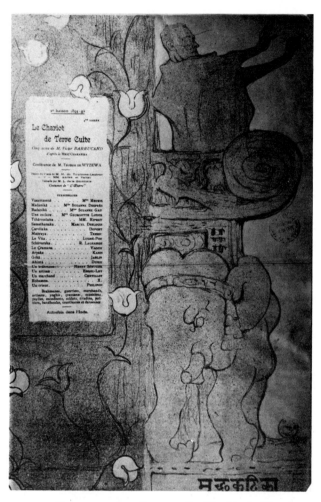

Figure 1.13   Program for *The Little Clay Cart*, an adaptation of the Sanskrit drama by Victor Barracund for Lugné-Poë's Théâtre de l'Oeuvre in the season of 1894–1895. The program and some of the settings were designed by Toulouse-Lautrec. Courtesy Bibliothèque de l'Arsenal, Paris.

propriate theatrical aids, for the purpose of creating a quasi-religious experience—set the tone for the antirealistic works of the 1890s.

As with naturalism, symbolism made no marked impression in the theatre until an "independent" group, modeled on the Théâtre Libre appeared. In 1890, Paul Fort (1872–1962), a seventeen-year-old poet, founded the Théâtre d'Art, where by 1892 he had presented works by forty-six authors, ranging from readings of poems and adaptations of portions of the *Iliad* and the Bible to new plays. Most of the programs were given only one performance, and the actors, primarily amateurs, were often inadequate. Unlike Antoine, Fort received predominantly hostile critical notices, perhaps because his productions seemed incomprehensible to those accustomed to illusionism.

When Fort left the theatre in 1892, his work was carried on by the Théâtre de l'Oeuvre, headed by Aurélien-Marie Lugné-Poë (1869–1940). An actor and stage manager at the Théâtre Libre for a time, Lugné-Poë was converted to the idealist outlook after seeing and appearing in some of the productions at the Théâtre d'Art and while sharing an apartment with the painters Edouard Vuillard, Maurice Denis, and Pierre Bonnard. The Théâtre de l'Oeuvre gave its first performance in 1893. From that time until 1897 Lugné-Poë used a similar style for virtually all of his productions. Guided by the motto "the word creates the decor," he reduced scenery to simple compositions of lines and color painted on backdrops. Using settings by Toulouse-Lautrec, Denis, Vuillard, Bonnard, Odilon Redon, and others, Lugné-Poë sought to create a unity of style and mood rather than of milieu.

The opening production, *Pelléas and Mélisande*, was typical. Few properties and little furniture were used; the stage was lighted from overhead and most of the action passed in semidarkness; a gauze curtain, hung between the actors and the audience, gave the impression that mist enveloped the stage; backdrops, painted in grayed tones, emphasized the air of mystery; costumes were vaguely medieval, although the intention was to create draperies of no particular period. The actors spoke in a staccato chant like priests and, according to some critics, behaved like sleepwalkers; their gestures were strongly stylized. Given this radically new approach, it is not surprising that many spectators were mystified.

Lugné-Poë's repertory was made up primarily of French plays but with these he mingled some works by Ibsen, Hauptmann, Sanskrit dramatists, and others. Of the French dramas, those by Maeterlinck were the best. Maurice Maeterlinck (1862–1949), after coming to Paris from Belgium, turned to playwriting in 1889 and by 1896 had written *The Intruder* (1890), *The Blind* (1890), and *The Death of Tintagiles* (1894). Of his early work, the best known is *Pelléas and Mélisande* (1892), in which a young woman, after marrying a prince who has found her in a forest, falls in love with his brother and dies of grief. The interest does not reside in the triangular relationship, however, but in the mood of mystery which envelops it and which is evoked through a multitude of symbols, such as a wedding ring dropped into a fountain, doves that fly away from a tower, subterranean pools and grottoes, enveloping shadows, and blood stains that cannot be washed away. In the early 1890s Maeterlinck argued that the most dramatic moments are those silent ones during which the mystery of existence, ordinarily obscured by bustling activity, makes itself felt. After 1896, Maeterlinck revised his view and modified his style to include more straightforward action. The most famous of his later plays is *The Blue Bird* (1908), an allegory about the search for happiness.

In 1896 Lugné-Poë presented Alfred Jarry's (1873–1907) *Ubu Roi*, sometimes called the first absurdist drama. Jarry's play is related to symbolist works in being antirealistic but its moral topsyturvydom more nearly resembles that of the naturalists' *comédies rosses*, although it completely avoids their scientific bias and realistic techniques. *Ubu Roi* shows in all its grotesqueness a world without human decency. Its central figure, Ubu, is violent, stupid, totally devoid of moral scruple; he is the epitome of all that Jarry found inane and ugly in bourgeois society, of all that is monstrous and irrational in man. The action of the play shows how Ubu makes himself king of Poland and keeps his power by killing and torturing all those

Figure 1.14   Jarry's *Ubu Roi* at the Théâtre Antoine, 1908. Gémier directed the play and appeared as Père Ubu. From *Figaro* (16 February 1908).

who oppose him; eventually he is driven from the country but he promises to continue his exploits elsewhere. Jarry wrote two other plays about Ubu, *Ubu Bound* (1900) and *Ubu the Cuckold* (published 1944), but these were not produced during his lifetime. At first Jarry's influence was negligible, but in the 1920s he attracted a following among the surrealists and since World War II his grotesque vision of man has won him a place of honor as a major prophet of the absurdist movement.

The first major phase of the antirealistic movement came to an end in 1897 when Lugné-Poë broke with the symbolists after concluding that most of their plays were immature and that his commitment to a single style of production was too limiting. His decision was influenced by his admiration for Ibsen, whose plays he found unadaptable to the extreme stylization favored by the symbolists.

The Théâtre de l'Oeuvre closed in 1899, but Lugné-Poë was to revive it in 1912 and again after World War I and to continue his work there until 1929. Nevertheless, it is his symbolist productions of the 1890s that constitute his most significant contribution to the theatre. Through tours with his company and articles written about his work, Lugné-Poë influenced almost every departure from realism between 1893 and 1915.

Appia and Craig

At about the time that Lugné-Poë was closing down the Théâtre de l'Oeuvre in 1899, two other men, Appia and Craig, working independently of each other, were beginning to lay the theoretical foundations of modern nonillusionistic theatrical practice. Adolphe Appia (1862–1928), born in Switzerland, first came into contact with the theatre through his musical studies. Deeply impressed by Wagner's music-dramas and theoretical writings, Appia recognized that the usual mounting of the operas did not properly embody Wagner's theories. After years of thought, he published *The Staging of Wagner's Musical Dramas* (1895), *Music and Stage Setting* (1899), and *The Work of Living Art* (1921). In these, he set forth ideas about theatrical production that were eventually accepted almost universally.

Beginning with the assumption that artistic unity is the fundamental goal of theatrical production, Appia sought to analyze failures to achieve it. He concluded that stage presentation involves three conflicting visual elements: the moving three-dimensional actor; the perpendicular scenery; and the horizontal floor. In painted two-dimensional settings he found one of the major causes of disunity and recommended that they be replaced with three-dimensional units (steps, ramps, platforms) that enhance the actor's movement and blend the horizontal floor with the upright scenery. Above all, however, Appia emphasized the role of light in fusing all of the visual elements into a unified whole. Since to him light was

the visual counterpart of music, which changes from moment to moment in response to shifting moods, emotions, and action, Appia wished to orchestrate and manipulate light as carefully as a musical score. Attempts to implement this theory, which require control over the distribution, brightness, and color of light, have led to much of modern stage-lighting practice. Appia also argued that artistic unity requires that one person control all of the elements of production. Thus, his ideas strengthened the role of the director.

In 1906 Appia met Emile Jacques Dalcroze (1865–1960), who, next to Wagner, was to be the greatest influence on Appia's work. Dalcroze was the inven-

Figure 1.15   Design by Adolphe Appia for the sacred forest in Wagner's *Parsifal*, 1896.

tor of "eurythmics," a system under which students were led to experience music kinesthetically by responding physically to the rhythms of musical compositions. Under Dalcroze's influence Appia came to believe that the rhythm embedded in a text provides the key to every gesture and movement to be used on the stage and that the proper mastery of rhythm will unify all the spatial and temporal elements of a production into a satisfying and harmonious whole. Appia worked with Dalcroze on a few productions at Dalcroze's school at Hellerau, and for this school Appia designed the first theatre of modern times to be built without a proscenium arch and with a completely open stage.

In the 1920s Appia began to win his long-delayed recognition. In 1923 he staged *Tristan and Isolde* in Milan and in 1924–1925 two parts of the *Ring* cycle

Figure 1.16   Craig's setting for *Hamlet* at the Moscow Art Theatre, 1912. The screens were supposed to be sufficiently mobile that the appearance of the setting could be changed quickly and without closing the front curtain. Unfortunately they never functioned as envisioned. From *Moscow Art Theatre, 1898–1917*, Moscow (1955).

in Basel. Nevertheless, it was not through practice but through theory that Appia was to exert lasting influence on the modern theatre.

Gordon Craig (1872–1966), son of Ellen Terry and Edward Godwin, began his career as an actor in Irving's company. His first important practical experience as a designer was gained in his mother's company at the Imperial Theatre in London in 1903. An exhibit of his work in 1902 and the publication of his book, *The Art of the Theatre* (1905), created such controversy that within a few years he was well known throughout Europe. In 1904 he designed a play for Brahm in Berlin, in 1906 one for Eleanora Duse in Florence, and in 1912 one for the Moscow Art Theatre. Everywhere controversy followed him. He continued to set forth his provocative and original ideas in *On the Art of the Theatre* (1911), *Towards a New Theatre* (1913), *The Theatre Advancing* (1919), and *The Mask*, a periodical issued sporadically between 1908 and 1929. In 1908 he settled in Florence, where he ran a school for a time. Although Appia had set forth many of the same ideas, it was Craig who publicized them. To many conservative producers, Craig seemed as dangerous "a crank" as Ibsen had in the 1880s.

Craig thought of the theatre as an independent art and argued that the true theatre artist welds action, words, line, color, and rhythm into a product as pure as that of the painter, sculptor, or composer. He acknowledged the kind of theatre in which a craftsman-director, beginning with a literary text, coordinates the work of several other craftsmen, but he sought a higher form in which the master-artist, without the medium of a literary text, would create every part of a wholly autonomous art.

Craig's influence was felt most heavily in design, perhaps because he conceived of the theatre primarily in visual terms. He argued that the public goes to see rather than to hear a play. His own drawings show a marked predilection for right angles and an obsession with parallelism. Their most notable feature, however, is height and the resulting sense of grandeur. Perhaps Craig's favorite project was the

Figure 1.17   Design by Gordon Craig for *Electra*, 1905. From City of Manchester Art Gallery, *Exhibition of Drawings and Models by Edward Gordon Craig* (1912).

blamed the overemphasis upon the spoken word. Similarly, he often blamed starring actors for the low state of the theatre, since they sought to aggrandize themselves and to interject their own conceptions between those of the director and the public. Consequently, he once suggested that ideally the master-artist should use an *Ubermarionette*, a superpuppet without any ego but capable of carrying out all demands. No idea voiced by Craig aroused a greater storm.

Although Appia and Craig arrived at many of the same ideas, there were also important differences. Appia's artist was to be primarily an interpreter of the composer-dramatist's work; Craig's was a full-fledged artist in his own right. Appia assigned a hierarchy to the theatrical elements; Craig refused to do so. Appia thought in terms of successive settings (a different setting for each locale); Craig sought a single setting capable of expressing the spirit of the entire work or of reflecting changes through mobility.

Appia and Craig were often denounced as impractical men who knew little of the workaday theatre and whose ideas were useless in practice. But they championed ideals and goals that practical men of the period could not provide. Together they forced their contemporaries to reconsider the nature of the theatre as an art, its function in society, and its elements (both separately and in combination). They influenced the trend toward simplified decor, three-dimensional settings, plasticity, and directional lighting—toward evocation rather than literal representation. At first highly controversial, their theories were to prevail after World War I.

Strindberg and Freud

The first decade of the twentieth century also brought works of another type that were to be a major influence on modern drama: the nonrealistic plays of the Swedish dramatist, August Strindberg (1849–1912). Strindberg had already established his reputation as a realistic dramatist with *The Father*

mobile setting. Throughout most of his life he experimented with screens, out of which he hoped to create a setting that by invisible means, could move in ways analogous to the actor and to light.

Craig always refused to assign a hierarchy to the theatrical elements and blamed many faults of the past on the dominance of one or another part. Thus, he often denounced the dramatist, upon whom he

(1887) and *Miss Julie* (1888), both of which demonstrate his preoccupation with what he considered to be the elemental and inevitable conflict between men and women. *Miss Julie* especially won high praise for its emphasis upon heredity and environment, its unusual setting (a triangular view of one corner of a kitchen), and its use of pantomimes to replace intermissions. Many critics considered it an excellent exemplar of naturalistic principles.

Powerful as these plays are, they were not to be as influential as those Strindberg wrote after undergoing a bout with insanity during the 1890s. Partially because of his recent experiences and partially under Maeterlinck's influence, Strindberg now began to write "dream plays," of which he said: "The author has tried to imitate the disconnected but seemingly logical form of the dream. Anything may happen; everything is possible and probable. Time and space do not exist. On an insignificant background of reality, imagination designs and embroiders novel patterns, free fancies, absurdities and improvisations. The characters split, double, multiply, vanish, solidify, blur, clarify. But one consciousness reigns above them all—that of the dreamer; and before it there are no secrets, no incongruities, no scruples, no laws." In such plays as *To Damascus* (a trilogy, 1898–1901) and *The Dream Play* (1902) Strindberg reshaped reality according to his own subjective vision. Time and place shift frequently and without regard for logical sequence, the real and the imaginary blend, and the seemingly commonplace is invested with a sense of significance. In these late works Strindberg treats with great compassion alienated man, lost and rootless, seeking meaning in an incomprehensible universe, trying to reconcile the most disparate elements: lust and love, body and spirit, filth and beauty.

From 1907 to 1910 Strindberg was associated with August Falck (1882–1938), an actor and producer, at the Intimate Theatre in Stockholm. Seating only 161, this theatre was intended as a home for Strindberg's plays, and for it he wrote five "chamber plays," of which the best known is *The Ghost Sonata* (1907),

a work which echoes many of the ideas found in *The Dream Play*.

By the time Strindberg died in 1912 he was one of the most famous writers in the world. Although his plays have never been widely popular in the theatre, they have never ceased to be a source of controversy and inspiration. His vision of man as tortured and alienated was to attract many later writers, and his dramatic devices were to show others how psychological states and spiritual intuitions might be externalized. As the first dramatist to make extensive use of the unconscious, he was to be a major influence on subsequent playwrights.

Strindberg's acceptance was probably aided by widespread interest in the psychoanalytic theories of Sigmund Freud (1856–1939), who in such books as *The Interpretation of Dreams* (1900) and *Three Contributions to the Theory of Sex* (1905) sought to analyze the structure of the mind, to describe its functionings, and to suggest means for dealing with abnormal behavior. Freud's explanation of human behavior, with its emphasis upon the unconscious mind, dreams as a key to understanding suppressed desires, and the human propensity for telescoping experience, gave strong authority for Strindberg's dramaturgy. Furthermore, just as Comte, Zola, and others had placed primary emphasis upon social environment as a determinant of human behavior, Freud turned attention toward equally powerful psychological causes. His interest in aggression and sexual drives as keys to human behavior also did much to break down taboos about suitable subjects for drama.

Freud's pervasive influence on modern drama is also explained in part by his quasi-scientific explanation of behavior that in idealist drama had been attributed to "the mystery of fate," "intuition," or other equally vague and subjective concepts. By locating the source within the human mind, Freud made it possible for realistic dramatists to portray behavior previously considered nonrealistic or irrational because it had no verifiable basis. Freud's conception of reality which intermingles the rational and irrational, the conscious and unconscious, the objective and subjective, the real and the fantastic, was to break down many of the barriers between realistic and nonrealistic drama.

Idealist Theatre and Drama in Germany

In Germany, a number of dramatists, most notably Hauptmann and Sudermann, eventually were to write alternately in realistic and nonrealistic styles. But others, among them Hofmannsthal and Wedekind, fall more clearly into the antirealist camp. Hugo von Hofmannsthal (1874–1929) is usually considered an exponent of neo-romanticism, a movement which in Germany roughly parallels symbolism in France. His early plays are mostly short, as in *The Fool and Death* (1893) and *The Adventurer and the Singing Girl* (1899), and written in a verse that led many critics to praise him as the finest poet since Goethe. Around 1900 he underwent a crisis during which he came to believe that words are meaningless. Although he moved beyond this belief, he thereafter reworked existing materials, as in *Elektra* (1903), *Everyman* (1912), and *The Great World Theatre* (1922), or wrote opera librettos, such as *Die Rosenkavalier* (1911) and *Ariadne on Naxos* (1912), in collaboration with Richard Strauss. Some of his plays continue to be mainstays of the Salzburg Festival.

Franz Wedekind (1864–1918) is more nearly related to Strindberg than to the French symbolists. After working as a journalist, publicist, and actor, Wedekind toured Germany in a repertory of his own plays, which were never widely appreciated during his lifetime. Wedekind's first important play, *Spring's Awakening* (1891), is the story of two adolescents' struggle with sexual awareness. One commits suicide, and the other is saved from a similar fate only by the mysterious "Man with the Mask." The play is interesting in part because of its intermingling of naturalism and symbolism, of brutal frankness and lyri-

cal expression. Wedekind's interest in sexual themes continued in *Earth Spirit* (1895) and *Pandora's Box* (1904), both treating the same protagonist, Lulu, who cannot distinguish between lust and love; in the first play Lulu prospers, but in the second she gradually descends until she is murdered by Jack the Ripper. Many of Wedekind's other plays also show his preoccupation with sex, but in such late works as *Samson* (1914) and *Herakles* (1917) the treatment sometimes borders on lunacy. Wedekind's plays are of such uneven quality that it is difficult to judge them fairly. But after 1900 his reputation grew steadily and he exerted considerable influence on the expressionists, who were attracted both by his rebellion against conventional values and by his experiments with stylistic elements.

After 1900 German producers also came to be increasingly interested in nonrealistic staging. Some of the most important innovations were made at the Munich Art Theatre, founded in 1907 and headed by

Figure 1.18   Design by Julius Diez for Shakespeare's *Twelfth Night* at the Munich Art Theatre, 1908. Director Albert Heine. Courtesy Theatermuseum, Munich.

George Fuchs (1868–1949), a critic and theorist, with Fritz Erler (1868–1940) as designer. In two books, *The Theatre of the Future* (1905) and *Revolution in the Theatre* (1909) Fuchs expressed the need for a theatre to meet the needs of modern man and declared pictorial illusionism outmoded. Under the slogan "retheatricalize the theatre," he sought to unite all the arts in a new kind of expression.

For the project, Max Littmann (1862–1931) designed a theatre with an auditorium and sunken orchestra pit similar to those at Bayreuth. The stage, however, differed markedly from that at Bayreuth. The acting area could be extended into the auditorum by covering over the orchestra pit, while an adjustable inner proscenium, containing a door at stage level and a balcony above, made it possible to

Figure 1.19   Design by K. Walser for Max Reinhardt's production of Wedekind's *Spring's Awakening* at the Kammerspiele, Berlin, 1906. This design is for Act III, scene 6. Courtesy the Max Reinhardt Archive, State University of New York, Binghamton.

adjust the size of the stage opening. The stage floor was broken into sections, each of which was mounted on an elevator, permitting the floor to be arranged into levels. The stage was backed by four cycloramas, each of a different color, which could be changed electrically.

The most contoversial aspect of the productions was the acting, which typically was confined to the plane outlined by the inner proscenium, while the area back of this plane was reserved for scenery or for crowd scenes. The aim was to keep the performer close to the audience so as to establish a sense of community and to emphasize his plasticity by framing him against a simplified background.

Erler sometimes used the adjustable proscenium as the principal scenic element; sometimes he used it in combination with other pieces, but often he employed it merely as a frame for the area behind it. His effects were achieved primarily with simple forms, painted drops, and the play of colored light.

Like Appia and Craig, Fuchs believed that rhythm fuses all the elements of production. Unlike them, however, he placed the actor in front of the setting rather than within it and so tended to mute the three-dimensionality they so avidly sought. Still, as the work of the Munich Art Theatre became widely known, Fuchs's theories reenforced those of Appia and Craig and helped to establish the trend toward stylization in all theatrical elements.

Ultimately, virtually all of the ideas and innovations—whether realistic or idealistic—introduced between 1875 and 1900 came together in the work of Max Reinhardt (1873–1943). On stage as an actor from the age of nineteen, Reinhardt was brought to the Deutsches Theater by Otto Brahm in 1894. While acting with Brahm's troupe, Reinhardt experimented with staging at a cabaret and developed a strong appreciation for its intimate atmosphere. His

first experience as a producer was gained between 1902 and 1905 at the Kleines Theater, where he presented nearly fifty plays drawn from many countries and styles. His major work began in 1905, when he succeeded Brahm as director of the Deutsches Theater. In 1906 he opened the Kammerspiele, a small theatre, in conjunction with the larger house. The flexibility in programming and style of production

Figure 1.20   Design by Ernst Stern for Reinhardt's production of Friedrich Freska's pantomime *Sumurun*, at the Kammerspiele, Berlin, 1910. Courtesy Harvard Theatre Collection.

which this arrangement permitted was to influence almost all state theatres in Germany and eventually the educational theatre in America.

Reinhardt's influence came in large part through his diversity. Unlike major producers who preceded him, almost all of whom had used the same style for every play they presented, Reinhardt believed that each play requires a different style. His eclecticism, therefore, reconciled many conflicting movements, for with him each style had its uses. With Reinhardt,

Figure 1.21   John Martin-Harvey in the title role of Sophocles' *Oedipus Rex* as staged by Max Reinhardt at Covent Garden, London, 1912. Courtesy the Max Reinhardt Archive, State University of New York, Binghamton.

each new production became a problem to be solved, not through the employment of proven formulas but through clues found within the work itself. Furthermore, his conception of theatrical style included the physical arrangement of the theatre and the spatial relationship of the audience to the performers. In his view, some plays required intimate surroundings, others large spaces; some needed a proscenium, others an open platform. For example, he staged *Oedipus Rex* in a circus, because this arrangement seemed most appropriate to the spirit of Greek tragedy. He was to extend such experiments with styles of production and theatre architecture after World War I.

Reinhardt believed that the director must control every element of production. For each play he prepared a *Regiebuch* (or promptbook) in which he recorded each detail of movement, setting, properties, sound, lighting, and costume. Some critics charge that Reinhardt's actors were mere puppets that he manipulated, while others maintain that Reinhardt was so sensitive that he knew exactly how to help each performer. In any case, Reinhardt worked closely with his actors to achieve performances that became world-famous for their stylistic excellence. Among his actors, the best known were Alexander Moissi (1880–1935), noted especially for his Shakespearean and Greek roles; Max Pallenberg (1859–1934), a versatile comic actor; Albert Bassermann (1867–1952), famous for his performances in Ibsen's plays and later as an actor in U. S. films; Werner Krauss (1884–1959); and Emil Jannings (1887–1950).

Reinhardt also worked closely with his scene designers, notably Ernst Stern (1876–1954), Alfred Roller (1864–1935), Oscar Strnad (1879–1935), and Emil Orlik (1879–1932). Often his productions centered around a motif, a ruling idea, or the staging conventions of a past period; they ranged through every style from naturalism to extreme stylization. Reinhardt has been accused of debasing the ideas of others, but he did more than anyone to make new movements and techniques acceptable to the general public.

The Nonrealistic Theatre in England

In England, few playwrights departed markedly from the realistic mode. Oscar Wilde (1856–1900), a member of the "Art-for-Art's Sake" or "Aesthetic" movement which paralleled French symbolism, rejected the idea that drama should be utilitarian or that the popular audience is a suitable judge of merit. He suggested that we should seek to turn life into a work of art rather than to make art imitate life. Nevertheless, of Wilde's plays only *Salomé* (1893), resembles French symbolist drama, although his phenomenally popular comedy, *The Importance of Being Earnest* (1895), illustrates his general outlook through its parody of the stock devices of comedy and its epigrams which puncture the conventional sentiments of his time. On the surface, *Lady Windermere's Fan* (1892), *A Woman of No Importance* (1893), and *An Ideal Husband* (1895) appear to be much like Pinero's social dramas, but a closer examination will show that Wilde deliberately lets the machinery of his plots show until the plays become near-parodies.

J. M. Barrie (1860–1937), after beginning as a journalist and novelist, turned to drama in 1892 and wrote regularly for the stage until 1936. Through all of his work shines an optimistic, whimsical view of life in which humor is infused with sentiment. His most successful play is *Peter Pan* (1904), a sentimental fantasy which romanticizes childhood and the child's view of reality. Other popular works by him include *The Admirable Crichton* (1902), *What Every Woman Knows* (1908), and *Dear Brutus* (1917).

While few English plays departed from the realistic mode, several innovations in staging were to lead away from illusionism. Many of these stemmed from interest in staging Shakespeare's works. An early step toward more simplified staging was taken by Frank Benson (1858–1939), who, after acting with Irving, founded his own troupe in 1883 and continued to tour the provinces in a Shakespearean repertory until 1933. Benson produced almost all of the plays

Figure 1.22 J. M. Barrie's *Peter Pan*, the original production at the Duke of York's Theatre, 1904. Seen here is the pirate's ship. Courtesy Theatre Museum, Victoria and Albert Museum.

seen at the annual festival at Stratford-on-Avon (instituted in 1879) between 1886 and 1913, and after 1900 gave a few performances in London each year. Benson began by producing plays in the style of Irving, but by 1900 he had reduced the scenic background to a few stock settings and was placing primary emphasis upon the actors. Although his solution was at best a compromise, Benson helped to make simplified staging acceptable to the public.

A more drastic reform was sought by William Poel (1852–1934). After his debut as an actor in 1876, Poel worked for Benson and others before undertaking those experiments with staging Shakespeare's plays for which he is now remembered. In this work, Poel had, between 1894 and 1905, the support of the Elizabethan Stage Society, of which he was the guiding spirit.

Figure 1.23   Poel's production of *Measure for Measure* in 1893. Shown here is Act II, scene 2. Note the costumed spectators on either side of the stage. Courtesy Theatre Museum, Victoria and Albert Museum.

In staging Elizabethan drama, Poel did not always use the same solution but he is now considered noteworthy almost entirely because of his attempts to reconstruct the Elizabethan public stage. He also popularized several conventions: dressing the actors in Elizabethan garments to reflect Shakespeare's own day rather than the historical epoch of the dramatic action; using costumed pages to draw the curtains of the inner stage and to arrange properties and furniture; and employing an on-stage audience to emphasize the audience-actor relationships of the Elizabethan era. But, above all, Poel desired continuity of action and lively pace. Although his productions did not generate much enthusiasm, they demonstrated the advantages of unbroken playing and of concentrating attention upon text and performers. Poel's approach represents another form of antiquarianism, one which sought to substitute the theatrical conditions of a past era for historical accuracy in the older

sense. It is typical of similar approaches then being tried in several countries. At the Royal Court Theatre in Munich in 1889, Karl von Perfall and Jocza Savits had attempted to approximate the Elizabethan plan on a picture-frame stage by using a deep apron behind which a playing space was enclosed by an architectural facade with several doors and at center back a curtained inner stage where furniture and realistic scenic pieces could be set and revealed as needed. This and a similar attempt made in Munich in 1909–1910 by Julius Klein and Eugene Kilian differed little from the solution used in 1840 by Immermann. In a somewhat similar vein, Antoine staged a number of seventeenth-century French plays at the Odéon between 1907 and 1910 for which he sought to reproduce the playing conditions and conventions of the original productions.

Many of the earlier experiments in staging Shakespeare's plays were synthesized by Granville Barker in productions at the Savoy Theatre in London between 1912 and 1914 of *A Winter's Tale*, *Twelfth Night*, and *A Midsummer Night's Dream*. Barker, who had worked for Poel before going to the Court Theatre, amalgamated Poel's continuous staging with the visual simplicity advocated by Craig and others. He remodeled the Savoy Theatre by adding an apron and doors forward of the proscenium. Back of the proscenium the stage was divided into a main acting area and a modified inner stage, raised a few steps and equipped with curtains. This division of the stage into three parts allowed a continuous flow of action and eliminated the extensive cutting and rearrangement of the scripts usual in illusionistic staging. Barker employed such artists as Norman Wilkinson (1882–1934) and Albert Rutherston (1884–1953) to design scenery and costumes. Settings were composed primarily of painted, draped curtains, while the costumes were of no certain period. Such bright colors as magenta, scarlet, and lemon replaced the somber tones usual in Shakespearean productions. The forest of *A Midsummer Night's Dream* (presented in 1914) contained no three-dimensional trees; rather, it was suggested by painted drapery.

Figure 1.24   Harley Granville Barker's production of *A Midsummer Night's Dream* at the Savoy Theatre, London, 1914. Note that the forest is represented by trees painted on draperies and that Titania's bower is formed of gauze hanging from a wreath. Courtesy Theatre Museum, Victoria and Albert Museum.

Similarly, Titania's bower was made of gauze suspended from a crown of flowers. The fairies were gilded and directed to move like marionettes in order to set them off from the mortals. Although many conservative critics were deeply offended by Barker's productions, his approach set the tone for work that would be done after the war.

The Irish Renaissance

Around 1900 Ireland began to assert its artistic independence from England. From the time of Henry VIII onward, England had ruled Ireland, although it had never been able to suppress Roman Catholicism or to command the full loyalty of the people. As elsewhere in Europe, in Ireland nationalistic sentiment became especially strong during the nineteenth century, and as a result its Gaelic and Celtic heritage assumed increasing importance. This interest eventually made its way into the theatre.

Although Dublin had been one of the major English theatrical centers since the seventeenth century, no attempts were made to create an indigenous Irish drama until the 1890s. The first significant step was taken in 1898, when the Irish Literary Society was established in Dublin. Between 1899 and 1902, this group produced seven short plays and demonstrated the possibility of creating an Irish theatre. The leaders of the Society were William Butler Yeats (1865–1939), Lady Augusta Gregory (1863–1935), George Moore (1853–1933), and Edward Martyn (1859–1923).

Meantime, another organization, the Ormond Dramatic Society, headed by W. G. Fay (1872–1947) and Frank Fay (1870–1931), was also presenting plays with an Irish flavor and eventually the two amalgamated to form the Irish National Theatre Society. An appearance by the new group in London in 1903 won the support of Miss A. E. F. Horniman, who acquired a building for the company and remodelled it into the Abbey Theatre, opened in late 1904. Until 1910 Miss Horniman also provided the troupe with a subsidy.

Originally the group gave only three performances a month, but after it obtained a permanent home it began to present a different play each week. Not until 1908, however, was it able to pay royalties or actors' salaries. Nevertheless, its finest achievements came before 1910, after which many of its best authors and actors began to defect.

Of the Abbey's playwrights, three—Yeats, Lady Gregory and Synge—were most important. Yeats wrote about thirty plays between 1892 and 1938. Much of his early work resembled that of the French symbolists, many of whom he had known in Paris. Of

Figure 1.25   William Butler Yeats's *The Hour Glass*. Design by Gordon Craig. From Yeats, *Plays for an Irish Theatre* (1911).

the early plays, the best known is probably *Cathleen ni Houlihan* (1902), in which the spirit of Ireland, incredibly old but forever lovely, is embodied in the figure of an old woman who is transformed into a young girl. Around 1910 Yeats ceased to write specifically for the Abbey and soon afterwards came under the influence of Japanese Noh drama. Thereafter he made increasing use of masks, dance, music, and chant. Among the late works, one of the best is *At the Hawk's Well* (1917), in which a chorus describes the action as two characters await the appearance of waters that will confer immortality. Yeats disliked realistic drama and sought to arouse a community of feeling and ideals among spectators through poetic plays based on Celtic myth or legend.

From the first there were two conflicting styles at the Abbey: the poetic-mythic (best represented by Yeats) and the realistic-domestic (best represented by

Lady Gregory). Most of Lady Gregory's dramatic writing was done between 1902 and 1912, although she did not cease altogether until 1926. She was most at home in one-act peasant comedies, such as *The Spreading of the News* (1904). But she also virtually invented the Irish folk-history play based primarily on oral tradition, as in *Kincora* (1905). Only rarely did she venture into the fully serious realm, as in *The Gaol Gate* (1906). Though she does not rank in critical stature with Yeats, she was far more successful than he was with audiences, perhaps because she wrote about familiar subjects and in a familiar style.

It remained for John Millington Synge (1871–1909) to fuse the two styles represented by Yeats and Lady Gregory, for he made the mythic seem familiar, raised the familiar to the level of myth, and wrote in a lilting, poetic prose fashioned from speech familiar to the Irish people. But Synge was also the most controversial of the Abbey's writers. *In the Shadow of the Glen* (1903) was denounced as a slander on Irish womanhood because it showed a wife happily leaving home to go away with a tramp after her husband has ordered her from the house. Here as in others of his plays Synge is concerned with the conflict between a repressive life and the urge toward joy and freedom. *The Playboy of the Western World* (1907) aroused even greater wrath, for its story, in which a young man becomes a village hero after boasting of killing his father, was considered an insult to the national character. Wherever it played riots occurred. Not all of Synge's plays were controversial. Many critics consider *Riders to the Sea* (1904) to be the finest short play in the English language. In it Maurya loses the last of her six sons to the sea, but she achieves a new peace, since fate can do no more to her. Although Synge is now considered the finest Irish dramatist of his day, at the time his plays did much to create dissension in the company and motivated many actors and playwrights to desert the Abbey. Consequently, although in the 1920s the Abbey was to recapture some of its former glory with the plays of Sean O'Casey, its major contribution had been made by 1915.

Russian Idealism

In Russia, the revolts against realism were centered at first around *The World of Art*, a periodical begun in 1898 by Sergei Diaghilev (1872–1929). In addition to keeping Russians abreast of events in the artistic centers of Europe, the magazine sought to encourage Russian artists and composers. Diaghilev's major contribution, however, was to stem from ballet. After Petipa retired, Prince Sergei Volkonsky, Director of the Imperial Theatres, and Mikhail Fokine (1880–1942), choreographer at the Mariinsky Theatre, introduced several innovations. Fokine disliked the long narrative works that Petipa had favored, and sought more limited subjects that offered greater opportunity for novel choreographic design.

Using music by such composers as Igor Stravinsky, he emphasized complex rhythms and an overall harmony of mood.

Meanwhile, Diaghilev had been arranging exchanges of art with other countries, and in 1909 he took opera and ballet companies, including Fokine's, to Paris for a six-week season. The ecstatic response led Diaghilev to form his Ballets Russes, which then toured throughout Europe. Everywhere they were praised both for their dancing and for their scenic design. When the Revolution came, many members of the company remained in the West.

The scenic style of the Ballets Russes did not depend upon any new technical devices, for it relied upon painted wings and drops. Nevertheless, it departed markedly from illusionism, since line, color, and decorative motifs were considerably stylized to reflect moods and themes rather than specific periods or places. Costumes also emphasized exaggerated line, color, and mass. Thus, although the artists drew on familiar forms and decorative motifs,

Figure 1.26   Leon Bakst's design for the Ballets Russes' *Tamar*, 1912. From the souvenir program.

they created a sense of exoticism and fantasy through stylization. The influence upon European scenic art of the Ballets Russes' designers—among them Leon Bakst, Alexandre Benois, Alexander Golovin, Mstislav Dobuzhinsky, and Natalie Gontcharova—is incalculable. Bakst and Benois later settled in Paris and continued to work there.

During the 1890s the symbolist ideal began to be expounded in Russia but not until about 1905 did it make a deep impression. From that time until 1917 it was to be the major literary mode. Shortly after 1900 Stanislavsky became interested in Maeterlinck and in 1904–1905 presented a bill of his short plays. This experience helped to convince Stanislavsky that his company needed to enlarge its approach, and in 1905 he established a studio to experiment with nonrealistic styles. To supervise the work, Stanislavsky employed Vsevelod Meyerhold (1874–1940), a former member of the Moscow Art Theatre who had left in 1902 to form his own troupe. A number of productions were planned for the new studio, but Meyerhold's subordination of the actors to his directorial concepts displeased Stanislavsky so much that he discontinued the experiment.

Nevertheless, the Moscow Art Theatre went on to produce other nonrealistic works, including Maeterlinck's *The Blue Bird* in 1908 and *Hamlet* in 1912, the latter with scenery by Gordon Craig. It also encouraged Leonid Andreyev (1871–1919), Russia's foremost nonrealistic dramatist. After beginning in the realistic mode, Andreyev was converted to symbolism in 1907, the year in which he wrote his most famous play, *The Life of Man*, an allegory which seeks to summarize the human experience. Stanislavsky staged it against black curtains, using rope to outline windows, doors, and walls, and with considerable stylization in acting. Andreyev later turned to writing in a more concrete style, although *He Who Gets Slapped* (1915), a drama with a circus background, demonstrates his continuing penchant for allegory.

In 1911 the Moscow Art Theatre established the First Studio, under the direction of Leopold Sullerzhitsky (1872–1916), primarily to give training in the Stanislavsky system, but also to encourage nonrealistic approaches. Here a number of future leaders, notably Richard Boleslavsky, Mikhail Chekhov, and Eugene Vakhtangov, received their training. But, if Stanislavsky experimented with nonrealistic approaches, any marked departure from realism was ultimately unacceptable to him since all tended to "dematerialize" the actor.

The most important early experiments with nonrealistic staging in Russia were undertaken in the company maintained by Vera Kommissarzhevskaya (1864–1910). On the stage from 1891, she attracted an enormous following and opened her own theatre in St. Petersburg in 1904. Interested in new approaches, she employed Meyerhold when he left Stanislavsky. For his production of Ibsen's *Hedda Gabler*, Meyerhold assigned each character a costume of distinctive color and devoid of realistic detail. Furthermore, each character was restricted to a limited number of sculpturesque gestures and a pose to which he always returned. The setting and furniture were greenish-blue and white. Ibsen's stage directions were completely ignored. For Wedekind's *Spring's Awakening*, Meyerhold placed everything to be used in the production on stage at once and spotlighted each area as needed. When audiences did not respond favorably to these and other experiments, perhaps because Meyerhold did not exploit the considerable talents of Kommissarzhevskaya, Meyerhold was asked to leave. Immediately afterward he was employed by the Director of Imperial Theatres. With the state troupes he continued his experiments. When he staged Molière's *Don Juan* at the Alexandrinsky Theatre in 1910, he removed the front curtain and footlights, extended the forestage into the auditorium, kept the house lights on throughout the performance, used stagehands to change properties and scenery, and set the actors' dancing movements to Lully's music. After the enormous success of this production, he went on to stage several operas, among them Wagner's *Tristan and Isolde*.

Between 1910 and 1914 Meyerhold also established studios where he experimented with circus and *commedia dell'arte* techniques. In one studio the performers mingled with the audience and converted the entire auditorium into an acting area. Actors worked out their own scripts and experimented with geometrically patterned movement, improvisation, and rhythm. Meyerhold also became interested in Oriental theatre and began to turn the scenic background into a mere apparatus for acting—a collection of steps and levels. He was to continue and extend his work after the Revolution. In these early years Meyerhold clearly believed that the director is the major creative force in the theatre and that a script is merely material to be molded and reworked as the director wishes. His was the most persistent exploration of the possibilities and limitations of the theatre as a medium of expression to be found anywhere at that time.

At Kommissarzhevskaya's theatre Meyerhold was succeeded by Nikolai Evreinov (1879–1953). Although equally opposed to realism, Evreinov sought to enlarge the actor's place in the theatre by emphasizing flamboyance, theatricality, and the grotesque. Evreinov is probably most famous for his "monodramas," the basic principle of which was first set forth in his "Apology for Theatricality" in 1908. He suggested that man's inborn theatrical instinct leads him into "role playing" and makes him seek to transform reality into something better. Consequently, he argued, the theatre should not imitate life, but life should seek to become like theatre at its best. In his "monodramas," he aimed to help the audience achieve its desires by making it the alter-ego of the protagonist. Through identification, the audience supposedly participated directly in the experience and was led to perceptions of the higher reality. In staging the monodramas, Evreinov sought to treat everything as seen through the mind of the protagonist. Lighting, sound, and scenery reflected the character's changing moods and emotions. The most famous of the monodramas was *The Theatre of the Soul* (1912). Although never very popular, Evreinov's monodramas contributed to expressionism and to motion picture techniques. Evreinov considered illusionism mistaken and in several ways sought to provide examples of more profitable alternatives: he

staged two seasons of works from the Middle Ages and the Spanish Golden Age; he conducted experiments with *commedia dell'arte*; and he promoted cabaret theatre.

Theodore Kommisarzhevsky (1874–1954) worked with his sister, Evreinov, and others before opening his own theatre in 1910. Probably the most balanced Russian producer, he sought to remain faithful to each playwright's intention, an attempt which led to a thoroughgoing eclecticism. His eclecticism extended further than that of Reinhardt, however, for he adopted a working method that might be called "internal eclecticism." Rather than choosing a historical period or single style for a play and then staying consistently within it, Kommissarzhevsky believed that each character and action has its own qualities for which the director must find some meaningful visual metaphor that will set up the right associations for contemporary audiences. Thus, his productions often combined elements from many periods and styles. Kommissarzhevsky was associated with numerous theatres between 1910 and 1919 (when he emigrated to the West); at one time he was head of four theatres and a training school. He later was to continue his work in France, England, and America.

Alexander Tairov (1885–1950) worked for a number of producers before opening his own theatre, the Kamerny (or Chamber) Theatre in Moscow in 1914. Tairov argued that there is no relationship between art and life and that the theatre must be viewed as analogous to the sacred dances of an ancient temple. Like Meyerhold, he viewed the text as an excuse for creativity, although he objected to Meyerhold's suppression of the actor, who, according to Tairov, is the basic creative force in the theatre. Because he was concerned with rhythmical movement, Tairov's settings were essentially architectural, being composed primarily of sculptural elements, steps, and levels. Productions were approached as if they were musical compositions; speech was a compromise between declamation and song, and movement always tended toward dance. The effect was nearer to ritual than to the usual dramatic performance. By the time

Figure 1.27 Tairov's production of Wilde's *Salomé* at the Kamerny Theatre, 1917. Costumes and setting by Alexandra Ekster. Each costume combined materials of varying color and texture to create the effect of figures taken from stained glass windows.

of the Revolution, Tairov had staged fourteen plays drawn from a wide variety of countries and dramatic types. Most productions featured his wife, Alice Koonen, his ideal interpreter. Tairov was to continue his work after the Revolution.

By 1917, Russian experimenters had introduced techniques far removed from those employed by Stanislavsky in 1898. Some methods were as determinedly nonrealistic as have ever been devised. One of the least advanced countries of Europe at the end of the nineteenth century, Russia had witnessed some of the most daring theatrical experiments, although, with the exceptions of the Ballets Russes and the Moscow Art Theatre, the work had made little impact outside its borders.

The Revival of Idealism in France

After the closing of the Théâtre de l'Oeuvre in 1899, Paris settled once more into its somewhat complacent conviction that it was the artistic capital of Europe. Antoine's productions became the standard, and nonrealistic experiments were few and sporadic. Thus, the appearance of the Ballets Russes in 1909 came almost as a revelation. A new wave of experimentation was given further impetus by the publication in 1910 of *Modern Theatre Art* by Jacques Rouché (1862–1957). After describing the work of Fuchs, Erler, and Reinhardt in Germany, of Meyerhold, Stanislavsky, and Kommissarzhevskaya in Russia, and the theories of Appia and Craig, Rouché went on to call for similar experiments in France. Not only was his book widely read and discussed, Rouché himself set out to implement his ideas at the Théâtre des Arts between 1910 and 1913. Rouché did not aim at extreme stylization, but sought a simplicity in which color and line characterize a milieu and mood without calling attention to themselves. He found his ideal designer in Maxime Dethomas (1867–1929). Rouché was the first French producer to be truly eclectic. He went on to become director of the Opéra, where between 1914 and 1936 he renovated the repertory and brought to it a new generation of scene designers.

Rouché's work had important consequences. Lugné-Poë revived the Théâtre de l'Oeuvre, where he presented a series of plays with designs by Jean Variot, who reenforced Rouché's influence. More important, Rouché inspired Jacques Copeau (1879–1949) to open his own theatre. A dramatic critic, Copeau gained his first practical experience at the Théâtre des Arts when his adaptation of *The Brothers Karamazov* was produced there in 1911. Copeau was convinced that Rouché's suggested reforms put too much emphasis upon visual elements and that no significant progress could come except through the drama itself.

In 1913 Copeau published a manifesto for a new theatre. In it, he adopted a position almost opposite to that of Meyerhold and Tairov, for he argued that the director's primary task is the faithful translation of the dramatist's script into a "poetry of the theatre." Furthermore, he stated that the actor, as the "living

Figure 1.28   *Hamlet* at the Theatre de l'Oeuvre, 1913. Directed by Lugné-Poë and Gémier. Setting by Jean Variot. The structure in the foreground remained throughout, and set pieces were changed behind the central opening. From *Le Théâtre* (1913).

Figure 1.29   Scene from Copeau's adaptation of Dostoyevsky's *The Brothers Karamazov* at Rouche's Théâtre des Arts, 1911. At center Charles Dullin is seen as Smerdiakov. Setting by Maxime Dethomas. From *Le Théâtre* (1911).

presence" of the author, is the only essential element of theatrical production, and that a rejuvenation of the drama depends upon a return to the bare platform stage.

Copeau assembled a company of ten actors, including Louis Jouvet, Charles Dullin, Suzanne Bing, Romain Bouquet, and Valentine Tessier, all of whom were to be significant in the postwar theatre, and retired to the country to perfect his first productions. Meanwhile, with the assistance of Francis Jourdain, Copeau converted a small hall into the Théâtre du Vieux Colombier, seating only 400. It had a forestage forward of an inner proscenium, but no machinery except for a set of curtains and asbestos hangings which could be moved on rods to effect rapid changes of locale. To these curtains were added only the most essential furniture and set pieces. In 1913–1914, before the war forced him to stop, Copeau presented fifteen plays, including works by Shakespeare, Molière, Heywood, Claudel,

and others. In 1917 Copeau was asked to revive the troupe and take it to New York. There between 1917 and 1919 he presented plays for U. S. audiences before returning to Paris to reopen his theatre. It is impossible to overrate the importance of the Théâtre du Vieux Colombier, for with its formation the leadership of the French theatre passed from Antoine to Copeau, who was to dominate the postwar theatre in France.

The Theatre in Italy and Spain, 1875–1915

Between 1875 and 1915, both Italy and Spain were more emulative than innovative. Italy's major

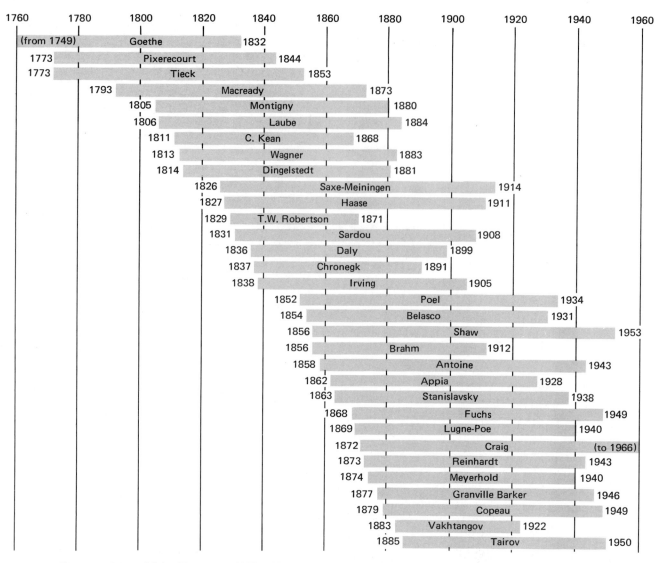

Figure 1.30   Major Directors, 1800–1920.

creative energies continued to be poured into opera. In drama, realism arrived first in the works of Paolo Ferrari (1822–1889), a writer in the vein of Dumas *fils*, and then through the "Verist" (or naturalistic) school. Neo-romanticism found its major exponent in Gabriele D'Annunzio (1863–1938), who, under the influence of Maeterlinck, wrote such plays as *The Dead City* (1898), *La Gioconda* (1898), and *Francesca da Rimini* (1902).

The strong Italian acting tradition was continued by Eleanora Duse (1859–1924). On the stage from the age of four, she became Rossi's leading lady in

1879. After touring South America in 1885, she formed her own company and played throughout the world. She retired in 1909, but returned to the stage in 1921 and died in Pittsburgh while on tour. Duse played an extremely wide range of roles, many of them favorites of Bernhardt, with whose flamboyance her quiet style contrasted sharply. Noted for subtlety, she used simple means to convey complex conceptions. She scorned makeup and prided herself on her ability to make the physical adjustments required by each role unaided by external means. To many discerning critics, she was the greatest of modern actresses.

In Spain, the realistic drama found its first important exponent in José Echegaray (1848–1927), notably in *The Son of Don Juan* (1892), patterned on Ibsen's *Ghosts*, and *The Great Galeoto* (1881), a play about the power of gossip to ruin lives. After the war of 1898 had stripped Spain of her last shreds of glory, a new movement, "the Generation of '98," sought to revitalize literature. The most famous of the new writers was Jacinto Benavente (1866–1954), a versatile dramatist who composed nearly 300 works ranging through every style and form. Of his realistic plays, the best is probably *The Passion Flower* (1913), the story of a man's love for his stepdaughter, while of the nonrealistic works *The Bonds of Interest* (1907), a philosophical work using *commedia dell'arte* conventions, is the best known.

The modern movement in Spain was helped considerably by the Teatro Intim, founded in imitation of the "independent theatres" of Europe by Adria Gual (1872–1932) in 1898 at Barcelona. Here a cross section of drama from Aeschylus to the present was offered for more than thirty years. With his experiments in production styles, Gual brought many of the new trends to Spain.

Theatre in the United States, 1895–1915

The new trends made little impact on the American theatre prior to 1915. By 1895, the traveling road show had become the usual source of theatrical entertainment in the United States. While a few resident troupes remained, the long-run hit had become the goal, and New York was virtually the only theatrical center. These conditions brought many new problems. Perhaps the most obvious difficulties were those connected with booking. The manager of a local theatre now had to go to New York to arrange a season of attractions. If he wished

Figure 1.31   Eleanora Duse in the title role of D'Annunzio's *Francesca da Rimini* at the Teatro Constanzi, Rome, 1902. From *Le Théâtre* (1902).

to schedule a forty-week season, he often had to deal with forty different producers, each of whom was negotiating with many other local managers. Thus, booking was difficult and haphazard and, because producers often defaulted on their agreements, local theatres were frequently faced with sudden cancellations. To remedy these ills, new approaches evolved. Theatres in a restricted area joined together to arrange bookings, and agents began to serve as middlemen between managers and producers.

In this confusion, a small group of men saw the possibility of gaining control of the American theatre. In 1896 Sam Nixon and Fred Zimmerman of Philadelphia, Charles Frohman, Al Hayman, Marc Klaw, and Abraham Erlanger of New York formed the "Theatrical Syndicate." Of these men, only Frohman was directly involved in theatrical production, the others being booking agents or theatre owners. The new organization began by offering a full season of stellar attractions, on the condition that local managers book exclusively through the Syndicate. This offer was welcomed by many managers, for it permitted them to deal with a single agent and to obtain outstanding productions. Managers who refused to deal with the Syndicate were systematically eliminated through simple, if ruthless, maneuvers. The Syndicate did not seek to gain direct control over all theatres in the country; rather, it concentrated on key routes between large cities, for unless productions could play along the way, touring was financially impossible. Where it could not gain control over key theatres, the Syndicate built rival houses and booked into them the finest productions at reduced prices until the competing theatres were bankrupt. New York producers who refused to cooperate were denied bookings and many actors were "blackballed," since the Syndicate would not send on tour any production in which they appeared. By 1900, the Syndicate was in effective control of the American theatre. Now in a position to influence the choice of plays, it refused to accept works not likely to appeal to a mass audience and favored productions that featured stars with large personal follow-

ings. As a result, between 1900 and 1915, the American theatre became largely a commercial venture.

Of the Syndicate members, Charles Frohman (1854–1915) was by far the most important, since he was the only one directly involved in theatrical production. Working his way up from program seller to business manager and agent, Frohman had entered management in 1889. In 1893 he opened the Empire Theatre in New York, where he maintained a fine stock company for many years. In 1896, he extended his interests to London and later controlled five theatres there. At the height of his power he employed some 10,000 persons. As an entrepreneur, Frohman was guided by two convictions: public taste is infallible, and stars are necessary to attract audiences. Thus, he sought to provide the mass public with works that would please, and he launched many new stars.

Despite the Syndicate's strength, it did not go un-

Figure 1.32   Mrs. Fiske and Holbrook Blinn in Edward Sheldon's *Salvation Nell*, 1908. Courtesy Hoblitzelle Theatre Arts Collection, University of Texas, Austin.

opposed. James A. Herne, Mr. and Mrs. Harrison G. Fiske, James O'Neill, David Belasco, and others held out, although with the exception of the Fiskes all eventually came to terms with the Syndicate. Minnie Maddern (1865–1932) was on the stage from the age of three and had achieved considerable fame by 1889, when she married Harrison Grey Fiske (1861–1942), a dramatist and editor of the most influential theatrical newspaper of the day, *The New York Dramatic Mirror*. After she returned to the stage in 1893, Mrs. Fiske championed the new realistic drama and was the first American to give Ibsen an extensive hearing through her productions of *A Doll's House*, *Hedda Gabler*, *Rosmersholm*, *Pillars of Society*, and *Ghosts*. When the Syndicate closed its theatres to her, she and her husband leased the Manhattan Theatre, where from 1901 to 1907 they produced many outstanding plays in which they sought to subordinate stars to ensemble effect. As a performer, Mrs. Fiske relied upon direct observation of life and a close study of psychology. She moved away from lines of business and encouraged actors to play as wide a range of roles as possible. She probably did more than any other American performer of her day to pave the way for the modern theatre.

James O'Neill (1847–1920), now remembered as the father of Eugene O'Neill, was one of the United States' most popular actors from the 1880s until World War I. Despite great promise, he became identified with the leading role in *The Count of Monte Cristo*, which he first played in 1883, and rarely appeared in other works.

But the most significant opposition to the Syndicate came from David Belasco (*c.* 1854–1931), a producer and dramatist who shared many of Frohman's ideals. Born in San Francisco, he was on the stage as a child and wrote his first play at the age of twelve. By the time he left California in 1882, he had written or adapted over one hundred works and had staged some 300. In New York he served as manager of the Madison Square Theatre after MacKaye left it, and later was MacKaye's stage manager at the Lyceum. Between 1887 and 1890 he collaborated with Henry

C. DeMille (1850–1893) on four very successful plays for the Lyceum, and during the 1890s continued to build his reputation as a dramatist with such hits as *The Girl I Left Behind Me* (1893), *The Heart of Maryland* (1895), and *Zaza* (1899). Although he had produced plays occasionally during the 1890s, it was not until 1902 that he acquired his own theatre. In 1907 he opened the Stuyvesant Theatre (renamed the Belasco in 1910), where every modern improvement was installed. Here he continued his work until 1928. Belasco never maintained a stock company and always worked on the single-play principle.

As a producer, Belasco is now remembered for three reasons: his power as a star-maker, his realism in staging, and his opposition to the Syndicate. Like Frohman, Belasco depended much on stars, many of whom he coached carefully and for whose capabilities he tailored plays. Among his stars were Mrs. Leslie Carter (1862–1937), featured in many of Belasco's works from 1895 to 1905; Blanche Bates (1873–1941), noted especially for her appearances in Belasco's *Madame Butterfly* (1900) and *The Girl of the Golden West* (1905), and later in many of Frohman's produc-

Figure 1.33   David Belasco's production of *The Governor's Lady* showing the replica of Childs Restaurant which he erected on stage. From *Le Théâtre* (1912).

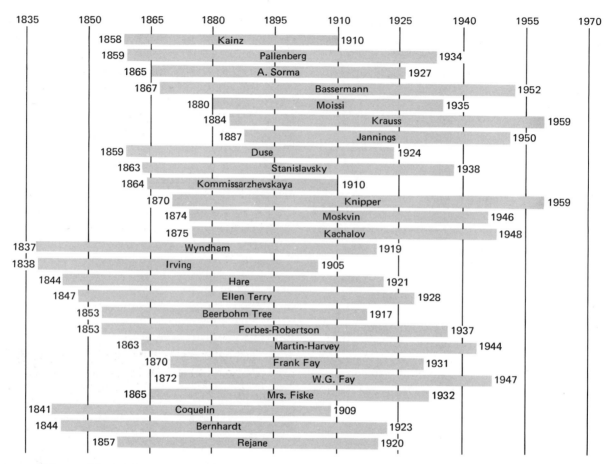

Figure 1.34   Major Actors, 1875–1915.

tions; Frances Starr (1886–1973), a versatile actress who starred in such works as Belasco's *The Rose of the Rancho* (1906) and Eugene Walter's *The Easiest Way* (1909); and David Warfield (1866–1951), a burlesque performer until Belasco transformed him into a leading dramatic actor in such plays as *The Auctioneer* (1902), *The Return of Peter Grimm* (1911), and *The Merchant of Venice* (presented in 1922).

Above all, Belasco is now remembered for his staging. Like Daly and MacKaye, Belasco insisted upon controlling every aspect of his productions. With him, naturalistic detail reached the peak of its development in the United States. For *The Governor's Lady* (1912), a Childs Restaurant was reproduced on stage and the Childs chain stocked it daily with food which was consumed during the performance. For *The Easiest Way*, Belasco bought the contents of a boardinghouse room, including the wallpaper, and had it transferred to his stage. His crowd scenes were famous for their authenticity and power. In collaboration with Louis Hartman, he experimented extensively with stage lighting. In *Madame Butterfly*, the passage of night was shown realistically through a twelve-minute sequence that moved through sunset to night to dawn. Around 1915, Belasco replaced footlights with spotlights mounted in the auditorium and developed new color media. In his search for perfection, however, Belasco remained firmly within the nineteenth-century tradition, for he sought merely to bring the maximum of illusion to a repertory in the Boucicault tradition.

Belasco first came into conflict with the Syndicate when he sought to take *The Auctioneer* on the road in 1902. Further difficulties led to a court battle in 1906. By 1909 Belasco's productions were in such demand that the Syndicate was forced to accept Belasco's terms, even though he refused to book exclusively through it. Its concessions to Belasco marked the first important break in the Syndicate's power.

The willingness of the Syndicate to make concessions had been hastened by the rise of the Shuberts. Three brothers, Sam (1876–1905), Lee (1875–1954), and Jacob J. (1880–1963), after beginning in Syracuse, New York, leased a theatre in New York City in 1900. When the Syndicate closed its theatres to their productions in 1905, the Shuberts began to establish a rival chain. By this time, the high-handed methods of the Syndicate had created much dissatisfaction, and the Shuberts were welcomed by many local managers as allies. By 1908 several theatres had defected to the Shuberts, and the revolt accelerated after 1910 when the National Theatre Owners Association was formed. The struggle between the Shuberts and the Syndicate reached its peak in 1913, after which the Syndicate's grip was broken. Further weakened by the death of Charles Frohman in 1915, the Syndicate ceased to be an effective force after 1916. Unfortunately, the Shuberts became as dictatorial and monopolistic as the Syndicate had been. As producers, they were noted for lavish musicals with little substance. Although they largely gave up producing plays after 1945, they continued to control "the road" until 1956, when the government ordered them to sell many of their theatres. Despite this divestiture, the Shubert organization remains one of the most powerful forces in the American theatre.

Under the conditions that governed the American theatre between 1895 and 1915, it is not surprising that significant playwriting did not flourish. Probably the most successful dramatist was Clyde Fitch (1865–1909), who, after being commissioned by Richard Mansfield to create *Beau Brummel* (1890), wrote about sixty plays, of which the most important were *Barbara Frietchie* (1899), *Captain Jinks of the Horse Marines* (1901), *The Girl with the Green Eyes* (1902), *The Truth* (1907), and *The City* (1909). During the season of 1900–1901, ten of Fitch's works were being played in New York or on the road. A careful observer, Fitch reflected the life of his times. Noted for his quiet, intense scenes, he probably failed to achieve true depth because of the haste with which he wrote. As the first American playwright to publish his works regularly, he established a pattern continued until the present.

During the first decade of the century William

Figure 1.35   The first act of William Vaughan Moody's *The Great Divide*, with Henry Miller and Margaret Anglin, Princess Theatre, New York, 1906. Courtesy Hoblitzelle Theatre Arts Collection, University of Texas, Austin.

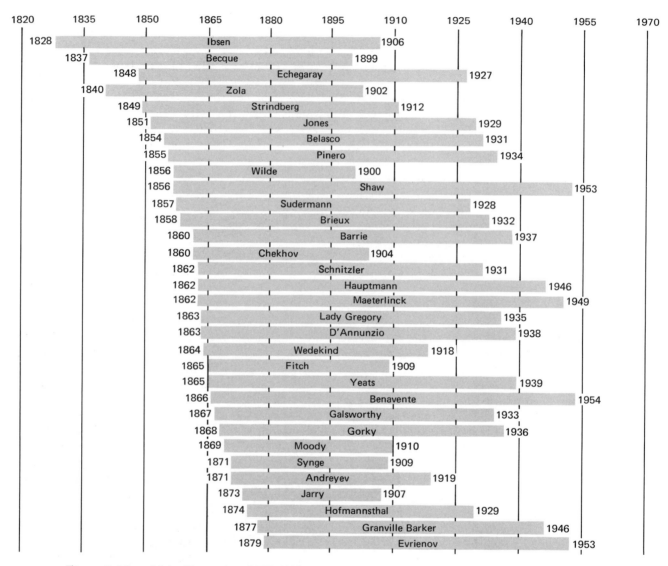

Figure 1.36   Major Dramatists, 1875–1915.

Vaughan Moody (1869–1910) seemed the dramatist with greatest promise. Moody was a professor at the University of Chicago and a poet of stature when he began writing closet dramas about 1900. His first produced work, *The Great Divide* (1906), performed by Henry Miller and Margaret Anglin, was considered a landmark because it combined considerable literary merit with an exciting action which dramatized the "great divide" between the effete and self-conscious East and the rough and open-hearted West. Moody's only other play to reach the stage, *The Faith Healer* (1909), was not well received, perhaps because of its rather unconvincing protagonist. Moody's early death blighted the hopes of those who saw in his work the source of a truly significant American drama.

By 1915 the theatre was beginning to decline in popularity. While increased ticket prices were partially responsible, effective competition, most notably from spectator sports and motion pictures, was also appearing. Soon after Thomas A. Edison demonstrated the "kinetoscope" in 1894, "penny arcades" began to show short motion pictures. Only one person at a time could be served, however, until George Eastman's flexible film and Thomas Armat's projector made it possible to show movies to an assembled audience.

In 1905 the first of the "nickelodeons" was opened in McKeesport, Pennsylvania, and by 1909 there were 8,000. The early theatres seated only about one hundred and offered only short films. In 1914 the Strand Theatre in New York, with its 3,300 seats, began the trend toward larger houses. But it was not until D. W. Griffith's *The Birth of a Nation* (1915) surpassed Belasco's realism and melodramatic power that films became a serious competitor to the theatre. With their superior ability to capture spectacle and their markedly lower admission costs, motion pictures began to draw away that audience that had sought illusionism and thrills in the theatre. Unfortunately, the commercialization of the theatre had alienated a large part of the more discriminating spectators, leaving no effective buffer against disaster.

The competition from films did not bring an overnight revolution. In 1915 there were still about 1,500 legitimate theatres outside of New York and the number of theatrical productions on Broadway continued to increase until the season of 1927–1928. The invention of sound motion pictures in 1927 and the depression of 1929 dealt serious blows, however,

and by 1930 only 500 theatres remained outside of New York. Thereafter, the number steadily declined.

Although these new directions were not readily apparent in 1915, it was already clear to many that the old production methods were outmoded and that commercialization had gradually reduced the repertory to works calculated to appeal to the mass audience. Reassessment, new methods, and changing ideals were in the offing.

Major Technical Innovations, 1875–1915

Between 1875 and 1915 several important technical innovations were introduced, the majority in Germany. Many were motivated by the need to shift the heavy three-dimensional settings which were replacing the wings and drops designed for movement by the chariot-and-pole system. One of the most important of the new devices was the revolving stage. The first one was installed at the Residenz Theater in Munich in 1896 by Karl Lautenschläger (1843–1906). Its ability to accommodate several settings and to change them merely by revolving the turntable, led to its wide adoption after 1900. Another solution, the rolling platform stage, was introduced by Fritz Brandt (1846–1927) at the Royal Opera House in Berlin around 1900. With it, settings could be mounted on a large platform offstage and then moved on stage by means of rollers set in tracks. The elevator stage also was widely adopted. At the Munich Art Theatre, the Burgtheater, and elsewhere, the stage was divided into segments, each of which could be adjusted to create a variety of levels for the action or to raise heavy objects from beneath the stage. A still more complex arrangement was installed in the Dresden state theatre by Adolf Linnebach (1876–1963) in 1914 by combining sliding platforms with elevators. These complex mechanical devices were supplemented with flying, manual shift-

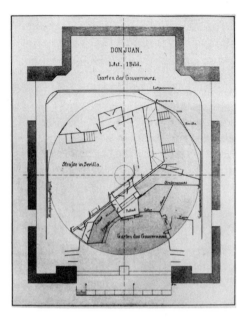

Figure 1.37   The first revolving stage as used for Mozart's *Don Giovanni* at the Residenz Theater, Munich, in 1896. At right is a plan showing two settings in place: the Commandant's Garden, and a street in Seville. At left is a drawing of the setting for the first of these. Courtesy Theatermuseum, Munich.

ing, and with small wagons mounted on casters. The new stage machinery was adopted more widely in Germany than elsewhere probably because of two factors: the expense, absorbed in Germany by the state; and the decline of realism before the devices were widely adopted elsewhere, for the growing emphasis upon simplified settings made complex machinery less essential.

Many German theatres of this period also installed a plaster dome (or *kuppelhorizont*) which curved around and over the stage to give the effect of infinite space and eliminated the need for overhead and side masking pieces. To fulfill the same function, other theatres used a cloth cyclorama hung from a batten which curved around the stage.

Many experiments with stage lighting also were conducted. Light bridges and other new mounting positions were tried. After 1907, improvements in the filaments of incandescent lamps made it possible to increase wattage. By 1913, 1,000-watt lamps were available in Europe, and color media and spotlights were beginning to be common. Consequently, footlights were gradually replaced by spotlights mounted in the auditorium. One of the most ambitious lighting systems of the period was devised by Mariano Fortuny (1871–1949), who directed strong lights against colored silk panels, which reflected the light onto a *kuppelhorizont* and then onto the stage. With elaborate machinery for changing the panels and controlling the light, the system gave the most subtle variations of any then known, but its complexity and cost prevented its widespread adoption. Nevertheless, it is indicative of the growing interest in lighting as an important element of design.

Auditoriums also underwent considerable change, largely under the influence of Wagner's theatre at Bayreuth. Boxes tended to disappear and the number of balconies to decrease (sometimes there was none); center aisles were eliminated to improve sight lines. As the interest in breaking down the barriers between performers and audience grew, the apron stage returned to favor and in a few instances the proscenium arch was eliminated. Thus, the Italianate theatre, dominant since the seventeenth century, was challenged for the first time.

By 1915 the standards of production that had been accepted almost universally in 1875 had begun to seem outmoded. Although pictorial realism still dominated the popular theatre, it had been undermined by a host of experiments. A common theme ran through all of the experiments: the need for unified production, a strong director, and artistic integrity, so that the theatre might once more assume the role it had played in ancient Greece as a source of insight and a place of communion. Although the war interrupted developments, it provoked reassessments, out of which new convictions and renewed vigor came in the postwar years.

Looking at Theatre History

One way of studying theatre history is through reconstructing specific productions. Obviously, one cannot recapture a performance completely, but one can regain much more than might be expected. Such an approach requires that one collect information about the entire context: the prevailing theatrical conditions and conventions, the dramatist, the script, the director, the actors, the theatre building, the settings, the costumes, the lighting, the music, the rehearsals, the performances, the audiences, and the critical response. One needs also to read any accounts left by participants or eyewitnesses and to gather all the visual evidence that has survived. With such materials in hand, one can gain a reasonably complete understanding of the elements that went into the production and can trace the performance, scene by scene. Such study will illuminate not only the specific production but the theatre of that age.

Among the best sources of information about productions are prompt scripts, especially those made after 1850, for before that time few details about blocking and stage business were recorded in the prompt-copy, as such matters were considered to lie within the actor's domain. But since the mid-nineteenth century prompt scripts usually have recorded highly specific information about almost all production elements.

Charles Shattuck has published a list of the Shakespearean promptbooks that are available in libraries and collections in *The Shakespeare Promptbooks: A Descriptive Catalogue* (Urbana, Ill., 1965). In addition, Shattuck's studies of specific Shakespearean productions are models of how performances can be reconstructed. These include *William Charles Macready's "King John"* (Urbana, Ill., 1962) and *The Hamlet of Edwin Booth* (Urbana, 1969). Although his are full-length books, other reconstructions need not be so thorough to be enlightening.

A study of the critical responses to plays and production styles between 1875 and 1915 can be very revealing. Saxe-Meiningen's work was readily accepted because its realism was essentially an intensification of trends with which the audience was already familiar and of which it approved. In 1881 the company appeared in London. Reviewers were not impressed by all aspects of the productions, since they thought that in some areas the English did as well or better, but they found much to recommend as models for emulation. Here are portions of a review of *Julius Caesar* (see the illustration on page 544):

> *It may . . . be maintained that no spectacular play of Shakespeare, such as "Julius Caesar" may claim to be considered, has ever been put upon our stage in a fashion equally effective. . . . the principal gain is in the manner in which those who are little or nothing more than supernumeraries wear the costumes of a bygone age, and take intelligent part in actions and movements of which they can have had no experience in real life. . . . the openly manifested desire to obtain an ascendancy over his fellows, which has been the disgrace of the English actor, is kept out of sight. . . .*
>
> *In the case of "Julius Caesar" the most noteworthy features consisted of the arrangement of the tableaux and the disposition of the supernumeraries when as in the case of the oration of Antony over the body of Caesar, strong and growing emotion has to be expressed. From the picturesque standpoint these things were perfect.*
>
> *The Athenaeum,* June 11, 1881, p. 796.

A study of critical responses can also help us to understand the great uproar caused by scripts or productions that now seem uncontroversial. As a playwright, Ibsen was a special focus for contention. Here are some of Clement Scott's responses to *Ghosts* when it was first produced in London:

> *If people like the discussion of such nasty subjects on the stage . . . if it is desirable to drive decent-minded women out of the playhouse, and to use the auditorium as a hospital-ward or dissecting-room, let it be so. . . . But in our hurry to dramatize the Contagious Diseases Act let us first set about writing a good play. Who in their senses can say that*

> *Ghosts is a good play? . . . If, by the examples we have seen, Ibsen is a dramatist, then the art of the dramatist is dead indeed. . . .*
>
> *The Illustrated London News,* 21 March 1891.

Similarly, when Granville Barker attempted to do away with illusionistic scenery in his Shakespearean productions, he met considerable derision. Here are portions of a review of *A Midsummer Night's Dream* written in 1915 (for an illustration of one setting, see page 573):

> *Let it be said that it represented the last cry in the new stage decoration. . . . The . . . changes of scene were indicated by curtains that waved, to the loss of all illusion. . . . No human being . . . can be expected to be anything but worried and annoyed by pink silk curtains that are supposed to be the roofs of houses, or green silk curtains that are supposed to be forest trees. . . . I hope this is not indicative of what will happen when stage setting ceases to be scenery and becomes only decoration.*
>
> Review by G. C. D. Odell, reprinted in his *Shakespeare from Betterton to Irving* (New York, 1920), II, 467–468.

Probably the most extreme departure from the realistic mode was seen at Paris's Théâtre de l'Oeuvre, where more startling than the abandonment of illusionistic scenery was the highly stylized acting:

> *The most simple and sensible things take on a different appearance in passing through the mouths and gestures of the l'Oeuvre's actors under the direction of Lugné-Poë. They have a continual ecstatic air of perpetually being visionaries. As if hallucinatory, they stare before them, far, very far, vaguely, very vaguely. Their voices are cavernous, their diction*

choppy. They seem to be attempting to give the air that they are fools.

Moniteur Universel, 5 March 1894.

Perhaps the most notable feature of the period between 1875 and 1915 was the attempt to redefine the "art of the theatre." In this effort, the leaders were Appia and Craig. Here are some excerpts from one of Appia's essays. After pointing out the weaknesses of the nineteenth-century theatre (which he blames on the disparity between the static, two-dimensional painted scenery, the flat stage floor, and the three-dimensional, moving actor), he goes on to ask:

> *What would happen if we begin with . . . the plastic, moving human body? . . . An object is three-dimensional to our eyes only because of the light that strikes it. . . . [Furthermore] human movement . . . requires obstacles if it is to be fully expressive. Therefore, the actor's mobility cannot be used to artistic advantage except when it is integrally related to objects and the floor. Thus the two basic conditions required for the artistic use of the human body on the stage are: light that reveals its plasticity, and its harmonization with the setting so as to enhance its attitudes and movements. . . .*
>
> *The effects of lighting are limitless. . . . [When it is used properly] the actor no longer walks about in front of painted light and shade; he is enfolded in an atmosphere destined for him. . . .*
>
> *Scenic illusion may be defined as the living presence of the actor.*
>
> *. . . [If we are to create the appropriate scenic illusion] we must greatly simplify [the setting] . . . completely rearrange the stage floor, and above all make adequate provisions for lighting. . . .*

"Comment Reformer Notre Mise en Scène," *La Revue*, 50 (June 1, 1904), 342–349.

Craig wished to establish that theatre can be an autonomous art created by a master artist, rather than an assemblage of other arts put together by craftsmen:

> *The Art of the Theatre is neither acting nor the play, it is not scene nor dance, but it consists of all the elements of which these things are composed: action, which is the very spirit of acting; words, which are the body of the play; line and colour, which are the very heart of the scene; rhythm, which is the very essence of dance. . . .*
>
> *When [the director] interprets the plays of the dramatist by means of his actors, his scene-painters, and his other craftsmen, then he is a craftsman—a master craftsman; when he will have mastered the uses of actions, words, line, colour, and rhythm, then he may become an artist. Then we shall no longer need the assistance of the playwright—for our art will then be self-reliant.*

On the Art of the Theatre (Chicago: Browne's Bookstore, 1911), pp. 138, 148.

During this period, Stanislavsky began to evolve his system of acting, probably the most influential of all times. In *My Life in Art*, he tells how his system took shape over many years, beginning in 1906 when he became concerned over his inability to remain fresh in his roles:

> *How was I to save my roles from bad rebirths, from spiritual petrifaction, from the autocracy of evil habit and lack of truth? There was the necessity not only of a physical make-up but of a spiritual make-up before every performance. [pp. 460–461]*

As he experimented with a system capable of meeting the actor's problems, his ideas began to attract others:

For the young people who came to seek my help I founded a Studio [in 1911]. . . . here we gathered all who wanted to study the so-called Stanislavsky System. . . . I began to give a full course of study in the shape in which I had at that time formed it. Its aim was to give practical and conscious methods for the awakening of superconscious creativeness. [p. 531]

About his system, Stanislavsky warned:

My system cannot be explained in an hour or in a day even. It must be systematically and practically studied for years. It does good only when it becomes the second nature of the actor, when he stops thinking of it consciously, when it begins to appear naturally, as of itself. [p. 529]

> Constantin Stanislavsky, *My Life in Art*, trans. J. J. Robbins (New York: Theatre Arts Books, 1948).

The Theatre in Europe and the United States between the Wars

The period between 1915 and 1940 was bounded by the two most destructive and costly wars of modern times. World War I grew out of problems inherited from the nineteenth century: the desire of each ethnic and language group to have its own nation; the competition among the great powers for territory, markets, and spheres of influence; military alliances that had been formed to insure a balance of power; and secret diplomacy that created suspicion among nations. The war utilized not only the largest armies ever assembled up to that time, but new and improved instruments of destruction—tanks and other mechanized vehicles, airplanes and bombs, submarines and torpedoes. Some 8,300,000 people died and more than $337 billion were spent. To many thoughtful people the war seemed an exercise in madness.

The war ended in a wave of optimism as republics replaced monarchies, as small ethnic groups were allowed to form their own nations, and as a League of Nations and a World Court were established to arbitrate national disputes. But optimism soon declined because of the great economic problems created by human and material destruction and because of the vindictive treatment of the losing nations. Rampant inflation in the 1920s was followed by severe depression in the 1930s. In several countries conditions became so chaotic that dictators were able to gain complete control: Mussolini of Italy in 1922, Stalin of Russia around 1928, Hitler of Germany in 1933, and Franco of Spain in 1939. During the 1930s, conflicts —over ideologies, territorial claims, and imperialistic designs—increased steadily. The League of Nations proved ineffective, and the great powers set about rearming. In 1939 the tensions erupted into a second World War that was to be even more destructive than the first.

World War I seems to have had a liberating effect, however, in many realms, perhaps most notably in moral standards, codes of dress and behavior, women's and workers' rights, and artistic experimentation.

Figure 2.1   Europe *c.* 1925.

German Theatre and Drama, 1915–1940

During World War I the German theatre continued without interruption and, unlike its English, French, and American counterparts, did not turn primarily to popular entertainment. When Germany became a republic at the end of the war, the former "royal" theatres were rechristened "state" theatres, but there were few changes in organization or policy, for they continued to offer seasons composed of varied plays performed by permanent companies. After 1920, as economic conditions worsened and inflation skyrocketed, nonsubsidized groups found it increasingly difficult to survive except by abandoning the repertory system in favor of new works tailored to popular tastes. Eventually most of the private theatres were taken over by municipalities, thereby increasing governmental involvement in theatre.

Of the prewar producers, Max Reinhardt remained the most important. While continuing his management of the Deutsches Theater and the Kammerspiele, he also remodeled the Circus Schumann into the Grosses Schauspielhaus (seating more than 3,500), where between 1919 and 1922 he presented a series of monumental productions, most notably the *Oresteia*, *Julius Caesar*, and *Danton's Death*. The venture ultimately failed, perhaps because the theatre's great size discouraged subtlety and because the compromises demanded by the combined open and picture-frame stages were never entirely satisfactory.

From 1922 to 1924 Reinhardt maintained his headquarters in Austria, where he had annually produced von Hofmannsthal's *Everyman* and *The Great*

Theatre of the World at the Salzburg Festival since its founding in 1920. In 1922 he became director of Vienna's Theater in dem Redoutensaal, converted from an imperial ballroom of the 1740s, where against a background of screens he presented plays and operas of the eighteenth century. The intimacy of this theatre contrasted markedly with the immensity of the Grosses Schauspielhaus. Although he retained and extended his Austrian enterprises, in 1924 Reinhardt returned to Berlin where he continued his manifold activities until Hitler's rise to power forced him to flee in 1933. Between 1905 and 1933 Reinhardt had personally directed 136 plays and through his experiments with production styles and theatre architecture had exerted a pervasive influence on the German stage. In the United States after 1933 Reinhardt directed a few plays and films, but he never fully adjusted to his new situation.

Reinhardt's postwar activities were essentially continuations of practices he had begun before 1914.

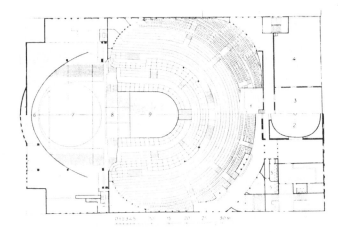

Figure 2.2   Plan of Reinhardt's Grosses Schauspielhaus, remodeled from a circus building. At left note the full proscenium stage, complete with revolving stage. Forward of the proscenium are a platform and arena. The theatre seated about 3,500. From Barkhin, *Architectura Teatra*, Moscow (1947).

Figure 2.3   Reinhardt's Redoutensaal theatre, Vienna, 1922, created within the ballroom of an eighteenth century palace. Note that the stage has been erected without disturbing the walls of the ballroom. There is no proscenium arch or curtain. From *Le Théâtre* (1922).

But other directors championed a new mode—expressionism—which for a few years dominated the German stage. The term *expressionism* first gained currency in France around 1901 as a label used to distinguish the kind of painting done by Van Gogh and Gauguin from that of the impressionists, who sought to capture the appearance of objects as seen under a certain light at a particular moment. In contrast, expressionism was thought to emphasize strong inner feelings about objects and to portray life as modified and distorted by the painter's own vision of reality.

Around 1910 expressionism as a term was introduced into Germany, where shortly afterward it was picked up by critics and popularized as a label for tendencies already underway in literature and the arts. Since almost any departure from realism soon came to be labeled "expressionism," the movement is difficult to define. Nevertheless, its basic premises may be outlined. An anthropomorphic view of existence led expressionists to project human emotions and attitudes into all objects, and to seek truth in man's spiritual qualities rather than in external appearances. Expressionists opposed realism and naturalism on the grounds that they focused attention upon surface details and implied that the observable phenomena of contemporary materialistic and mechanistic society respresent fixed truths. The expressionists argued that external reality is alterable and should be changed until it harmonizes with man's spiritual nature, the only significant source of value. Many expressionists sought merely to focus attention upon these inner qualities, but others took a more militant view and worked to transform social and political conditions so that they would no longer mechanize and distort man's spirit and prevent his attainment of happiness.

Since the expressionists' "truth" existed primarily within the subjective realm, they had to seek new artistic means to express it. Distorted line, exaggerated shape, abnormal coloring, mechanical movement, and telegraphic speech were devices commonly used to lead audiences beyond surface appearances.

Often everything was shown through the eyes of the protagonist, whose view might alter emphases and impose drastic interpretations upon the events. Most expressionist plays were structurally episodic, their unity deriving from a central idea or argument, often one suggesting the possibility of a future Utopia.

The first true expressionist play—*The Beggar* by Reinhard Johannes Sorge (1892–1916)—was published in 1912. It shows the struggle between established conventions and new values, between the older and younger generations, and the attempt of a visionary poet to achieve fulfillment in a materialistic and insensitive society. Much the same idea is found in Walter Hasenclever's (1890–1940) *The Son* (1914), in which the protagonist threatens to kill his father

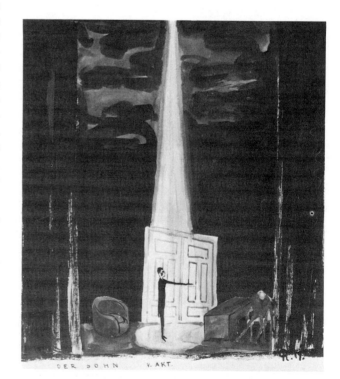

Figure 2.4   Setting by Otto Riegbert for Hasenclever's *The Son* at Keil in 1919. Courtesy Theatermuseum, Munich.

because his freedom to experience life in all its glory is restricted by his puritanical and hypocritical parents; it was probably intended as a symbolic treatment of the need to rid the world of those old values and social forms standing in the way of the "new man."

With the coming of World War I, expressionism began to change as its emphasis moved from personal concerns to warnings of impending universal catastrophe or pleas for the reformation of man and society. For example, Hasenclever's antiwar play *Antigone* (1916) suggests that love is the only path to happiness but that it cannot be followed until unjust and autocratic rulers are overthrown. Similarly, Fritz von Unruh's (1885–1970) *One Race* (1918) shows how mistaken values and deeds (especially war) have dehumanized man, and it ends with a plea to storm "the barracks of violence" as a prelude to a better world.

In 1918 widespread revolution overthrew the German government and brought an end to the war and the monarchy. Until that time few expressionist

Figure 2.5   Jessner's production of Shakespeare's *Richard III* at the Berlin State Theatre in 1919. Setting by Emil Pirchan. Courtesy Theatermuseum, Munich.

plays had been produced in Germany because of the strict censorship. Beginning in 1913 a few private readings and dramatic performances had been presented by Herwarth Walden (1878–1941) under the sponsorship of his periodical *The Storm*. But no public performance of an expressionist play was given until 1916, and when the war ended only a few plays had been seen and these only by limited audiences. When peace came, however, expressionism flourished. For example, the ten German-language expressionist periodicals of 1917 had grown to forty-four in 1919. Similarly, beginning in 1919 theatres began to take expressionist plays into their repertories and until 1924 the new mode was to remain dominant. But the optimism that accompanied the end of the war (and that seemed to promise the possibility of achieving the expressionists' ideals) soon gave way to disappointment and disillusionment. By 1924 expressionism was virtually dead. This shift from optimism to pessimism is especially evident in the work of the two major expressionist playwrights —Kaiser and Toller.

Georg Kaiser (1878–1945) began his playwriting career in 1911 but his first important work in the expressionist vein was *From Morn to Midnight* (1916), in which a machine-age Everyman searches for the meaning of life only to become a martyr to callousness and greed. But, though the world is not yet ready for the hero's message, Kaiser seems to believe that he has pointed the way. He next wrote a trilogy of plays—*Coral* (1917), *Gas I* (1918), and *Gas II* (1920). In the first, the protagonist gradually comes to recognize the primacy of the soul, and in the second his son sets out to regenerate society. Though in neither play is the protagonist fully successful, both works are essentially optimistic about the future. But in *Gas II* Kaiser seems to have despaired of man, and when the play ends, the world is undergoing a cataclysmic destruction. After this time Kaiser abandoned the expressionist mode.

Ernst Toller (1893–1939) wrote his first play, *Transfiguration* (1918), while serving a prison term for antiwar activities. It shows the gradual evolution of its hero from a naive patriotic soldier to ardent antiwar revolutionary seeking to help man fight his oppressors. Toller's most influential work was to be *Man and the Masses* (1921), the story of a woman's struggle to aid workers, and her defeat by those who place ideological position above humanitarian principles. By the time Toller wrote *Hurrah, We Live!* (1927) his disillusionment was complete. It shows former idealists, now settled into comfortable lives, repeating the mistakes they once rebelled against. In protest against such madness the protagonist commits suicide.

Between 1919 and 1924 expressionism also became a major style of production, especially as applied by Jessner and Fehling. Leopold Jessner (1878–1945) had worked in Hamburg and Königsberg before becoming director of the Berlin State Theatre in 1919. Here he won international fame for his imaginative use of flights of steps (*Jessnertreppen*) and platforms as the major compositional elements in his productions. His principal designers, Emil Pirchan and Cesar Klein, discarded representational scenery for stylized pieces which, along with costumes and lighting, were selected primarily for their emotional and symbolic qualities. Jessner's production of *Richard III* is typical of his approach; the blood-red costumes and light used at the peak of Richard's power dissolved into white costumes and light as Richmond's forces came to the fore. Despite his fame as an expressionist director, Jessner worked primarily with the classics. In 1933 he emigrated to the United States.

Unlike Jessner, Jürgen Fehling (1890–1968) made his reputation with expressionist drama, beginning with Toller's *Man and the Masses* at Berlin's Volksbühne in 1921. Fehling sought to arouse intense emotional response in spectators. In his production, bankers fox-trotted to the sound of jingling coins; the workers did a wild dance, which, set to the tune of a concertina and accompanied by constantly shifting colored lights, gave the impression of a witches' sabbath; throughout, the masses were used to create striking effects with movement and sound. Fehling was more eclectic than Jessner, both in the kinds of plays he directed and in the devices he used. He remained in Germany under the Nazis and served as director of the Berlin State Theatre.

As expressionism declined, a more militant approach, eventually to be called "Epic Theatre," arose. Its first major practitioner, Erwin Piscator (1893–1966), after working with the Proletarian Theatre in 1920 and the Central Theatre from 1921 to 1924, was appointed a director at the Volksbühne, where between 1924 and 1927 he sought to create a "proletarian drama," as opposed to merely producing standard plays for a working-class audience. His reshaping of texts into propaganda, however, aroused such controversy that he resigned in 1927 to found the Piscator Theatre. There in 1927–1928 he perfected many of the techniques later associated with Epic Theatre. For Toller's *Hurrah, We Live!*, a reworking of Alexei Tolstoy's *Rasputin*, and an adaptation of Jaroslav Hacek's novel, *The Good Soldier Schweik*, Piscator used filmed sequences, cartoons, treadmills, segmented settings, and other devices to draw strong parallels between the dramatic events and real-life situations, thus arguing the need for social and political reforms. Piscator left Germany in 1933 and in 1939 went to the United States, where

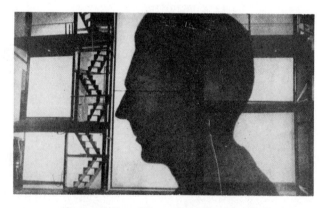

Figure 2.6   Piscator's setting for Toller's *Hurrah, We Live*. From *Theatre Arts* (1932).

borrowing freely from various sources; not exclusive in opinion, taste, etc.

until 1951 he taught at the New School for Social Research and staged a number of plays in New York and elsewhere.

Despite Piscator's pioneering work, Epic Theatre is now associated primarily with Bertolt Brecht (1891–1956), the movement's major theoretician and dramatist. Brecht entered the theatre as a director in Munich and later worked as a *dramaturg* for Reinhardt in Berlin. As a playwright, he experimented with dada and expressionism in such early plays as *Baal* (1918) and *Drums in the Night* (1922) before arriving at his more characteristic style with *Man is Man* (1926). His first major success came with *The Three-Penny Opera* (1928), which, with music by Kurt Weill and settings by Caspar Neher (1897–1962), ran for 400 performances. In 1933 Brecht went into exile, during which he wrote most of his major works: *The Private Life of the Master Race* (1935–1938), twenty-eight scenes demonstrating Nazi inhumanity; *Mother Courage* (1937), emphasizing both the endurance and the brutalization of a woman during the Thirty Years' War; *Galileo* (1938–1939); *The Good Woman of Setzuan* (1938–1940), *Herr Puntila* (1940–1941), *The Resistible Rise of Arturo Ui* (1941), and *The Caucasian Chalk Circle* (1944–1945), Brecht's last major play. Because of his exile, Brecht's works were little produced until he returned to Germany in 1947, but since then they have been increasingly important throughout the world.

Although Brecht's plays have gained a devoted audience, his theory is equally well known. Brecht called his approach "epic" in order to indicate its broad sweep and its mixture of narrative and dramatic techniques. He wished to assign the spectator an active role in the theatre by making him watch critically rather than passively. Consequently, he arrived at the concept of "alienation" (*verfremdungseffekt*), or making stage events sufficiently strange that the spectator will ask questions about them. To create this thoughtful contemplation and to prevent the spectator from confusing stage events with real-life events, Brecht wanted the theatrical means (such as lighting instruments, musicians, scene changes) to

Figure 2.7 Brecht's *Drums in the Night* as presented at the Kammerspiele in Munich, 1922. Directed by Otto Falckenberg, setting by Otto Riegbert. Courtesy Theatermuseum, Munich.

be visible. He also deliberately separated episodes by inserting songs and narrative passages between them. Through these and other devices he called attention to the theatrical nature of the experience and sought to create the alienation that he thought would induce critical evaluation of the dramatic situations. Brecht hoped in this way to lead the audience to relate what they saw on the stage to social and economic conditions outside the theatre; ultimately, he wished the audience to apply its new perceptions by working for changes in the social and economic system.

Unlike Appia and Craig, Brecht did not believe that all the theatrical elements should be synthesized into a master work with a completely unified effect. This, he suggested, was a redundant use of the various elements, each of which should make a different comment on the action. He also rejected Stanislavsky's approach to acting and advised performers to think of their roles "in the third person" so that

School of Fine Arts and of Arts and Crafts in which he attempted to break down the traditional barriers between the artist and the craftsman and to unite architecture, painting, sculpture, and other arts into a communal expression. Ultimately the Bauhaus wished to shape daily surroundings into a "master art work" in which everything from the landscaping to the house, its furnishings, decorations, and even its kitchen utensils are conceived as parts of a total design for living. It sought to make the functional artistic and the artistic functional. It wished to end the elitist status of art, under which it had been confined primarily to museums or the homes of the wealthy, and to make it a part of daily life.

From 1923 until 1929 the Bauhaus' stage workshop was under the direction of Oskar Schlemmer (1888–1943), who was concerned primarily with three-dimensional figures in space. Rather than trying to adjust stage space to the natural form of man, he sought to unify the human body with the abstract stage space, and consequently he attempted to alter the human shape through three-dimensional costumes that transformed actors into "ambulant architecture" and to control their movement through mathematical precision. Schlemmer ignored the verbal element, but he systematically analyzed each visual element (empty space, the human figure, movement, light, and color) both in isolation and in various combinations. Like much of the Bauhaus' work, Schlemmer's can probably best be viewed as a form of basic research, the results of which can be applied in various ways to practical problems. Since the 1950s his experiments have been especially influential on dance.

In theatre architecture, the Bauhaus' most important work was done by Gropius, who in 1927 designed a "total theatre" for Piscator. Although never built, its design has continued to be influential on theatre architecture. According to Gropius, there are only three basic stage forms—the arena, thrust, and proscenium—and in his total theatre he sought to accommodate all. He mounted a segment of seats and an acting area on a large revolvable circle for-

Figure 2.8   Brecht's *Threepenny Opera*, the original production at the Theater am Schiffbauerdamm, Berlin, 1928. Directed by Erich Engel, setting by Caspar Neher. Courtesy Theatermuseum, Munich.

through their acting they would comment on the characters' motivations and actions. Brecht's theories have been subjected to many conflicting interpretations, but they have stimulated directors throughout the world.

Still another experiment of the 1920s—the Bauhaus—was to have considerable international impact. In 1919, Walter Gropius (1883–1969) established at the Staatliches Bauhaus in Weimar a

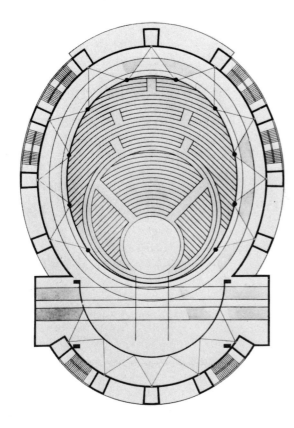

Figure 2.9 Gropius's "total theatre." Note that the white circle (a playing area) joins the proscenium to form a thrust stage. This circle (along with the seating shown on the larger circle) can be revolved to place the acting area in the middle of the auditorium to create an arena stage. Note the ramp, which also may be used for acting, that completely surrounds the auditorium. Note also the projectors (the beams of which are represented by triangular lines) place around the auditorium and back of the cyclorama, thus making it possible to enclose the audience within a projected setting. From Barkhin, *Architectura Teatra*, Moscow (1947).

ward of the proscenium. When this acting area was moved to a position contiguous with the proscenium, it formed a thrust stage, and when rotated 180 degrees it became an arena. From the wings of the proscenium stage ran an open platform which continued completely around the edge of the auditorium. It could be used as an acting area, and scenery could be shifted on it by means of wagons. A wide stage house also permitted rolling platforms to move horizontally. Spaced around the perimeter of the auditorium were twelve columns between which could be mounted screens. A translucent cyclorama at the rear of the proscenium stage also provided a surface for projections, and other screens were mounted in the auditorium above the heads of the spectators. Gropius declared that he wished to place the audi-

ence in the midst of the action and "to force them to participate in experiencing the play."

The Bauhaus was always controversial and when the Nazis came to power it was forced to close. Its members dispersed throughout the world, but their influence upon design and architecture (especially furniture, interior decor, and the steel and glass buildings of our cities) has been so pervasive that its source is seldom recognized.

Although Epic Theatre and the Bauhaus now seem the major German contributions of the 1920s, at the time another movement—usually called *Neue Sachlichkeit* or neorealism—dominated the theatre. It came into being around 1923 in reaction to the excesses of expressionism and consequently concentrated on such mundane problems as the difficulties of adjusting to peacetime, the overly rigid legal system, and the traumas of adolescence and school life. Unfortunately, though neorealistic plays were numerous, few now bear reading. Among the best writers were Friedrich Wolf (1888–1953), with *Cyanide* (1929), an attack on abortion laws, and *The Sailors of Cattaro* (1930), a documentary drama about an uprising in the Austro-Hungarian navy during World War I; and Ferdinand Bruckner (1891–1958), with *The Malady of Youth* (1926), about the disillusionment of young people, and *The Criminals* (1928), a study of the legal system. (Bruckner later won international fame with his plays about historical figures, such as *Elizabeth of England*.) The best of the neorealist writers was Carl Zuckmayer (1896–1977). His *The Merry Vineyard* (1925), an earthy comedy set against the background of a wine festival, was a resounding success. His most enduring work has been *The Captain of Köpenick* (1931), a satirical treatment of Prussian bureaucracy, showing how a petty criminal takes over a town merely by putting on a military officer's uniform and thereby commanding unquestioning obedience.

With the advent of Hitler in 1933, many important theatre artists left Germany. Many of those who remained underwent what has been called an "inner emigration" by writing or staging historical works or by deliberately distancing their work from the contemporary scene. The Nazis encouraged plays about the Teutonic past and a production style calculated to evoke a grandiose, larger-than-life picture of an all-powerful, all-Nordic world. But theatrical personnel were seldom overtly required to comply with Nazi ideology, and several were able to retain relative independence. For the most part, however, the German theatre between 1933 and 1945 was subordinated to political demands.

Theatre and Drama in France, 1915–1940

World War I severely curtailed theatrical activities in France. Practically all able-bodied actors were inducted and others spent much of their time performing for the armed forces. The Parisian companies were so depleted that even the Comédie Française had to fill out casts with students from the Conservatoire. The wartime mood turned the theatre toward popular entertainment, a direction which continued to dominate the "boulevard theatres" after the war. Of the boulevard producers, the most successful was probably Sacha Guitry (1885–1957), author of about 150 plays, most of which he produced, directed, and starred in.

At the opposite extreme, a series of revolts against tradition—fauvism, cubism, futurism, constructivism, dada, and surrealism—helped to break the hold of realism and to turn attention to new forms. During the war many artists and political dissenters sought refuge in Switzerland, where dada, the most extreme of the revolts, was launched in 1916. The principal spokesman for dada was Tristan Tzara (1896–1963), who published seven manifestoes between 1916 and 1920. Dada was grounded in a thorough-going skepticism about a world that could produce a global war. Since insanity seemed to them the world's true state, the dadaists sought in their actions to replace logic and reason with calculated madness and in their art to substitute discord and chaos for unity, balance, and harmony. They presented a number of programs composed of lectures, readings, "sound poems," dances, visual art, and short plays. Often several things were going on simultaneously. As the war drew to a close, the dadaists dispersed. For a time, the movement thrived in Germany, but it received its greatest support in Paris. But everywhere it had begun to decline by 1920 and shortly afterwards disappeared. Much of what it stood for was to resurface in the 1960s and to be developed under other names.

In France, dada was succeeded by surrealism, which drew much of its inspiration from the works of Jarry and Apollinaire. Guillaume Apollinaire (1880–1918), friend to almost all *avant-garde* writers and painters after 1900 and the principal spokesman for cubism, influenced surrealism largely through his play, *The Breasts of Tiresias* (1903, revised and produced in 1917), subtitled a "drame surréaliste." Purporting to be a plea for the repopulation of France, the play concerns Thérèse, who after releasing her breasts (balloons, which float away) is transformed into Tiresias. Her husband, now forced to take over her functions, eventually discovers the means of creating children (sheer willpower) and becomes the parent of more than forty thousand offspring. This work exemplifies many of Apollinaire's theories; he rejected everyday logic and suggested that comedy, tragedy, burlesque, fantasy, acrobatics, and declamation should be mingled with music, dance, color, and light to create a new form of expression.

André Breton (1896–1966) soon assumed leadership of the surrealists and issued the movement's first "manifesto" in 1924. Freud's considerable influence upon Breton is evident in his definition of surrealism as "pure psychic automatism, by which is intended to express, verbally, in writing, or by other means, the real process of thought. Thought's dictation, in the absence of all control exercised by the reason and outside all esthetic or moral preoccupation." Thus, the subconscious mind in a dreamlike state represented for Breton the basis of artistic truth. After his conversion to communism in 1926, Breton sought to make surrealism more militant, and his second manifesto (1929) denounced many of the movement's former members. Thereafter, surrealism declined, although its crowning achievement did not come until 1938, when an international exhibition of painting demonstrated the movement's considerable accomplishments.

Surrealism's impact on the theatre was essentially indirect. The most effective uses of its techniques were made by Jean Cocteau (1892–1963), who began his theatrical work with *Parade* (1917), a ballet staged by the Ballets Russes, and *The Ox on the Roof* (1920), a pantomime performed by the Fratellini family of circus clowns. His finest plays, *Antigone* (1922), *Orpheus* (1926), and *The Infernal Machine* (1934), based on the Oedipus legend, are reworkings of myths. Cocteau's power came in part from the manner in which he juxtaposed the familiar with the legendary. For example, in *Orpheus* the protagonists are a modern young married couple, but the introduction of a mysterious glazier and a horse who delivers messages evokes a sense of mystery and significance, by means of which the ancient myth is given contemporary rel-

Figure 2.10   Jean Cocteau's surrealistic play, *Antigone*, as produced by Charles Dullin at the Atelier, Paris, in 1922. From *Le Théâtre* (1923).

evance. Although Cocteau never escaped the charge of charlatanism, he was a source of inspiration to other artists throughout his life.

Many of the new movements in the visual arts came into the theatre through the Ballets Russes, which commissioned settings from artists such as Picasso, Matisse, Juan Gris, Marie Laurencin, and Braque. The Ballets Suédois, which played in Paris between 1920 and 1925 under the direction of Rolf de Maré (1888–1964), also commissioned settings from Léger, de Chirico, and Picabia. This company extended the traditional conceptions of ballet as well through such works as Cocteau's *The Married Couple of the Eiffel Tower* (1921), in which dialogue was spoken by actors costumed as phonographs.

Of all the *avant-garde* figures between the wars, Antonin Artaud (1896–1948) was to be the most important. Associated with the theatre from 1921, Artaud had worked with Lugné-Poë, Dullin, and Pitoëff before founding the Théâtre Alfred Jarry in 1926 in association with Roger Vitrac, a surrealist playwright. Devoted entirely to nonrealistic drama, this theatre lasted only two seasons. Artaud's significant contributions were to be made after 1931, when the stimulation of a Balinese dance troupe motivated him to formulate his theory of the theatre, published in 1938 as *The Theatre and Its Double*.

According to Artaud, the theatre in the Western world has been devoted to a very narrow range of human experience, primarily the psychological problems of individuals or the social problems of groups. To Artaud, the more important aspects of existence are those submerged in the unconscious, those things that cause divisions within people and between people and lead to hatred, violence, and disaster. He believed that if given the proper theatrical experiences man can be freed from ferocity and can then express the joy that civilization has forced him to repress, for the theatre can evacuate those feelings that are usually expressed in more destructive ways. Or, as Artaud put it, "the theatre has been created to drain abcesses collectively."

Artaud was certain that his goals could not be reached through appeals to the rational mind. Rather, it would be necessary to operate directly upon the senses (for the conscious mind has been conditioned to sublimate many human impulses) and break down the audience's defenses. Artaud sometimes referred to his as a "theatre of cruelty," since in order to achieve its ends it would have to force the audience to confront itself. The cruelty he advocated is not primarily physical but moral or psychological.

Artaud's intention to operate directly on the nervous system led him to suggest many innovations in theatrical practice. Among these was the replacement of the traditional theatre building with remodeled barns, factories, or airplane hangars. He wished to locate acting areas in corners, on overhead catwalks, and along the walls. He was much impressed by Eastern practices and argued that the West needed to develop symbolic and ritualistic devices similar to those used in the Orient. In lighting, he called for a "vibrating, shredded" effect, and in sound he favored shrillness, abrupt changes in volume, and the use of the human voice to create harmonies and dissonances. Thus, Artaud wanted to assault the audience, to break down its resistance, to purge it morally and spiritually, and he sought to do this through devices "addressed first of all to the senses rather than to the mind," for "the public thinks first of all with its senses."

Like Appia and Craig, Artaud was a visionary rather than a wholly practical man, and like them he was at first little appreciated. Many of their ideas are similar, but Artaud differed drastically in his conception of the theatre's ultimate purpose. Appia and Craig tended to value art for its own sake, whereas Artaud saw in it the salvation of mankind. Theirs is a world of idealized beauty, his a region of cruel torment. Consequently, as the post–World War II view of man darkened, the influence of Appia and Craig declined as that of Artaud increased.

Somewhere between the commercial and *avant-garde* figures were Gémier, Hébertot, and Copeau. Firmin Gémier (1869–1933) began his acting career with Antoine in 1892 and later worked with groups ranging from the Théâtre de l'Oeuvre to melodrama troupes. Perhaps for this reason, Gémier was to follow an eclectic approach not unlike that of Reinhardt. From 1906 until 1922 he served as director of the Théâtre Antoine, and from 1922 until 1930 as director of the Odéon. Under Gémier, the Odéon became almost an *avant-garde* theatre, in part because his designer, René Fuerst, drew upon practically all of the recent movements. Despite Gémier's fine work as a director, his significance probably lies in his continuing attempts to bring the theatre to all the people.

The desire to make cultural activities available to the common man had led in the 1890s to the Volksbühnen of Germany and the less ambitious "people's theatres" of France. In 1903 Romain Rolland's *The Theatre of the People* outlined a program under which local groups would perform plays for their fellow citizens as in Greek times. Attracted by this movement, Gémier sought to make the best professional productions available to provincial audiences through his Théâtre Ambulant, which between 1911 and 1913 toured through France with a tent theatre. In 1920 Gémier persuaded the government to create the Théâtre National Populaire. Given only a token subsidy, Gémier had to rely on other companies to contribute occasional productions to the TNP. Although it never became a significant force during Gémier's lifetime, the TNP was to become one of France's finest theatres after World War II. Gémier's interests in a popular theatre also led him into other experiments. In 1919 he took over the Cirque d'Hiver, where he staged *Oedipus, King of Thebes* by Bouhélier and *The Great Pastoral*, a Provençal nativity play. In this and other ways, Gémier's work in France paralleled that of Reinhardt in Germany.

Jacques Hébertot (1886–1971) exerted his primary influence as an entrepreneur. In his three contiguous theatres, the Théâtre des Champs-Elysées, the Comédie des Champs-Elysées, and the Studio des Champs-Elysées, between 1920 and 1925, he employed the most imaginative directors of his age. Furthermore, he imported such companies as the Mos-

Figure 2.11 Stage of the Vieux Colombier as adapted for Shakespeare's *Twelfth Night*. From *Theatre Arts Magazine* (1924).

cow Art Theatre, the Kamerny, and others. Thus, Hébertot made the best of both domestic and foreign theatre available to the Parisian public.

The most pervasive influence on the theatre between the wars was exerted by Jacques Copeau, who reopened the Vieux Colombier in 1919 and rededicated himself to the ideals he had set forth before the war. Unlike Gémier, Copeau thought it impossible to maintain high standards while appealing to the masses. Consequently, he was often accused of snobbery and of treating the theatre as a religion. Eventually, Copeau found it difficult to reconcile his high standards with a full schedule of public performances; in 1924 he left Paris to open a school in Burgundy, where he hoped to perfect his ideas.

Although Copeau performed for only five years after the war, his ideals were to be continued by four other producers—Jouvet, Dullin, Pitoëff, and Baty—who dominated the Parisian theatre until World War II. In 1927 they formed an alliance, commonly called the Cartel des Quatre, under which they agreed to counsel each other, to share publicity, and to negotiate jointly with theatrical unions.

Louis Jouvet (1887–1951) began his career in Rouché's Théâtre des Arts where he met Copeau, for whom he acted minor roles in 1913–1914. Accompanying Copeau to New York in 1917, he remained with him until 1922 when Hébertot employed him as a director. After achieving a major success with Romains' *Dr. Knock* in 1923, Jouvet formed his own company in 1924, taking into it many members of Copeau's recently disbanded troupe. Jouvet did not prosper, however, until 1928, when he began his collaboration with Giraudoux. In 1934 he moved his company to the Théâtre de l'Athénée, a boulevard house, where he remained until 1941, after which he went into voluntary exile until 1945. Jouvet, like Copeau, put primary emphasis upon the text. Above all, he respected language and its nuances. He demanded lucid analysis and careful attention to detail from his actors. In the early years he designed his own scenery, which was always tasteful without being innovative. At the Athénée, he usually worked

Figure 2.12   Bérard's setting for Jouvet's production in 1937 of Molière's *School for Wives*. From *Décor de Théâtre dans le Monde depuis 1935*.

Figure 2.13   Pitoëff's production of *Romeo and Juliet*. Note the strong emphasis on triangular shapes and converging lines, giving an expressionistic effect. From *Theatre Arts* (1935).

with Christian Bérard (1902–1949), one of the finest designers of the period.

Charles Dullin (1885–1949) had played at many minor theatres before joining Rouché and then Copeau. After returning to Paris in 1919, he worked for Gémier before establishing his own theatre, l'Atelier, in 1922. He remained in this small, out-of-the-way theatre until 1939. Dullin was extremely eclectic, presenting works ranging from the Greeks to the present and from tragedy to farce. Through painstaking analysis of the text, he sought to let each play dictate the proper approach to it. His aim was to capture the "inner poetry" through honesty and unity. He refused to do any play that he thought depended upon machinery or upon a director's tricks. Nevertheless, he put considerable emphasis upon visual design and employed some of the best artists of his time: Louis Touchagues, Lucien Coutaud, Georges Valmier, Jean-Victor Hugo, Michel Duran, and André Bar-

sacq. Music, dance, and mimed spectacle also figured prominently in practically all of his productions. Dullin's perennial hope of attracting a wider audience led him in 1941 to become director of the Théâtre Sarah Bernhardt, a very large house, where he struggled along until 1947. His last years were spent in Geneva as director of the theatre section of the Maison des Arts. Ultimately, Dullin's impact on the theatre was to come in large part through his school, in which such significant later figures as Barrault and Vilar received their early training.

Georges Pitoëff (1884–1939) had performed widely in his native Russia before emigrating to Switzerland in 1914. He and his wife, Ludmilla (1896–1951), who had studied at the Conservatoire, came to

Paris in 1922 and worked for Hébertot until 1925, after which they formed their own company, played in a number of Parisian theatres, and toured abroad. Pitoëff was noted for his knowledge of foreign drama, of which he was the principal producer in France. As a director, Pitoëff placed primary emphasis upon the text. For him, the most powerful element was perhaps rhythm, which he sought to find and project for each character and scene. He designed his own scenery, which ranged stylistically from the abstract to the realistically pictorial. Characteristically, however, he used a few indispensable set pieces which he invested with symbolic significance. Of all the members of the Cartel, Pitoëff was probably the most versatile and experimental.

Gaston Baty (1882–1951) was the only member of the Cartel who was not an actor and who did not place primary emphasis upon the text. He began his career under Gémier in 1919, managed the Studio des Champs-Elysées from 1924 to 1928, and then settled in the Théâtre Montparnasse in 1930. After 1935, Baty became extremely interested in marionettes, as a result of which his productions became increasingly stylized. Through much of his career Baty was assisted by Marguerite Jamois (1903–1964), who starred in many of his productions and directed others. To Baty, the director was the major theatrical artist. In his productions a mysterious and poetic world, created by the skillful manipulation of mood, seemed to lurk behind a realistic surface. His emphasis upon costumes, scenery, properties, music, and lighting was sometimes criticized, but he was also known as the "magician of the *mise-en-scène.*"

The influence of Copeau was reenforced in the 1930s by several new groups. In 1930 students from Copeau's school formed the Compagnie des Quinze under the direction of Michel Saint-Denis (1897–1971), Copeau's nephew, and from 1931 to 1933 they played at the Vieux Colombier. After the company disbanded, Saint-Denis opened the Theatre Studio in London, which, in combination with his directing work at the Old Vic and elsewhere, served to carry Copeau's influence into the British theatre. Léon Chancerel (1886–1965), another of Copeau's students, worked primarily with student groups in schools and universities and with children's theatre. His Compagnie des Comédiens-Routiers (1929–1939) played primarily for Boy Scout groups, while his Théâtre de l'Oncle Sébastien (1935–1939) presented plays for children.

Three other directors, Barsacq, Dasté, and Jacquemont, were also to be of considerable importance. André Barsacq (1909–1973) had studied at the School of Decorative Arts and with Dullin before becoming one of Paris's leading scene designers. In 1937, he joined with Dasté and Jacquemont to form the Compagnie des Quarte Saisons, but left in 1940 to assume control of the Atelier when Dullin relinquished it. Barsacq continued to direct that theatre until his death, maintaining Dullin's high standards.

Figure 2.14   Scene set in a box at the opera in Baty's production of his own adaptation of *Madame Bovary* (1936). The actors are Lucien Nat and Marguerite Jamois. From *Theatre Arts* (1936).

Figure 2.15   André Barsacq's setting for Dullin's production of *Volpone*, 1929. From *Décor de Théâtre dans le Monde depuis 1935*.

Jean Dasté (1904–   ), Copeau's son-in-law and pupil, was a member of the Compagnie des Quinze before joining the Compagnie des Quatre Saisons. In 1940 he went with Barsacq to the Atelier, where he was one of the theatre's principal directors. Maurice Jacquemont (1910–   ) was trained by Chancerel and had worked with several companies before the formation of the Compagnie des Quatre Saisons, with which he continued until 1942. In 1944 he became head of the Studio des Champs-Elysées, a position he was to hold until 1960.

Copeau returned to a more active role in the theatre during the 1930s. In addition to directing both in Paris and abroad, he was associated with the Comédie Française after 1936 and served as its director in 1939–1940 until dismissed by the Vichy government. Under Emile Fabré's direction between 1915 and 1936, the Comédie Française had steadily declined, in large part because of low subsidy and political interference. After 1936, the new director, Edouard Bourdet, was able to make many improve-

ments. Not only was the subsidy doubled, but Bourdet imported Copeau, Dullin, Jouvet, and Baty to direct several revivals. For the first time in its history the Comédie Française came to list each play's director on its programs. By the time the war began, the prestige of the company was fully revived.

Although France produced few truly outstanding playwrights between the wars, a number achieved considerable renown. Henri-René Lenormand (1882–1951) was one of the first French writers to emphasize the subconscious mind and the relativity of time and space through such works as *Time is a Dream* (1919) and *The Eater of Dreams* (1922). Henri Ghéon (1875–1944) sought to revive religious drama and for many years toured with his Compagnons de Notre-Dame. Of his approximately one-hundred plays, the best known are *The Poor Under the Stairs* (1921) and *Christmas in the Market Place* (1935). André Obey (1892–1975) was associated with the Compagnie des Quinze, which produced his first plays, *Noah* and *The Rape of Lucrece*, in 1931. Perhaps his best work is found in *Man of Ashes* (1949), a retelling of the Don Juan story. Armand Salacrou (1899–   ) was one of the most versatile dramatists of the period, ranging through surrealist fantasies, light comedy, drama, and historical plays. He came to public attention with *Patchouli* (1927) and did his best work with *The World Is Round* (1935), a history in miniature of the recurrent struggle between the flesh and the spirit.

Of the satirical writers, the best were Jules Romains (1885–1972), whose *Doctor Knock, or the Triumph of Medicine* (1923) shows the exploitation of man's anxieties about his health, and Marcel Pagnol (1895–1974), whose *The Merchants of Glory* (1925) satirizes the business schemes built around the war dead, and *Topaze* (1928), the story of a schoolmaster who prospers only after he abandons his principles. Pagnol is now better known for his romantic trilogy about Marseilles waterfront life, *Marius* (1929), *Fanny* (1931), and *César* (1937). Surrealistic farce was exploited by Fernand Crommelynck (1888–1970), whose *The Magnificent Cuckold* (1921) tells of a man who, upon becoming suspicious of his wife's fidelity, insists on testing it endlessly but never to his satisfaction; and Roger Vitrac (1899–1952) who derided all traditional values in *Victor, or Children in Power* (1928) and *The Secret Hawker* (1936). Vitrac's reputation has grown considerably since 1963 when *Victor* was revived in Paris to critical acclaim. Marcel Achard (1899–1974) excelled in stylized romantic comedy, notably *Voulez-Vous Jouer avec Moi?* (1923), *Jean de la Lune* (1929), and *The Pirate* (1938), in which, typically, a devoted lover subdues the frivolity of a coquette.

The plays of the Belgian dramatist Michel de Ghelderode (1898–1962) resemble those of Jarry, the surrealists, and expressionists, and his theories recall those of Artaud. Throughout his more than thirty plays runs his vision of man as a creature whose flesh overpowers his spirit. Corruption, death, and cruelty are always near the surface, although behind them lurks an implied criticism of degradation and materialism and a call to repentance. But in his works faith is apt to be approached through blasphemy and suffering through ludicrous farce. Like Artaud, Ghelderode downgrades language in favor of spectacle. Place is apt to shift rapidly and unexpectedly; characters are usually exaggerated and many are descended from the clowns of music hall, circus, and fair. His scorn for traditional dramaturgy is shown by the labels he applied to his works: "tragic farce," "burlesque mystery," "tragedy for the music hall," and so on. Of his many dramas, the best known are *Escurial* (1927), *Chronicles of Hell* (1929), *Pantagleize* (1929), and *Hop, Signor* (1935). Since 1949, when he came to the attention of the absurdists, Ghelderode's reputation has steadily risen.

Probably the most important French dramatist between the wars was Jean Giraudoux (1882–1944), a novelist and member of the Foreign Service, who in 1928 began his theatrical career with a dramatization of his novel *Siegfried*. In Jouvet, Giraudoux found his ideal interpreter and he wrote most of his important works for him: *Amphitryon 38* (1929), *Judith* (1931), *The Trojan War Shall Not Take Place* (1935),

Figure 2.16   Jouvet's production of Giraudoux's *The Trojan War Shall Not Take Place*. Jouvet is seen at the right. From *Theatre Arts* (1936).

and *Ondine* (1939). Giraudoux often took his subjects from familiar sources but gave them novel interpretations, for he delighted in pointing out the simple in the complex and the surprising in the familiar. His works turn on antitheses—peace and war, fidelity and infidelity, life and death, liberty and destiny—and their reconciliations. His dramas take place at the moment when men are faced with a choice between two contradictory positions; he explores the contradictions and usually suggests means whereby they can be reconciled, often through some novel perception. Language, which he considered the highest expression of human reason, is Giraudoux's primary means. Writing at a time when the playwright had been subordinated to the director, Giraudoux sought to reaffirm the literary worth of drama. He wrote in a euphonious and highly expressive prose, with a marked disposition for fantasy, irony, and humor. Throughout all his work runs a deep faith in man.

Giraudoux's position of preeminence was to be challenged after the war by Jean Anouilh (1910–), who began as Jouvet's secretary and turned to writing in 1932 under Giraudoux's inspiration. His first success came in 1937 with *Traveller Without Baggage*, presented by Pitoëff. Most of Anouilh's later works, such as *Carnival of Thieves* (1938), *Rendezvous in Senlis* (1941), and *Antigone* (1943), were produced by Barsacq. Anouilh has divided his plays into the serious, or "black" pieces, and the comic, or "red" pieces. In the former, typically a young, idealistic, and uncompromising protagonist is able to maintain his integrity only by choosing death. *Antigone* is perhaps the best-known example. In the "red" plays, although the characters are in many ways similar, a fairy-tale atmosphere permits a happier resolution. Anouilh was to be one of France's most prolific writers after World War II.

With the coming of war in 1939 and the surrender of Paris to the Nazis, theatrical activities were at first seriously curtailed. Some major figures went into exile and those who remained were subject to close surveillance. For the most part, the theatre was reduced to politically inoffensive plays or popular entertainments, but a few productions were to attain true eminence despite all strictures.

Italian Theatre and Drama, 1915–1940

Many major Italian artists during this period were adherents of futurism, a movement launched in Italy in 1909 by Filippo Tommaso Marinetti (1876–1944). Like the expressionists, the futurists rejected the past and wished to transform man. But, whereas the expressionists associated the past with soul-destroying materialism and industrialism, the futurists deplored the veneration of the past as a barrier to progress. Consequently, they glorified the energy and speed of the machine age and sought to embody them in artistic forms. From 1910 onward they gave performances during which they proclaimed their manifestoes, gave concerts, read poems, performed plays, and exhibited works of visual art—at times several of these simultaneously. Sometimes they moved about among the spectators, using various parts of a room sequentially or concurrently. They especially outraged audiences with their demands that libraries and museums be destroyed as the first step toward creating a more dynamic future.

Among the art forms championed by the futurists were "picture poems" (or concrete poetry), kinetic sculptures, collages, and *bruitisme* (or "dynamic music," based on the sounds of everyday life). As for theatre, they denounced past practices and declared music halls, nightclubs, and circuses to be better models on which to base future forms. They found earlier drama too lengthy, analytic, and static and proposed instead a "synthetic drama" which would compress into a moment or two the essence of a dramatic situation. In 1915–1916 they published seventy-six of these short plays.

During World War I futurism lost many followers because it glorified war as the supreme example of energy. After the war it received new vitality, per-

Figure 2.17 A Futurist pantomime, *The Merchant of Hearts*, staged by Enrico Prampolini at the Théâtre de la Pantomime Futuriste in Paris, 1927. Note the mingling of performers with various non-human shapes and forms.

haps because many of its tenets were compatible with Mussolini's program of aggressive action. The principal exponent of futurism in the 1920s was Enrico Prampolini (1894–1960), who demanded that the painted scene be replaced by "stage architecture that will move." He also wished to substitute luminous forms for human actors. He conceived of the stage as a multidimensional space in which spiritual forces (represented by light and abstract forms) would play out a drama of semireligious significance.

After 1930 interest in futurism declined. Though it never became a major theatrical movement, it pioneered innovations that would be revived and extended in the 1950s: (1) the attempt to rescue theatrical art from a museum-like atmosphere; (2) direct confrontation and intermingling of performers and audiences; (3) the exploitation of modern technology to create multimedia performances; (4) the use of simultaneity and multiple focus; (5) an antiliterary and alogical bias; and (6) the breaking down of barriers between arts.

During World War I, a new school of writing, usually called "the theatre of the grotesque," appeared in Italy. Its name was derived from *The Mask and the Face* (1916), "a grotesque in three acts," by Luigi Chiarelli (1884–1947). Turning upon the contrast between public and private role-playing, this comedy tells the story of a man who, after confessing the murder of his wife because he thought her unfaithful, is tried and acquitted, although in actuality she is merely locked up at home. Of the many other writers who exploited this ironical vein, the best was probably Pier Maria Rosso di San Secondo (1887–1956), with *Marionettes, What Passion!* (1918) and *The Sleeping Beauty* (1919).

Luigi Pirandello (1867–1936) was by far the greatest Italian playwright of the period. After winning fame with his novels and short stories, Pirandello turned to playwriting in 1910 and after 1915 devoted himself increasingly to the theatre. From 1924 to 1928 he headed the Art Theatre of Rome, with which he presented many significant Italian and foreign plays. Here he was assisted by Marta Abba (1906–), who played leading roles, and a company which included Ruggero Ruggeri (1871–1954), one of Italy's most respected actors.

Pirandello's plays, of which the best are *Right You Are—If You Think You Are* (1916), *Six Characters in Search of an Author* (1921), *Henry IV* (1922), *Naked* (1922), *Each in His Own Way* (1924), *Tonight We Improvise* (1930), and *As You Desire Me* (1930), usually turn upon a question of fact that cannot be resolved because each character has his own version of the truth. Thus, Pirandello raises doubts about the validity of the scientific approach to truth—the direct observation of reality. He seems to suggest that "truth" is necessarily personal and subjective.

Pirandello was also concerned about the relationship between art and nature. Since nature demands continual change and since a work of art is fixed forever, he found the theatre the most satisfying form of art, for it necessarily differs at each performance. Thus, he likened the theatre to a living statue. Since for him even the most realistic play could only give a travesty of truth, he thought the only remedy lay in writing philosophical plays that show reality as ever changing. Pirandello made a profound impression on his age. Probably no other writer did so much to popularize the philosophical view that was to be espoused by dramatists of the post-World War II period.

Italy's most eclectic director between the wars was Anton Guilio Bragaglia (1890–1960), who from 1922 to 1936 ran the Teatro degli Independenti in Rome, where on a tiny stage he presented a wide-ranging program of works by Strindberg, Wedekind, Jarry, Maeterlinck, Pirandello, and others, including the futurists. For the most part, however, the Italian theatre was made up of touring companies playing the latest hits. A step toward improvement was taken in 1936 with the formation of the Academy of Dramatic Art in Rome under the direction of Silvio D'Amico. Here the principles of Stanislavsky, Copeau, and Reinhardt were taught. The coming of the war interrupted the Academy's work, however, and its impact was not to be felt until after 1945.

Theatre and Drama in Spain, 1915–1940

In the years between 1915 and 1940 the most significant Spanish drama of the immediate postwar years was written by Unamuno and Valle-Inclán. Miguel de Unamuno (1864–1936), one of Spain's most respected philosophers, first expressed his theory of drama in *The Tragic Sense of Life* (1913). His declaration that tragedy stems from a conflict between men's desire for immortality and skepticism about its possibility was to contribute much to existentialist drama following World War II. Because of censorship, Unamuno's plays, such as *Fedra* (1917) and *Dream Shadows* (1931), were not widely produced until after 1950. Similarly, the plays of Ramón del Valle-Inclán (1869–1936), perhaps because of their similarity to absurdist drama, have only recently come to the fore. Valle-Inclán, noted primarily as a novelist, wrote several verse plays, satirical dramas, and farces, of which the best are probably *Divine Words* (1913), *The Farce of the True Spanish Queen* (1920), and *The Horns of Don Friolera* (1925). Valle-Inclán labeled his method *esperpento*, or a systematic deformation designed to show the grotesque reality beneath the surface of Spanish life.

A new spirit began to enter Spanish literature with the "Generation of '27," a group which blossomed especially after censorship was eased under the second Republic, proclaimed in 1931. Of the new dramatists, the most significant were Lorca and Casona. Federico García Lorca (1899–1936) wrote his first play, *The Butterfly's Crime*, in 1920. After its failure, he cultivated his interests in symbolism, surrealism, music, painting, and Spanish folklore, and wrote a number of puppet plays. Following the performance of his *Mariana Pineda* in Barcelona in 1927 by Margarita Xirgu, one of Spain's outstanding actresses, Lorca resumed an active interest in the theatre.

But Lorca's major plays were written only after he had worked closely with a theatre group, La Barraca, a troupe composed of university students and subsidized by the government under its program to bring cultural events to the people. Formed in 1932, La Barraca played Golden Age dramas to rural audiences, and it was the enthusiastic response of these unsophisticated spectators that influenced Lorca to turn to similar themes of love and honor. The results may be seen in *Blood Wedding* (1933), *Yerma* (1934), and *The House of Bernarda Alba* (1935). Blending poetic imagery with primitive passions, these plays are usually considered the finest Spanish works since the Golden Age.

In many ways, the career of Alejandro Casona (1903–1966) paralleled that of Lorca. Between 1931 and 1936, he too directed a government-sponsored troupe, The People's Theatre, which toured Spanish villages. Casona's troupe played primarily short, humorous plays, but like Lorca, Casona was inspired by his experiences to write for this audience. *The Siren Washed Ashore* (1934) and *The Devil Again* (1935) show that blend of realism and fantasy for which Casona was to be noted. In all his works an air of optimism suggests that human problems can be solved.

The Civil War of 1936 brought profound changes. Lorca was killed and Casona emigrated to Argentina. Until 1939 the theatre served primarily as an instrument of propaganda for both sides of the conflict, and following the victory of Franco's forces it suffered from severe censorship. The plays of Lorca, Casona, and Unamuno were forbidden, and the Spanish theatre entered another period of isolation.

Theatre and Drama in Russia 1917–1940

The most drastic changes brought by World War I were felt in Russia, where the czar's policies had been unpopular for many years. The economic hardships created by the conflict fed the unrest, which in early 1917 broke into open rebellion and ended more than 300 years of rule by the Romanovs. Moderate socialists controlled the government at first, but in late 1917 the Communists seized power. Civil war continued, however, until the early 1920s, by which time more than twenty million people had died and Russia's economic resources were severely depleted. For several years thereafter the government was so preoccupied with rebuilding the nation that the theatre was left free to experiment with new forms.

The Communists viewed the theatre as a national treasure, formerly reserved for the middle and upper classes, to be made available to the proletariat. It was also considered a major tool of instruction and, as such, was placed under the authority of the Commissar of Education, Anatole Lunacharsky (1875–1932). Not only was attendance at professional productions encouraged, but amateur groups were organized among peasants, workers, and soldiers. By 1926, there were about 20,000 dramatic clubs among the peasants alone. Between 1918 and 1922, amateurs also figured prominently in the many mass spectacles that recreated major events in the Revolution. The most famous of these was *The Taking of the Winter Palace*, staged in 1919 by Evreinov on the site of the actual event with a cast of about 8,000 soldiers, sailors, and workers.

The new regime proceeded slowly in its nationalization of the theatre. By 1922–1923, only 33 percent of the theatre plants belonged to the state. By 1925–1926, the percentage had increased to 63, but the process was not to be completed until 1936. Similarly, it was long before theatrical personnel were subjected to political domination.

Many of the most enthusiastic supporters of the Revolution were members of the *avant-garde*, who saw in the new regime the opportunity to break with the past and to create new theatrical forms. Meyerhold soon emerged as the leader of this faction. In 1920 he was appointed head of the theatre section in the Commissariat of Education, a position that made him nominal head of the theatre in Russia. At the same time, he continued his own work as a director, staging *The Dawns* (written in 1898 by the Belgian symbolist, Emile Verhaeren) as a Soviet propaganda piece, in which real news bulletins were read from the stage and a public meeting was held with the audience taking part. When this production was denounced by the Central Committee of the Communist Party as foreign to the needs of the proletariat, Meyerhold resigned his government post, but later that year he was appointed head of the state's workshop for directors and in 1922 he acquired a theatre of his own. This series of events is indicative of the power of the *avant-garde* even in the face of official disapproval.

Between 1921 and 1930, Meyerhold perfected techniques with which he had experimented before the Revolution. He now developed more conscious and systematic methods, to which he applied such terms as *biomechanics* and *constructivism*. Biomechanics referred primarily to Meyerhold's approach to acting, intended to create a style appropriate to the machine age. His performers were trained in gymnastics, circus movement, and ballet in order to make them as efficient as machines in carrying out "an assignment received from the outside." Basically

Figure 2.18   Setting by Lyubov Popova for Meyerhold's production of Crommelynck's *The Magnificent Cuckold*, 1922. The action of this play occurs in and around a mill, suggested here by various wheels all of which turned at speeds that varied according to the rhythmical and emotional demands of the scene. This is a good example of Meyerhold's constructivist productions.

what Meyerhold had in mind is a variation on the James-Lange theory: particular patterns of muscular activity elicit particular emotions. Consequently, the actor, to arouse within himself or the audience a desired emotional response, needs only to enact an appropriate kinetic pattern. Thus, Meyerhold sought to replace Stanislavsky's emphasis on internal motivation with one on physical and emotional reflexes. To create a feeling of exuberant joy in both performer and audience, Meyerhold thought it more efficient for the actor to plummet down a slide, swing on a trapeze, or turn a somersault than to restrict himself to behavior considered appropriate by traditional social standards.

Constructivism was a term taken over from the visual arts, where it had first been applied about 1912 to sculpture composed of intersecting planes and masses without representational content. Similarly, Meyerhold frequently arranged nonrepresentational platforms, ramps, turning wheels, trapezes, and other objects to create a "machine for acting," more practicable than decorative.

Figure 2.19   Meyerhold's adaptation of Gogol's *The Inspector General*, 1926. Shown here is the "bribery" scene. The set could open at the back to allow wagons to move in and out.

Meyerhold applied his theories about biomechanics and constructivism most thoroughly in the years between 1922 and 1925, but he steadily softened them. His most famous production of the 1920s was Gogol's *The Inspector General*, presented in 1926. Meyerhold transferred the scene to a large city, reshaped all of the characters and invented several new ones. Costumes, scenery, and properties were based on stylized nineteenth century motifs, and the action was accompanied by period music. The most striking scene was one in which Meyerhold arranged fifteen doors around the stage, and an official emerged simultaneously from each door to offer the inspector a bribe.

Next to Meyerhold, the most influential Russian director of the 1920s was Tairov, who continued the methods he had introduced before the war. Following the Revolution, Lunacharsky had divided theatres into two groups: the well-established or "academic" theatres, which the government subsidized and allowed relative autonomy; and the unproven theatres, which were permitted to exist but given little encouragement. Thus, the government favored pre-Revolutionary groups, a practice bitterly opposed by Meyerhold. Under this scheme, the Kamerny Theatre was classified as an "academic" theatre. Until 1924, Tairov took little notice of the Revolution, producing such works as Wilde's *Salomé*, Scribe's *Adrienne Lecouvreur*, and Racine's *Phèdre* in the style he had always followed. Unlike most producers of the period, who clothed actors in uniform-like garments similar to those worn by the spectators, Tairov sought to lift audiences above the drabness of everyday life. After 1924, Tairov occasionally produced Russian classical and contemporary plays, but his theatre remained the principal link with the West. In addition to its predominantly Western repertory, the troupe also toured in Western Europe in 1923, 1928, and 1929. When Tairov turned to contemporary Russian works, he often ran into difficulties. In 1929 his production of Mikhail Levidov's *Plot of the Equals*, a play about the degeneration

Figure 2.20   Design by I. Nivinsky for Vakhtangov's production of Gozzi's *Turandot*, 1922.

of the French Revolution into the Reign of Terror, was removed after one performance. Thereafter, Tairov's influence declined.

Another important innovator in these early years was Yevgeny Vakhtangov (1883–1922), who had become the artistic leader of the First Studio of the Moscow Art Theatre after Sullerzhitsky died in 1916. Vakhtangov's reputation rests primarily upon four productions: Maeterlinck's *The Miracle of Saint Anthony* (performed by the Third Studio of the Moscow Art Theatre in 1921); Strindberg's *Erik XIV* (given at the First Studio in 1921); Ansky's *The Dybbuk* (performed by the Habimah Theatre in 1922); and Gozzi's *Turandot* (produced at the Third Studio in 1922).

Vakhtangov began as a faithful follower of Stanislavsky, but his strength came from his effective blending of the Moscow Art Theatre's realistic approach with Meyerhold's theatricalism. From Stanislavsky he preserved the emphasis upon concentration and the exploration of each character's biography and of hidden meanings; to this he added a heightened and stylized use of movement and design not unlike that of the German expressionists. In *Erik*

XIV, for example, which was conceived as a death knell for monarchy, all of the courtiers and bureaucrats were played as automatons while the proletariat were treated realistically. Vakhtangov's greatest achievement came with *Turandot*, throughout which the actors seemed to be improvising effortlessly. This production was retained in the repertory as a memorial to Vakhtangov, who died shortly after it opened. Because he worked with several student groups and trained so many actors, Vakhtangov's influence was considerable. His approach was continued by such associates and students as Yuri Zavadsky (1894–1977), Boris Shchukin (1894–1939), Reuben Simonov (1899–1968), Boris Zakhava (1896–1976), Nikolai Akimov (1901–1968), and Alexander Popov (1892–1961). Most of these men were to be important leaders into the 1960s. In the post-Stalinist era, Vakhtangov's methods were to offer the most acceptable alternative to Soviet realism.

In 1924 the First Studio became an independent organization, the Second Moscow Art Theatre, headed by Mikhail Chekhov (1891–1955), a nephew of Anton Chekhov. After entering the Moscow Art Theatre in 1910, Chekhov soon found the Stanislavsky method inadequate and later worked closely with Vakhtangov, winning considerable fame for his portrayal of Erik XIV. Chekhov thought that Stanislavsky's system restricted the actor to copying nature instead of emphasizing what might be. Thus, he came to stress inspiration above analysis as the actor's primary tool. His conceptions were always somewhat mystical, however, and in 1927 seventeen of his associates resigned from the troupe and published a denunciation. Chekhov then left Russia and settled in the United States, where he ran an acting school for many years and published *To the Actor*. The Second Moscow Art Theatre was dissolved in 1936.

Although the innovators of the 1920s attracted most attention, the conservative groups, notably the Maly Theatre in Moscow and the Alexandrinsky Theatre in Leningrad, were favored by political leaders and most of the public. Meyerhold disliked the Maly Theatre's realistic productions so much that in 1921 he recommended that the troupe be liquidated. In response, Alexander Yuzhin, the Maly's director, launched an attack on "formalism" that began a struggle not to be resolved until the 1930s.

Between 1917 and 1925, the Moscow Art Theatre played only a minor role in Russian theatrical life. It mounted only two new productions and its troupe was decimated in 1919 by the defection of several actors to the West. In 1922 it was granted permission to tour abroad, and in 1923–1924 the troupe performed in the United States to universal praise. When the company returned to Russia in 1924, it was at its lowest ebb. Its studios were alienated, and the company was so depleted that Stanislavsky had to add eighty-seven new members. Then the process of rebuilding began. In 1926 it achieved its first postwar success with Ostrovsky's *The Burning Heart*, and in 1927 presented Vsevelod Ivanov's *Armored Train 14–69*, its first important Soviet play. From this time, the company's fortunes steadily improved.

Around 1927 the Soviet attitude toward the theatre also began to change. After Lenin died in 1924, Stalin had gradually gathered power into his hands and in 1928 began his campaign to industrialize Russia and to collectivize farming. Concessions formerly granted dissident elements were withdrawn and the central government extended its power over all aspects of Soviet life. In 1927 a training program to equip party members to manage theatres was initiated and "artistic councils" within each theatre were given considerable power over repertory, style, and policy. Nevertheless, attacks on nonconformists in the theatre came primarily from the Russian Association of Proletarian Writers (RAPP), a radical group that sought to abolish everything not deriving directly from the proletariat. Its violence sufficiently alienated party leaders that it was disbanded in 1932 and replaced by the Union of Soviet Writers, headed by Gorky. At first, greater freedom seemed to be in store, but in 1934 "Socialist Realism" was declared the proper style for all art, and pressure began to be exerted to discourage "formalism." In 1936 all theatres were placed under the Central Direction of Theatres, and after 1938 the "stabilization" of companies made it almost impossible for workers to change jobs without specific government approval.

The new policies meant the gradual suppression of the *avant-garde* troupes and greater prestige for the Maly, Alexandrinsky (now renamed the State Academic Pushkin Theatre), and the Moscow Art Theatre, which after 1932 was called "the House of Gorky." The nonrealistic groups attempted to adapt to the new demands. Tairov began to alternate Soviet plays with productions in his older style. In 1933 he won considerable praise for his staging of Vishnevsky's *The Optimistic Tragedy*, but by 1937 he was so out of favor that his company was merged for a time with that of the Realistic Theatre. Reopening in 1939, the Kamerny gained approval for some productions but was sent to Siberia during the war years. Meyerhold adopted a style usually called "impressionistic," exemplified in his productions of Dumas' *Camille* in 1934 and Tchaikovsky's *Queen of Spades* in 1935. In neither did he alter the text or use biomechanics; both were given lavish, if somewhat stylized, decor and both were popular successes. Nevertheless, Meyerhold's completely nonpolitical interpretations displeased officials even more than his formalism, and in 1938 his theatre was closed. In 1939 he made his last official appearance; in a speech to the First All Union Congress of Directors he is reported to have admitted errors, but to have added: "The pitiful and wretched thing called socialist realism has nothing in common with art. . . . Where once there were the best theatres in the world . . . in hunting formalism, you have eliminated art." Shortly afterward he was arrested and disappeared.

Despite these repressions, stylization received official approval when it was used to convey clear political messages. The most significant experiments of the 1930s were those of Nikolai Okhlopkov (1900–1966) at the Realistic Theatre. Originating as the Fourth Studio of the Moscow Art Theatre in 1921, the Realistic Theatre attained independent status in

Figure 2.21   A production of *The Beginning* at Okhlopkov's Realistic Theatre in Moscow, 1932. Note the two levels and the placement of the audience.

1927. Okhlopkov, who had worked with both Meyerhold and Tairov, was appointed its director in 1932. He eliminated the platform stage and placed all action in the auditorium. Although he often used a central playing area, Okhlopkov also staged scenes around the periphery of the auditorium or on a bridge overhead. Realistic set pieces might be placed almost anywhere, and sound effects from many directions made the audience feel at the center of events. Okhlopkov preferred to work with dramatizations of novels, and all of his productions were "cinematic" in their rapid cutting from one scene to another. But while his selection of plays was acceptable, his production approach was considered too anarchic. For a time his theatre was merged with Tairov's. In 1943 he was named head of the Theatre of the Revolution, where he was to be one of the most important directors of the postwar period. Yuri Zavadsky's career followed a similar path. After Vakhtangov's death he operated a studio for a time, and in 1932 was appointed director of the Red Army Central Theatre. Here he did several fine productions, but in 1935, after refusing to merge his studio

with the larger troupe, he was exiled to the provinces until 1939. Zavadsky was succeeded at the Red Army Central Theatre by Alexei Popov, who was more responsive to official demands.

Considering the uncertainties of the early years and the political pressures of the 1930s, it is not surprising that few significant playwrights emerged. Gorky was the only pre-Revolutionary author who played an important role under the Communists and even he was alienated from the regime for many years. Consequently, his plays were little performed until 1927, after which they came to be considered models of appropriate style. After Gorky was named head of the Union of Soviet Writers in 1932, his works came to be almost obligatory parts of each theatre's repertory. After the Revolution, Gorky wrote only two plays and these not till the 1930s—*Yegor Bulichev and Others* (1932) and *Dostigayev and Others* (1933)—and even these concern life before the Soviet regime began.

In the years immediately following the Revolution, leadership passed to the futurists, militant ene-

Figure 2.22   Mayakovsky's *Bedbug* as produced by Meyerhold in 1929.

mies of old forms and strong advocates of a utilitarian art suited to the needs of a machine age. The major playwright of the movement was Vladimir Mayakovsky (1894–1930), a close friend of Meyerhold, who staged all of his plays. Mayakovsky's *Mystery-Bouffe* (1918) parodied the Bible and ended with the proletariat entering the promised land, while *The Bedbug* (1929) and *The Bathhouse* (1930) satirized Soviet bureaucracy. His last two plays were received so adversely that Mayakovsky committed suicide in 1930.

Most Soviet plays were either farces or melodramas upholding the Revolution and denouncing its opposers. Among the best of the early dramatists were Vsevelod Ivanov (1895–1963), with *Armored Train 14–69* (1927); Mikhail Bulgakov (1891–1940), with *The Days of the Turbins* (1925); and Constantin Trenyov (1884–1945), with *Lyubov Yarovaya* (1926).

Figure 2.23   Final scene from Trenyov's *Lyubov Yarovaya* at the Maly Theatre, Moscow, 1926. This was the first Soviet play to win widespread popularity.

Trenyov's play was the most popular of the early Soviet works, probably because it combined humor, melodrama, and sentiment. Of the later writers, the best were Nikolai Pogodin (1900–1962), with *Aristocrats* (1934) *The Man with the Gun* (1937), and *Kremlin Chimes* (1942); Alexander Afinogenov (1904–1941), with *Far Taiga* (1935) and *On the Eve* (1941); Alexander Korneichuk (1905–1972), with *Truth* (1937) and *The Front* (1942); and Vsevelod Vishnevsky (1900–1951), with *The Optimistic Tragedy* (1932) and *At the Walls of Leningrad* (1941).

By the beginning of World War II, the Russian theatre had been subjugated to political pressures. Nevertheless, no country in the world took its theatre more seriously as a medium of ideas and as an integral part of society.

English Theatre and Drama, 1915–1940

World War I brought major changes to the English theatre. With it, the actor–manager system virtually disappeared to be replaced by the commercial producer and the long run. During the war, popular entertainment dominated the stage. Tree's theatre, for example, the home of Shakespeare since 1900, was in 1916 given over to *Chu Chin Chow*, a musical version of *Ali Baba and the Forty Thieves*, which ran for 2,238 performances.

Probably the most significant occurrence of the war years was the emergence of the "Old Vic" as the principal producer of English classics. Built in 1818 as the Royal Coburg and later renamed the Royal Victoria, the Old Vic was taken over in 1880 by Emma Cons, a social reformer, who converted it into a "temperance Music Hall." In 1898 Miss Cons's niece, Lilian Baylis (1874–1937), became manager of the theatre and began to present operas. It was not until 1914, however, that Shakespearean plays were added. During the war years, the repertory was under the direction of Ben Greet (1857–1936), who, in the tradition of Frank Benson, had long been performing Shakespearean works for both English and American audiences.

After the war, Greet was succeeded by Robert Atkins (1886–1972) from 1920 to 1925, Andrew Leigh (1887–1957) until 1929, and Harcourt Williams (1880–1957) until 1934. In 1931 the Old Vic acquired the Sadler's Wells Theatre, and a ballet company was formed under the direction of Ninette de Valois (Edris Stannis, 1898–   ), who had been trained in the Diaghilev company and had later established her own school. Between 1931 and 1935, the opera and ballet company and the dramatic company alternated between the Old Vic and Sadler's Wells every week. When this arrangement became too cumbersome, drama was confined to the Old Vic, and opera and ballet to Sadler's Wells. The Sadler's Wells Ballet Company was to become the finest in England, and

Figure 2.24   The Old Vic's production of *The Tempest* in 1934. At the back as Prospero is Charles Laughton, in front of him Elsa Lanchester is seen as Ariel. Courtesy Debenham Collection, British Theatre Museum, London.

was rechristened the Royal Ballet after World War II, and its opera troupe developed into the present-day English National Opera Company.

When Miss Baylis died in 1937, it was feared that the Old Vic would close, but Tyrone Guthrie (1900–1971) was appointed administrator and operated it with distinction until 1945. Guthrie had made his debut as an actor in 1924, but had soon turned to directing. His first London production came in 1931, but his finest prewar work was done with the Old Vic. As a director, Guthrie was noted for his novel interpretations of standard works (sometimes considered merely bizarre by critics), and the restless and vital quality of movement. By 1939 the Old Vic was the most respected troupe in England. With its own theatre, a permanent company, and a policy of producing the finest plays at reasonable prices, it set a standard for the entire country.

Several other producers in London helped to raise the level of performance between the wars. Among these, the most important were the Lyric Theatre and the Gate Theatre. The Lyric Theatre, Hammersmith, one of the many houses built in the suburbs during the heyday of music halls, had fallen upon hard times when Nigel Playfair (1874–1934) leased it in 1918. Although Playfair presented many kinds of plays, his reputation rests upon his productions of Restoration and eighteenth-century works, most notably *The Beggar's Opera* (which opened in 1920 for a run of 1,463 performances), *The Way of the World* (1924), *The Rivals* (1925), *The Beaux' Stratagem* (1927), and *Love in a Village* (1928). Most of his productions were decorative, gay, stylized caricatures. For a time, the Lyric was the most fashionable theatre in London, but as Playfair's approach hardened into a formula, popularity declined, and in 1932 the company was dissolved. The Lyric was noted above all for its sense of style, first established by Claud Lovat Fraser (1890–1921), whose sensitive use of color and period motifs profoundly influenced others.

The Gate Theatre was opened in 1925 by Peter Godfrey (1899–1971), a former circus clown and

Figure 2.25 *The Beggar's Opera* at the Lyric Theatre, Hammersmith, 1920. Setting by Claud Lovat Fraser. The unit at front remained throughout, while pieces were changed behind the arches. Courtesy Theatre Museum, Victoria and Albert Museum.

Figure 2.26 Peter Godfrey's production of Kaiser's *From Morn to Midnight* at the Gate Theatre, London, in 1928. Courtesy Enthoven Collection, Victoria and Albert Museum.

Shakespearean actor. Unable to secure a license for the only hall he could afford, Godfrey ran his theatre as a private club. In nine years, he produced over 350 plays. His most characteristic productions were of expressionist plays or those with a psychoanalytic bias. Using set pieces against black drapes, unusual lighting effects, and stylized acting techniques, Godfrey was the principal exponent of expressionism in London. In 1934 the Gate Theatre passed to Norman Marshall (1901–　), who presented many works forbidden by the censor. He also did much to reestablish the intimate revue, which had declined since the 1920s.

Of the several important groups outside of London, perhaps the best was the Birmingham Repertory Company, which, under Barry Jackson's direc-

tion between 1913 and 1935, produced about 400 plays ranging through the entire history of drama. Between 1922 and 1934, Jackson also presented forty-two plays in London, many remarkably successful despite their departure from commercial formulas. Through his productions of *Hamlet* (1925), *Macbeth* (1928), and *Taming of the Shrew* (1928), Jackson began the vogue for playing Shakespeare in modern dress. When Jackson transferred ownership of his theatre to the City of Birmingham in 1935, it became England's first civic theatre.

Figure 2.27   *Gammer Gurton's Needle* at the Malvern Festival. Setting by Paul Shelving. From *Theatre Arts* (1933).

Jackson also founded the Malvern Festival in 1929, thereby giving considerable impetus to the summer festival movement. Operated primarily by the Birmingham Repertory Company until 1939, the Malvern Festival had no clear policy, some seasons being devoted to plays of a particular era, others to plays by specific authors, especially Shaw. All, however, were of high quality. The festival was discontinued between 1939 and 1949.

Two other provincial troupes—the Cambridge Festival Theatre and the Oxford Repertory Company—were outstanding. The Cambridge Festival Theatre was established by Terence Gray (1895–   ) in 1926 with the avowed purpose of undermining realistic acting and production, a policy that was followed consistently. The theatre had no curtain, proscenium arch, or orchestra pit. Scenery normally consisted of ramps or other constructions set against a cyclorama, upon which patterns of light were projected. The actors' movement was often described as "choreographic" and was always highly stylized. Gray thought the text an excuse for a director's improvisations. He performed *Romeo and Juliet* in flamenco costumes; put some characters in *Twelfth Night* on roller skates; and had the Judge in *The Merchant of Venice* play with a yo-yo. Gray's productions generated much controversy but had little immediate result. The theatre closed in 1933.

The Oxford Repertory Company, headed by J. B. Fagan (1873–1933) from 1923 to 1929, presented twenty-one plays a year drawn from many countries and periods. The schedule meant that productions were often rough, but all had vitality and clear interpretations. Little scenery was used, for the theatre had only a small stage fronted by a large apron, upon which most of the action transpired. The importance

Figure 2.28   Terence Gray's production of *Henry VIII* at the Festival Theatre, Cambridge, 1931. Note the abstract setting and the playing-card costumes.

of this company rests in part upon the many young actors, most notably Tyrone Guthrie, John Gielgud, Raymond Massey, Flora Robson, and Glen Byam Shaw, who received their first major experience under Fagan.

The Stratford-on-Avon seasons of Shakespeare's plays also gained in prestige after they resumed in 1919. Until 1934, most of the plays were directed by W. Bridges-Adams (1889–1965), who worked under adverse conditions. There were no shop or storage facilities, the Festival Committee controlled policy, and six plays were opened on six successive evenings. After the old theatre burned in 1926, the company played in a motion picture house until the present building was completed in 1932. Although the new auditorium was largely satisfactory, the stage was a conventional picture-frame structure; its sliding platform stages could not move entirely out of sight and the elevator stages only sank 8 feet. Such blunders have required several remodelings, the most recent in 1972. Bridges-Adams resigned in 1934 and was succeeded until 1942 by B. Iden Payne (1881–1976), whose most characteristic productions were in the style of Poel—using an Elizabethan structure and Elizabethan costumes. Other directors, most notably Theodore Kommissarzhevsky, brought novel conceptions to the plays. Kommissarzhevsky's production of *The Merchant of Venice* utilized *commedia dell'arte* conventions and his *The Merry Wives of Windsor* was given a Viennese background. London critics largely ignored the Stratford company, which did not achieve its current critical stature until after World War II.

The little theatre movement burgeoned in England after the First World War. The British Drama League, founded in 1919 and headed by Geoffrey Whitworth (1883–1951) until 1948, organized conferences, sent out costumes and properties, aided in play selection, and held annual festivals of plays.

During this period many performers of high merit appeared. Of the actresses, the best were probably Sybil Thorndike (1882–1976) and Edith Evans (1888–1976). Miss Thorndike began her career in

Ben Greet's company and after 1914 acted often with the Old Vic troupe. She was especially noted in the 1920s for her portrayal of Shaw's Saint Joan, although her performances ranged from Greek tragedy to modern comedy. Miss Evans began her career with Poel and gained fame as Millamant in the Lyric Theatre's production of *The Way of the World*. She also appeared frequently with the Old Vic, at the Malvern Festival, and in many London commercial theatres. Other outstanding actresses included Lilian Braithwaite (1873–1948), Marie Tempest (1864–1942), Flora Robson (1902–   ), Gertrude Lawrence (1898–1952), and Peggy Ashcroft (1907–   ).

Of the actors, the most important was John Gielgud (1904–   ), who made his debut in 1921 and won major acclaim with Hamlet in 1934. He soon be-

Figure 2.29   Laurence Olivier as Romeo, Edith Evans as the Nurse, and John Gielgud as Mercutio in Gielgud's production of *Romeo and Juliet*, 1935. From *Theatre Arts* (1936).

came one of England's major directors as well. In 1937–1938 he leased the Queen's Theatre, assembled a company that included Peggy Ashcroft, Michael Redgrave, and Alec Guinness, and produced a repertory of classics. By the time the war began, Gielgud was accepted as England's finest actor. Other outstanding performers included Cedric Hardwicke (1893–1964), who worked closely with Barry Jackson after 1922, Donald Wolfit (1902–1968), who played at the Old Vic, Stratford, and with his own company, and Maurice Evans (1901–   ), who played for Terence Gray and the Old Vic before emigrating to the United States in 1935. A number of young men, who would be of greater importance after the war, also established their promise: Laurence Olivier (1907–   ), who had played with the Birmingham Repertory Company, Gielgud, and the Old Vic; Michael Redgrave (1908–   ), on the stage after 1934; Ralph Richardson (1902–   ), Alec Guinness (1914–   ), who made his debut in 1934; Anthony Quayle (1913–   ), on the stage after 1931; and Glen Byam Shaw (1904–   ), who played with the Oxford Repertory Company and Gielgud.

Few major dramatists emerged between the wars, although a number of older ones, such as Shaw, Barrie, Galsworthy, and Pinero, continued to write. During the 1920s three authors—Maugham, Lonsdale, and Coward—excelled in sophisticated comedy. Somerset Maugham (1874–1965) wrote his first play in 1904 and until 1933 was one of England's most prolific playwrights. His major achievement came with his comedies of manners, *Our Betters* (1917), *The Circle* (1921), *The Constant Wife* (1927), and *The Breadwinner* (1930), in which sardonic humor and unusual personal outlooks never descend into trite happy endings. Often compared with Maugham, Frederick Lonsdale (1881–1954) drew a wide following with his amusing situations and effective dialogue in *The Last of Mrs. Cheyney* (1925), *On Approval* (1927), and *The High Road* (1929). Noel Coward (1899–1973) captured the spirit of the postwar era with such works as *Fallen Angels* (1925), *Hay Fever* (1925), *Bittersweet* (1929), *Private Lives* (1930),

and *Design for Living* (1932), in which unconventional behavior was combined with sophisticated wit.

Of the serious writers, J. B. Priestley (1894–   ) gained the greatest prestige. He began his dramatic career in 1932 with *Dangerous Corner* and went on to *Time and the Conways* (1937) and *An Inspector Calls* (1946). Although he wrote many kinds of plays, Priestley is most noted for his compression or distortion of time to illuminate characters and ideas. Of the sentimental and melodramatic school, Emlyn Williams (1905–   ) was perhaps the most successful. After writing two sensational plays, *A Murder Has Been Arranged* (1930) and *Night Must Fall* (1935), he presented *The Corn Is Green* (1938), a sentimental story about a Welsh teacher and her star pupil.

This period also brought several attempts to revive poetic drama. Gordon Bottomley (1874–1948) wrote

Figure 2.30 T. S. Eliot's *Murder in the Cathedral* at the Mercury Theatre, London, in 1935. Directed by E. Martin Browne. Robert Speaight is seen at right as Becket. Courtesy Debenham Collection, British Theatre Museum.

King Lear's Wife (1915), *Britain's Daughters* (1922), and *Laodice and Danae* (1930), and W. H. Auden (1907–1973) and Christopher Isherwood (1904–   ) collaborated on *The Dog Beneath the Skin* (1935) and *The Ascent of F6* (1936). The most lasting achievement was that of T. S. Eliot (1888–1965) with *Murder in the Cathedral* (1935), the story of Thomas à Becket's martyrdom. Eliot went on to write *The Family Reunion* (1939) and, after the war, several other verse plays. In general, however, the attempt to revive poetic drama was ineffective, primarily because of shortcomings in the plays rather than because of any opposition to poetry.

The revue was one of the most popular theatrical forms between the wars. C. B. Cochran (1873–1951), its most famous producer, began his work with "intimate revues" in 1914 and then turned to large-scale, lavish productions between 1918 and 1931. André Charlot (1882–1956) also presented many revues between 1916 and 1923, bringing Beatrice Lillie (1898–   ) to fame. The intimate revue was revived at the Gate Theatre in the 1930s, especially through the writing of Herbert Farjeon (1887–1945) and the performances of Hermione Gingold (1897–   ).

To Ireland, England's deep involvement in World War I offered the chance to throw off British rule. Consequently, in 1916 it began a rebellion which was put down after much bloodshed. But the demand for independence grew and in 1919 Ireland declared itself a republic. Three years of armed conflict ensued before a treaty was signed in 1923 which granted independence to all but six northern counties.

This struggle provides the context for the early plays of Sean O'Casey (1884–1964), Ireland's most important postwar playwright. O'Casey turned attention away from folk and legendary subject matter to the urban life of his time. The plays that established his fame—*The Shadow of a Gunman* (1923), *Juno and the Paycock* (1924), and *The Plough and the Stars* (1926)—were realistic in tone and dealt with the effects of the rebellion on the lives of ordinary people. After this time O'Casey adopted expressionistic techniques in such works as *The Silver Tassie* (1928), *Within the Gates* (1934), *Red Roses for Me* (1943),

and *Purple Dust* (1945). His change of style precipitated a break with the Abbey Theatre in 1928, after which O'Casey lived in England. O'Casey's works have been more widely read than produced, largely because, in spite of many powerful scenes, the dramatic action is sometimes obscure. Nevertheless, his characterizations, vivid use of language, and human compassion make him one of the finest writers of modern times.

Theatre and Drama in the United States, 1915–1940

The United States was able to remain aloof from World War I until 1917, when it was drawn into the conflict. Not only was it decisive in the outcome of the war, it was a leader in founding the League of Nations and in establishing independent states for the ethnic and language groups of Europe. Following the war, however, the United States entered another period of isolationism, during which it sought to divorce itself from foreign affairs and imposed tariffs to reduce imports. The economic results were disastrous for farmers and workers and ultimately were instrumental in bringing on the Great Depression of the 1930s. It was during the postwar period that women won the right to vote and that mass production and new developments in transportation and communication revolutionized American life.

During the 1930s the energies of the nation were devoted to overcoming economic problems. For the first time, the government assumed a key role in social planning and began such programs as social security and public works. By 1940, American life was vastly different from what it had been in 1915. The United States had become one of the world's great powers and an industrial giant. It had also won a measure of respect in artistic and cultural affairs for the first time.

Not until around 1915 did the United States begin to be aware of innovations that had long been underway in the European theatre. This awareness came about in large part through nonprofessional groups. Around 1912 several "little theatres" were established in emulation of the independent theatres of Europe. Among the most important of these were the Toy Theatre, opened by Mrs. Lyman Gale in Boston in 1912; the Chicago Little Theatre, formed by Maurice Brown in 1912; the Neighborhood Playhouse, established in New York by Irene and Alice Lewisohn in 1915; the Washington Square Players, formed in New York in 1915; the Provincetown Players, organized in Provincetown, Massachusetts, in 1915; and the Detroit Arts and Crafts Theatre, opened in 1916. By 1917 there were at least fifty of these groups. For the most part they depended upon unpaid volunteers for personnel and upon subscribers for financial support; most produced a series of plays each year, using techniques already widely accepted in Europe. The little theatre movement made its greatest contributions between 1912 and 1920 by preparing audiences to accept the new drama and production methods.

After 1920, the little theatres began to be indistinguishable from community theatres. Originating like its European counterpart in attempts to revive the spirit of ancient Greece, the community drama movement had begun in the United States around 1905. Its most ardent supporter was Percy MacKaye (1875– 1956), whose *The Civic Theatre* (1912) and *Community Drama* (1917) outlined a program and whose outdoor pageants provided texts designed to involve several thousand participants. Interest in mass spectacles soon declined, however, and after 1920 most local groups turned to the performance of recent Broadway hits. By 1925, nearly 2,000 community or little theatre companies were registered with the Drama League of America, an organization which encouraged local interest in drama. The number has continued to grow.

Drama programs also began to be introduced into colleges and universities. Although plays had been produced by students since the seventeenth century, no courses in theatre were offered until about 1900. The first important change came in 1903 when George Pierce Baker (1866– 1935) began to teach playwriting at Radcliffe College. Later opened to

Harvard University students, the course was enlarged in 1913 to include a workshop for the production of plays. Baker attracted many of the United States's most talented young men, including Eugene O'Neill, S. N. Behrman, and Robert Edmond Jones, instilled in them high standards, and helped them to acquire skills. In 1925 Baker moved to Yale University where he established a drama department which was to provide professional training for many later theatre workers. In 1914 at the Carnegie Institute of Technology, Thomas Wood Stevens (1880– 1942) instituted the country's first degree-granting program in theatre, and in 1918 Frederick Koch (1877– 1944) founded the influential Carolina Playmakers. Many other programs soon followed. By 1940 theatre education was an accepted part of most American universities.

In the years following 1910, the "new stagecraft," as the European trends were called in North America, began to find its way into the commercial theatre. Winthrop Ames (1871– 1937), who had gone

Figure 2.31 Robert Edmond Jones's design for Granville Barker's production of *The Man Who Married a Dumb Wife*, 1915. This setting is usually said to be the first important native expression of the "new stagecraft" in the United States. From *The Theatre* (1915).

to Europe in 1907 to study new developments there, was employed in 1909 to manage the New Theatre in New York, an ambitious nonprofit repertory company. The large theatre soon proved both financially and artistically unsatisfactory, however, and Ames then built the Little Theatre, seating only 300, where in the years preceding World War I he presented a number of plays in the new style. In 1912 he imported Reinhardt's production of *Sumurun*, which also aroused much interest in European ideas.

In 1912 the Boston Opera Company hired Joseph Urban (1872–1933), a well-established Viennese designer of the new school, to mount its productions. Urban later worked in New York, where he was famous for the fresh coloring and simplicity of his settings. In 1915 the New York Stage Society invited Harley Granville Barker to direct a series of plays for its members. For Barker's production of *The Man Who Married a Dumb Wife*, Robert Edmond Jones (1887–1954) provided settings usually considered the first native expression of the "new stagecraft." Jones was one of several young men, including Lee Simonson and Sam Hume, who had studied in Europe between 1912 and 1915 and had been impressed by the changing theatrical trends. In 1914 Hume arranged an exhibit of continental scene design which was shown in New York, Detroit, Chicago, and Cleveland. Hume later was associated with the Detroit Arts and Crafts Theatre; here his associate, Sheldon Cheney, in 1916 launched *Theatre Arts Magazine*, which until 1948 was to be the principal disseminator of new ideas in North America. Visits of the Abbey Theatre in 1911, the Ballets Russes in 1916, and Copeau's troupe from 1917 to 1919 also helped to stimulate interest in foreign movements. Nevertheless, when the war ended in 1918 the American theatre was only beginning to be aware of European practices.

The triumph of the new ideal owes most to the Provincetown Players, the Theatre Guild, and to Arthur Hopkins. After presenting a few programs on Cape Cod, the Provincetown Players moved to New York in 1916. In its early years the company concentrated upon plays by American playwrights and by 1925 had presented ninety-three plays by forty-seven authors. After 1923, the group split into two branches. One continued the older practices, while the other, under Eugene O'Neill, Robert Edmond Jones, and Kenneth Macgowan, performed foreign and period plays along with the noncommercial works of O'Neill and others. Although it succumbed to financial pressures in 1929, the Provincetown Players had served an important role as an experimental theatre both for new plays and for new production techniques.

In 1918 the Washington Square Players was disbanded, but some of its members then formed the Theatre Guild, a fully professional company, with the avowed purpose of presenting plays of merit not likely to interest commercial managers. After an uncertain beginning in 1919, it soon became the United States' most respected theatre, presenting a number of plays each year to an audience of subscribers. In 1928 it also began a subscription series in six other cities. The Guild was governed by a board of directors, and for a time maintained a nucleus company of actors. It adopted an eclectic approach to staging; its principal director, Philip Moeller (1880–1958), and its principal designer, Lee Simonson (1888–1967), drew upon several European movements, although their most typical style was a modified realism. During the 1930s the company gradually curtailed its activities because of financial problems and by World War II was merely another commercial producer investing in long-run hits.

In 1918 Arthur Hopkins (1878–1950) began a series of productions that were to mark him as the most adventurous of New York's commercial producers. Working with Robert Edmond Jones, Hopkins presented plays by Tolstoy, Ibsen, Gorky, Shakespeare, O'Neill, and others. In 1921 his production of *Macbeth* created a sensation with its expressionistic use of titled arches, and in 1922 *Hamlet*, starring John Barrymore (1882–1942), was declared one of the best productions of the century. After Hopkins and the Guild demonstrated the commercial viability of the

Figure 2.32   Robert Edmond Jones's setting for the banquet scene in *Macbeth*. Arthur Hopkins's expressionistic production, 1921. Note the masks above the stage. From *Theatre Arts Magazine* (1924).

"new stagecraft," it was gradually adopted by others and by 1930 had become the standard approach.

The "new stagecraft" was primarily a visual movement, and the total effect of most productions might best be described as "simplified realism." In addition to Jones and Simonson, the major influence on scene design was Norman Bel Geddes (1893– 1958), a visionary not unlike Appia. Geddes's plan for staging Dante's *The Divine Comedy* on a series of terraces (published in 1921) is still considered one of the most brilliant conceptions by an American designer. His penchant for steps, platforms, and imaginative light-ing was also seen in his productions of *Hamlet* (1931) and Werfel's *The Eternal Road* (1936), in which the platforms soared to a height of 50 feet. Other important designers included Cleon Throckmorton (1897– 1965), Mordecai Gorelik (1899–   ), Boris Aronson (1900– 1980), Aline Bernstein (1882– 1955), Howard Bay (1912–   ), Donald Oenslager (1902– 1975), and especially Jo Mielziner (1901– 1976), who was to be the United States' most prolifice and respected designer after 1945. While all did not follow the same style, they shared a respect for simplicity and a desire to capture the spirit of a text.

Figure 2.33   Norman Bel Geddes's project for staging Dante's *The Divine Comedy*. Courtesy Hoblitzelle Theatre Arts Collection, University of Texas, Austin.

Figure 2.34   Norman Bel Geddes's setting for *The Miracle* at the Century Theatre, New York, 1924. For this production, directed by Max Reinhardt, Bel Geddes converted the theatre into a cathedral. This sectional plan shows how the scenery and machinery were arranged. From *The Scientific American* (1924).

Continental influence continued to be felt in the 1920s through a series of visitors: the Moscow Art Theatre toured the United States in 1923–1924; Reinhardt presented *The Miracle* (with designs by Geddes) in 1924 and staged a season of plays in 1927–1928; and Copeau directed *The Brothers Karamazov* for the Theatre Guild in 1927. Two of Stanislavsky's actors, Richard Boleslavsky (1889–1937) and Maria Ouspenskaya (1881–1949), were induced to head the American Laboratory Theatre between 1923 and 1930. Here the Stanislavsky system was taught in a version later popularized by Boleslavsky's book *Acting, the First Six Lessons* (1933). Among the more than 500 students who studied at the American Lab-

oratory Theatre were Stella Adler, Lee Strasberg, and Harold Clurman.

Between 1925 and 1940 several groups tried to escape the commercial pattern. From 1925 to 1930 Walter Hampden (1879–1955) revived the actor–manager system with his repertory company. Although the depression forced him to give up his theatre in New York, Hampden continued to tour with his troupe for many years. Between 1926 and 1933 Eva Le Gallienne (1899–) managed the Civic Repertory Theatre, produced thirty-four plays and built up a subscription list of 50,000. Despite its excellent repertory and wide following, the company was always in debt and could not survive the depression.

The most distinguished troupe of the 1930s was the Group Theatre, launched in 1931 by Lee Strasberg (1901–), Harold Clurman (1901–1980), and Cheryl Crawford (1902–) on the model of the Moscow Art Theatre, whose methods and ensemble approach it emulated. With a company including Stella Adler (1904–), Morris Carnovsky (1898–), and Elia Kazan (1909–), it presented plays by Paul Green, Maxwell Anderson, Sidney Kingsley, Irwin Shaw, William Saroyan, and others, although its reputation rests especially upon its productions of Clifford Odets's dramas. Ultimately the troupe foundered because of disagreements over policy. In 1941 it was disbanded. Its influence has continued, however, through the work of many former members, several of whom were instrumental in popularizing the Stanislavsky system in the United States.

The depression motivated the creation of a unique experiment, the Federal Theatre Project, which was established in 1935 to combat unemployment. Headed by Hallie Flanagan Davis (1890–1969), at its peak it employed 10,000 persons in forty states. About 1,000 productions of all types were mounted, 65 percent of them free. In spite of its diversity, it is now remembered primarily for developing the "Living Newspaper," a cinematic form which integrated factual data with dramatic vignettes. Each script centered around a problem: *Triple-A Plowed Under* (1936) dealt with agriculture, *Power* (1937) with rural electrification, and *One-Third of a Nation* (1938) with slum housing. Most of the plays had as a central character the "little man" who, upon raising questions about a current problem, was led through its background, human consequences, and possible solutions. Much of the dialogue was taken from speeches, newspaper stories, or

Figure 2.35 Howard Bay's setting, a tenement house, for *One Third of a Nation*, "a living newspaper" about inadequate housing, staged by the Federal Theatre Project in 1938. From *Theatre Arts* (1938).

other documents. Many of the techniques were borrowed from Epic Theatre. The political tone of many works eventually alienated Congress, which in 1939 refused to appropriate funds for its continuance.

The Federal Theatre motivated the formation of the Mercury Theatre in 1937, when Orson Welles (1915–) and John Houseman (1902–) decided to present Marc Blitzstein's *The Cradle Will Rock* after it was withdrawn from production by the Federal Theatre. Welles had already established a reputation as an actor with his portrayal of Doctor Faustus and as an imaginative producer with *Macbeth*, which he set in Haiti and performed with an all-black cast. Between 1957 and 1939 the Mercury Theatre presented works by Büchner, Dekker, Shaw, and Shakespeare. Its greatest success came with *Julius Caesar*, played as a comment upon fascism.

The Federal Theatre also promoted black theatre,

Figure 2.36   Orson Welles's version of *Macbeth*, set in Haiti. It was produced by the Federal Theatre Project. Setting by Nat Karson. From *Theatre Arts* (1936).

which, though not extensive between the wars, was laying the foundations for later developments. In the years between 1890 and 1915 a few musicals had been written for black casts, a few stock companies had performed sporadically in New York and elsewhere, and (after 1910) one black performer—Bert Williams (1876–1922)—had won stardom on Broadway in musical pieces.

An important step was taken in 1915 when Anita Bush organized the All-Colored Dramatic Stock Company in New York, which, after one season, passed to the control of Robert Levy at the Lafayette Theatre. Most of the company's repertory was taken from Broadway, but it gave black actors their longest continuous employment in regular drama to that time. Around this time a few dramatists also began to write sympathetically about blacks. The first serious plays for black actors to be seen on Broadway were Ridgely Torrence's *Three Plays for a Negro Theatre* (1917), which not only marked a turning away from the stereotyped treatment of blacks but also the first time that blacks were welcomed into Broadway audiences. There followed such works as O'Neill's *The Emperor Jones* (in which a black actor played the leading role in a serious American play on Broadway for the first time), DuBose and Dorothy Heyward's *Porgy*, Marc Connelly's *The Green Pastures*, and Paul Green's *In Abraham's Bosom*, all by white authors.

There were as well several black authors, although they were given relatively little encouragement. Among the best of the plays were Willis Richardson's *The Chipwoman's Fortune*, Frank Wilson's *Sugar Cane*, Hall Johnson's *Run Little Chillun*, and Langston Hughes's *Mulatto*. There were also a number of musical plays, among the most successful of which were Noble Sissle and Eubie Blake's *Shuffle Along*, *Chocolate Dandies*, and *Runnin' Wild*. All of these plays helped such black performers as Richard Harrison, Frank Wilson, Rose McClendon, and Abbie Mitchell to demonstrate that they could compete with the best actors of the period.

Black theatre received a major boost from the Federal Theatre, which in several cities established black units that presented seventy-five plays in four years. Unfortunately, most of the hopes were dashed when the project ended in 1939. Since the archives of the Federal Theatre Project were rediscovered a few years ago, considerable attention has been paid to the black dramas found there.

By World War II many plays about black life had found their way onto the stage. Perhaps the most disturbing of these was *Native Son*, Paul Green and Richard Wright's adaptation of Wright's novel, which showed the terrible effects of social evils on

Figure 2.37   European and American Directors, 1915–1940. ▶

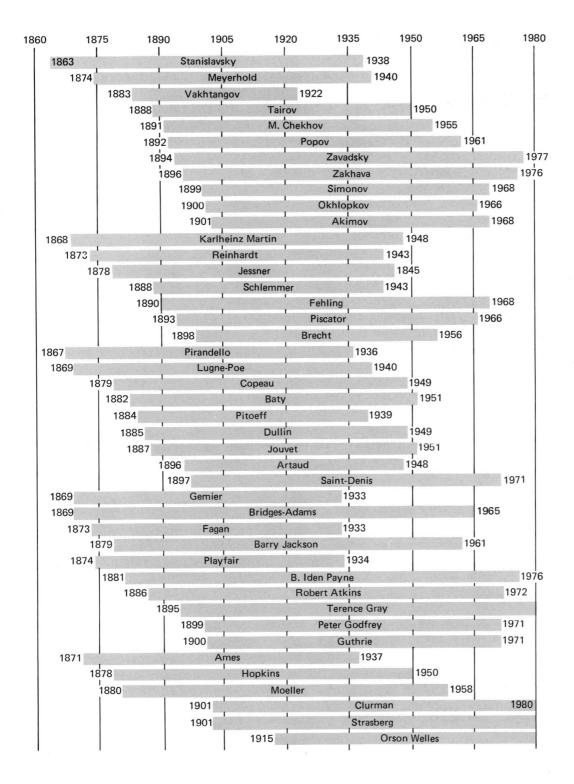

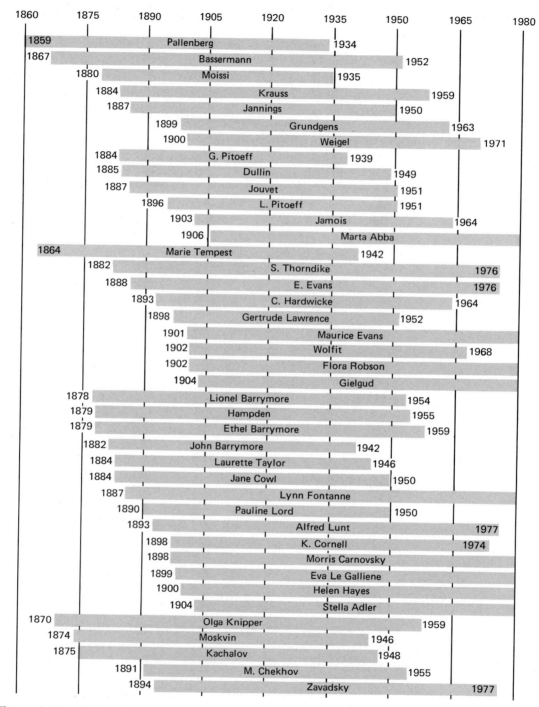

Figure 2.38   Major European and American Actors, 1915–1940.

the life of the protagonist. But, if there was still a long way to go, there had been much improvement since 1915. The black theatre artist had made his presence felt, even if he had not yet been permitted to demonstrate his full potential.

The depression also gave impetus to the "workers' theatre" movement, which had begun in 1926 with the Worker's Drama League. In 1932 a national organization was formed, later called the New Theatre League. Most of the member groups were amateur, but in 1933 a fully professional organization, the Theatre Union, was formed in New York and provided leadership for the entire movement. After the failure of the Theatre Union in 1937, the League declined and by 1942 had virtually ceased to exist. For the most part, the workers' theatres presented socialistic propaganda plays designed to arouse protest.

As the depression deepened, it became increasingly difficult for playwrights to get unusual works produced. Largely for this reason, the Playwrights' Company was created in 1938 by Maxwell Anderson, Elmer Rice, Sidney Howard, Robert E. Sherwood, and S. N. Behrman. In addition to their own plays, they also presented works by other authors. The Playwrights' Company was to be a major producing organization until 1960.

These dissident groups had little effect upon the basic pattern of the commercial theatre. The length of runs steadily increased, reaching a peak with *Tobacco Road* (1933), which played for seven years. The number of new productions also grew each season until 1927–1928, when about 300 plays were mounted, but rapidly declined after 1930, having fallen to eighty by 1939–1940. Theatrical production was complicated in these years by the emergence of powerful labor unions. The stage hands' union, the National Alliance of Theatrical Stage Employees, had achieved full recognition during the season of 1910–1911, and in 1918 the United Scenic Artists was formed. Actors Equity Association, founded in 1912, was recognized in 1919; it became a "closed shop" in 1924 and was able to establish a minimum-wage scale in 1933. The Dramatists' Guild, formed in 1912, became the bargaining agent for all playwrights in 1926. As each group bettered working conditions, it also demanded considerably higher pay for its members and thereby contributed to the economic problems of the theatre.

Between 1915 and 1940, American dramatists began to command international respect for the first time. Few were members of any particular movement, but most shared a dislike for romantic melodrama with realistic trappings. Only one American dramatist—O'Neill—achieved genuine stature. Eugene O'Neill (1888–1953), son of James O'Neill, turned to playwriting around 1912, attended Professor Baker's playwriting classes for a time, and in 1915 had his first works presented by the Provincetown Players. The group continued to encourage him through the 1920s by performing those works rejected by commercial producers. His first full-length play, *Beyond the Horizon*, brought him to Broadway in 1920. After 1934, although he continued to write, no new works were performed until 1946.

O'Neill wrote about twenty-five full-length plays of uneven quality. Many were artistic failures, and even the best often suggest that more was intended than achieved. Nevertheless, his protagonists' search for some significance in life gives the plays a tone of high seriousness. O'Neill also experimented with many novel theatrical devices and dramatic techniques. In *The Great God Brown* (1926), *Lazarus Laughed* (1926), and *Days Without End* (1934) he made use of masks; in *Strange Interlude* (1928) he employed lengthy "interior monologues" to express the characters' inner thoughts; in *Mourning Becomes Electra* (1931) he gained scope by adopting the trilogy form. O'Neill also ranged through many styles. The devices of expressionism were adopted for *The Hairy Ape* (1922) and *The Great God Brown*, those of symbolism for *The Fountain* (1922) and to a lesser extent for almost all the plays; those of realism for *Beyond the Horizon*, *Anna Christie* (1921), and *Desire Under the Elms* (1924). O'Neill's strength lay in complex characterization, strong dramatic situations, and seriousness of purpose.

Probably O'Neill's greatest rival was Maxwell Anderson (1888–1959), who after achieving renown for his anti-romantic war play, *What Price Glory?* (1924), turned to blank verse drama in *Elizabeth the Queen* (1930), *Mary of Scotland* (1933), *Winterset* (1935), and other plays. Although dramatically effective, Anderson's plays offered few new insights, being merely skillful retellings of familiar stories. Other serious playwrights included Elmer Rice (1892–1967) with *The Adding Machine* (1923), an expressionistic drama about the dehumanization of man, and *Street Scene* (1929), a naturalistic play set in the New York slums; Sidney Howard (1891–1939), with *They Knew What They Wanted* (1924), an anti-romantic comedy about three people who get their wishes by accepting compromises, *The Silver Cord* (1926), about a mother's attempt to retain her control over her newly married son, and *Yellow Jack* (1934), a semidocumentary play about the fight to control yellow fever; Paul Green (1894–1981), with his tragedies, *In Abraham's Bosom* (1926) and *The House of Connolly* (1931), and the expressionistic antiwar play, *Johnny Johnson* (1936); and Lillian Hellman (1905–   ), with such moral fables as *The Little Foxes* (1938), a story of rapacious greed among the rising industrialists of the new South around 1900.

The comedy of manners was well represented by Phillip Barry (1896–1949) with *Paris Bound* (1927) and *The Philadelphia Story* (1939), both treating divorce among the upper classes; and S. N. Behrman (1893–1973), with *Biography* (1932), *Rain from Heaven* (1934), and *End of Summer* (1936), all of which contrast tolerance with inhumanity. Among the writers of farce, the best was George S. Kaufman (1889–1961), who worked with a number of collaborators, most successfully with Moss Hart (1904–1961), on *You Can't Take it With You* (1936) and *The Man Who Came to Dinner* (1940). William Saroyan (1900–1981) glorified the simple life in such plays as *My Heart's in the Highlands* (1939), *The Time of Your Life* (1939), and *The Beautiful People* (1941), all of which depict eccentric characters living on the fringes of society who find beauty and redemption.

The drama of social consciousness was most persistently practiced by John Howard Lawson (1895–1977), whose *Roger Bloomer* (1923), *Processional* (1925), and *Internationale* (1928) were experimental in form and militantly propagandistic in theme. Clifford Odets (1906–1963) followed something of the opposite development, for his early plays, *Waiting for Lefty* (1935) and *Awake and Sing* (1935) call for group action, while his later works, *Paradise Lost* (1935) and *Golden Boy* (1937), take a more complex view of social conditions. Odets was essentially a chronicler of family relationships; his strength lay in his ability to create believable characters struggling to achieve more than life will give them.

Two of the finest dramatists of the 1930s were Sherwood and Wilder. Robert E. Sherwood (1896–1955) in *The Petrified Forest* (1935) created an allegorical cross section of American life, in *Idiot's Delight* (1936) depicted through melodramatic farce the horrors of war and the spiritual bankruptcy which gives rise to it, and in *Abe Lincoln in Illinois* (1938) sought to remind Americans of the high ideals upon which their country had been founded. Thornton Wilder's (1897–1975) reputation was created primarily by two plays, *Our Town* (1938), which seeks to point out the eternal patterns of human experience behind seeming progress, and *The Skin of Our Teeth* (1943), a testimonial to man's ability to survive all disasters. Wilder's frank theatricality and simplicity have won him a wide following both at home and abroad.

Much popular entertainment between the wars took the form of musical comedy and revues. Every year between 1907 and 1931, Florenz Ziegfeld (1869–1932) mounted a new edition of the *Ziegfeld Follies*, each more lavish than the last. Musical comedy, long merely the excuse for presenting beautiful chorus girls, began to move in a new direction after 1928, when Jerome Kern and Oscar Hammerstein II placed the major emphasis in *Showboat* upon a coherent story. This new direction reached its culmination in Richard Rodgers's and Oscar Hammerstein's *Oklahoma* (1943), in which music, story, dance, and setting were fully integrated to tell a semi-serious story. With the triumph of the new approach, the old type of musical largely disappeared.

Of the United States' many outstanding performers, only a few can be mentioned: Jane Cowl (1884–1950), on the stage from 1903 but most famous for her portrayals of Juliet, Cleopatra, and the heroines of Sherwood; Pauline Lord (1890–1950), especially remembered for her performances in *Anna Christie* and *They Knew What They Wanted*; Laurette Taylor (1884–1946), one of the most versatile actresses of her day, whose last major appearance was made as Amanda in Tennessee Williams's *The Glass Menagerie*; Ina Claire (1895–   ), who appeared in many *Ziegfeld Follies* before playing the heroines of Behrman's comedies; Helen Hayes (1900–   ), noted especially for her appearances in Barrie's plays, Anderson's *Mary in Scotland*, and

Housman's *Victoria Regina*; Katherine Cornell (1898–1974), who gave outstanding portrayals in *Candida*, *The Three Sisters*, *The Baretts of Wimpole Street*, and many other plays: Lynn Fontanne (1887?–   ), an English actress, who came to the United States in 1910 and whose later career was tied up with that of her husband, Alfred Lunt (1893–1977), with whom she appeared in *The Guardsman*, *Reunion in Vienna*, *Amphitryon 38*, and many other works.

World War II, like the first, interrupted the theatre's normal patterns. The war also raised serious doubts about a world that had created such horrors as the Nazi extermination camps and such destructive weapons as the atomic bomb. Out of the questioning would come new experiments in theatre and drama.

Looking at Theatre History

One of the ways of studying theatre history is through the theories of art that lie behind practice. Perhaps for no period is this more helpful than the twentieth century, which has seen artistic movements come and go with bewildering rapidity. The proliferation of movements was especially evident between 1910 and 1925. Many movements of that time introduced ideas and techniques that were to reappear in the theatre of the 1960s. Because they are often based on unfamiliar premises, modern artistic movements have seemed merely perverse, bizarre, or incomprehensible to those unaware of their goals. If we are to understand artistic movements, therefore, we must explore the perceptions about truth that underlie them. Only then will we see why they depict human experience as they do and why the techniques they employ are consistent with their intent. Understanding may not cause us to admire the artistic products of movements, but it will prevent us from reaching uninformed judgments. It will

also help us to understand the forces that have helped to create the extremely varied theatre of the twentieth century.

Immediately following World War I, the movement with the greatest impact on the theatre was expressionism. An excellent overview of the movement can be gained from John Willett's *Expressionism* (New York, 1970), but little of the theory has been translated into English. Here are some excerpts from a statement written by Yvan Goll in 1918 about his vision of a new "superdrama":

> [*It will depict*] *man's battle against everything that is thinglike and animallike around and within him. . . . The writer must recognize that there are realms quite different from that of the five senses. . . . His first task will be to destroy all external form. . . . Man and objects will be stripped as clean as possible and looked at through a*

magnifying glass for greater effect. . . . The theatre must not restrict itself to "real" life; it will become "superreal" when it learns what lies behind things. Pure realism was the worst mistake ever made in literature. . . . Art, if it wishes to educate, improve, or be effective in any way, must destroy everyday man . . . . to make him become once more the child he once was. The easiest way to do this is through the grotesque. . . . Consequently, the new theatre must use technological means that are equivalent to the ancient mask. . . . the phonograph to distort the voice, masks . . . which typify through . . . physical distortions [equivalent to] the inner distortions of the plot. . . . We are searching for the Superdrama.

Yvan Goll, Preface to *The Immortal Ones* (Cologne, 1920).

The futurists made less immediate impact than the expressionists, but in their manifestoes they set forth ideas that were harbingers of future developments. Here are some excerpts from a manifesto that glorifies the variety theatre.

Futurism exalts the Variety Theatre because: . . . .

4. The Variety Theatre is unique today in its use of cinema which enriches it with an incalculable number of visions and otherwise unrealizable spectacles. . . .

5. The Variety Theatre . . . naturally generates what I call "the Futurist marvelous," produced by modern mechanics [which includes] all the new significations of light, sound, noise, and language, with their mysterious and inexplicable extensions into the least-explored part of our sensiblity. . . .

8. The Variety Theatre is alone the audience's collaboration. It doesn't remain static like a stupid voyeur. . . . the action devel-

ops simultaneously on the stage, in the boxes, and in the orchestra. . . .

16. The Variety Theatre destroys all our conceptions of perspective, proportion, time, and space. . . .

"The Variety Theatre," September 29, 1913. From *Marinetti, Selected Writings*, edited and with an introduction by R. W. Flint (New York: Farrar, Straus and Giroux, 1971), pp. 116–122.

The most influential theoreticians of the theatre between the two world wars were Bertolt Brecht and Antonin Artaud. They were united in their dislike for conventional, realistic theatre, but divided in their conceptions of the ideal theatre. Brecht's theories took shape over many years. (His writings have been collected in John Willett's *Brecht on Theatre*.) Perhaps the most systematic statement of his theoretical views is "A Short Organum for the Theatre." In it Brecht states his dislike for the traditional theatre which lulls the spectator into a belief that social conditions are fixed, and he proposes to replace it with one which distances him (the Alienation effect) from the stage events in a way that will make him judge them critically:

42. . . . A representation that alienates is one which allows us to recognize its subject, but at the same time makes it seem unfamiliar. . . .

43. . . . The new alienations are only designed to free socially-conditioned phenomena from that stamp of familiarity which protects them from our grasp today.

47. In order to produce A-effects the actor has to discard whatever means he has learnt of getting the audience to identify itself with the characters which he plays. . . .

48. At no moment must he go so far as to be wholly transformed into the character played. . . . He has just to show the character. . . .

74. So let us invite all the sister arts of the drama, not in order to create an "integrated work of art" in which they all offer themselves up and are lost, but so together with the drama they may further the common task in their different ways; and their relations with one another consist in this: that they lead to mutual alienation.

> "A Short Organum for the Theatre," *Brecht on Theatre*, trans. by John Willett (New York: Hill and Wang, 1964), pp. 179–205.

Brecht later sought to clarify his position on alienation in acting with this note:

The contradiction between acting (demonstration) and experience (empathy) often leads the uninstructed to suppose that only one or the other can be manifest in the work of the actor (as if the Short Organum concentrated entirely on acting and the old tradition entirely on experience). In reality it is a matter of two mutually hostile processes which fuse in the actor's work. . . . His particular effectiveness comes from the tussle and tension of the two opposites, and also from their depth. . . .

> "Appendices to the Short Organum," *Brecht on Theatre*, pp. 276–281.

Artaud's major essays on theatre were collected in *The Theatre and Its Double* (1938). Here are some excerpts from his "Theatre of Cruelty, First Manifesto":

The theatre will never find itself again . . . except by furnishing the spectator with the truthful precipitates of dreams, in which his taste for crime, his erotic obsessions, his savergy, his chimeras, his utopian sense of life and matter, even his cannibalism, pour out, on a level not counterfeit and illusory, but interior. . . .

Every spectacle will contain . . . cries, groans, apparitions, surprises, theatricalities of all kinds, . . . costumes taken from certain ritual models; resplendent lighting, incantational beauty of voices, . . . physical rhythm of movements whose crescendo and decrescendo will accord exactly with the pulsation of movements familiar to everyone. . . .

We abolish the stage and the auditorium and replace them by a single site, without partition or barrier of any kind. . . . A direct communication will be reestablished between the spectator and the spectacle, . . . from the fact that the spectator placed in the middle of the action, is engulfed and physically affected by it. . . .

There will not be any set. . . .

We shall not act a written play, but we shall make attempts at direct staging, around themes, facts, or known works. . . .

Without an element of cruelty at the root of every spectacle, the theatre is not possible. In our present state of degeneration it is through the skin that metaphysics must be made to re-enter our minds. . . .

> Antonin Artaud, *The Theatre and Its Double*, trans. M. C. Richards (New York: Grove Press, 1958).

Theatre and Drama, 1940–1960

World War II was the most extensive war ever fought in terms of people killed, property destroyed, and the number of countries involved. It made use of the most deadly weapons yet devised, including bombers, ballistic missiles, and the atomic bomb.

The causes of the war were numerous, including problems left unsolved by World War I, the rise of totalitarian governments with their denial of civil liberties and, in some instances, programs of genocide, and the territorial ambitions of such countries as Germany, Italy, and Japan. The German extermination camps are one of the great blots on human history. At the end of the war Europe was divided into sectors, with the east dominated by Russia and the west dominated by the United States. There followed a "cold war" as the two nations sought to maintain or extend their influence. As a result, during the 1950s the world lived under the threat of an atomic war capable of ending life on earth. It was an age of anxiety and stress. The major stabilizing force was the United Nations, which replaced the League of Nations. It provided a forum for debate and international cooperation, but, like its predecessor, the U.N. was often ineffective, since a few major powers had the right to veto its actions.

The theatre was heavily influenced by the horrors of the war and the threats of impending disaster. Serious questions were raised about man's capacity to act responsibly or even to survive. Anxiety and guilt became major themes, although as in most periods much entertainment sought merely to distract audiences from cares.

French Theatre and Drama, 1940–1960

During the war years, the theatre in Paris was relatively prosperous. Productions were numerous and well attended, although with the exceptions of those by Dullin, Baty, Barsacq, and the Comédie Française, few were outstanding. The end of the war brought many stresses, as production costs rose and films and television drained away audiences. The new government, attempting to play a more decisive

Figure 3.1   Europe since World War II.

role than its predecessors, took steps to aid the theatre. In 1946 the Ministry of Arts and Letters began to subsidize productions of selected new plays and a few new companies; an annual competition was also inaugurated among the new troupes for the best production and direction. Furthermore, the state theatres were reorganized. The Opéra and Opéra-Comique were placed under a single management, and the Comédie Française and Odéon were merged, the

Odéon being called the Salle Luxembourg and the main house the Salle Richelieu. At first, the Salle Luxembourg was restricted to new or recent plays, but this scheme proved impractical and both branches came to present similar repertories. When Pierre Dux. (1908–   ), Administrator of the Comédie Française from 1944 to 1947, instituted new regulations designed to reduce his actors' film appearances and other outside commitments, many of the leading *sociétaries*, including Jean-Louis Barrault, Madeleine Renaud, Marie Bell, Renée Faure, and Aimé Clairond, resigned. As a result, the troupe lost much of its strength, and, although it slowly rebuilt under the administrations of Pierre-Aimé Touchard (between 1947 and 1953) and Pierre Descaves (between 1953 and 1959), its prestige suffered seriously.

The government also encouraged decentralization of the theatre, which by 1945 was restricted almost entirely to Paris. Consequently, subsidized regional dramatic centers began to be established in 1947. The first, the Dramatic Center of the East, was based at Strasbourg; a second was opened almost immediately at St. Etienne; in 1949, Le Grenier, a troupe which had been performing since 1945, was designated the Dramatic Center for Toulouse, and in the same year a fourth center was established at Rennes. Other centers were inaugurated at Aix-en-Provence (1952), Tourcoing (1960), and Bourges (1963). In addition to performing in its home theatre, each troupe made annual tours to towns in its region. Furthermore, both national and local authorities aided the many dramatic festivals founded after 1945, most notably at Avignon (beginning in 1947) and Aix-en-Provence (beginning in 1948). By the 1960s more than fifty festivals were being held annually.

Despite these steps toward decentralization, Paris continued to be the principal theatrical center and the boulevard theaters, with their long-run policy, the typical organizations. The most influential theatres, however, departed from this pattern. For a few years after the war, three members of the Cartel continued their work: Dullin remained Paris until 1947, Baty until 1951, and Jouvet from 1945 until his death in 1951. But by 1952 all of the members of the Cartel were dead. Of the younger prewar leaders, André Barsacq (at the Atelier after 1940) and Maurice Jacquemont (at the Studio des Champs-Elysées until 1960) were probably the most important. To this group should be added Marcel Herrand and Jean Marchat, who, after acting with Pitoëff's company,

had formed the Rideau de Paris in the 1930's. Upon Pitoëff's death in 1939, they took over his Théâtre aux Mathurins. Until 1952, they presented there excellent productions of foreign works, as well as many new French plays.

The major leaders in the postwar years were to be Barrault and Vilar. Jean-Louis Barrault (1910–   ), after studying with Dullin and working with Artaud and the pantomimist Etienne Decroux, had attained an enviable reputation as an actor in both the theatre and films before the war began. In 1940 he became a *sociétaire* at the Comédie Française, where in 1943 his production of Claudel's *The Satin Slipper* was the first important example of what came to be called "total theatre." Claudel's play, written between 1919 and 1924, had previously been considered unplayable because of its length and complexity, for the events span a century and occur in Spain, Italy, Africa, America, and at sea. At one point, the hemispheres converse, and at another the earth is represented as one bead on a rosary. A drama of love and salvation, *The Satin Slipper* was shaped by Barrault into a theatrical experience of such a high order that

Figure 3.2   Jean-Louise Barrault's production of Claudel's *Christophe Colomb* at the Théâtre Marigny (1953). Photograph by Agence de Presse Bernand.

it was to influence other directors for a long time. Although Barrault was later to refine his ideas, in 1943 he had already formulated his basic outlook. He has declared that the text of a play is like an iceberg, since only about one eighth is visible. It is the director's task to complete the playwright's text by revealing the hidden portions through his imaginative use of all the theatre's resources. Thus, Barrault arrived at something like a synthesis of Copeau's and Artaud's approaches.

In 1946, after resigning from the Comédie Française, Barrault (with Madeleine Renaud, whom he had married in 1936) formed the Compagnie Madeleine Renaud-Jean-Louis Barrault. With such major actors as Jean Desailly, André Brunot, Jacques Dacqmine, Edwige Feuillère, and Pierre Brasseur, Barrault produced about forty plays ranging from the *Oresteia* to contemporary *avant-garde* works before he gave up his Théâtre Marigny in 1956.

Jean Vilar (1912–1971), a fellow student of Barrault at Dullin's school, was much slower in achieving recognition, and had worked in a number of companies before being employed to organize the festival at Avignon in 1947. His work there and his fine performances in Paris (most notably as Pirandello's Henry IV in Barsacq's production) led in 1951 to his appointment as director of the Théâtre National Populaire, then on the verge of collapse. He assembled a company that included Maria Casarès, Georges Wilson, and Daniel Sorano, and was most fortunate in attracting Gérard Philipe (1922–1959), who, after a brief career in the theatre, had been one of France's major film stars. Although not immediately successful, by 1954 the TNP was one of the most popular troupes in France. Vilar's productions always placed major emphasis upon the actor, reenforced by costume and lighting. Scenery was usually restricted to platforms or a few set pieces. Vilar was the first producer to achieve wide popularity with the approach advocated by the Cartel (whose following had always been limited). Although the TNP's principal home was at the Palais de Chaillot in Paris, it also played at the Avignon Festival and toured

Figure 3.3 Vilar's production of Marivaux's *Triumph of Love* at the Théâtre Nationale Populaire (1956). Setting by Leon Gischia. Courtesy Agence de Presse Bernand.

throughout France. It soon commanded greater popular support there than any of the other state troupes, all of which played almost exclusively in Paris.

Many changes in the postwar theatre were intimately connected with experiments in dramaturgy, notably those of the absurdists. This movement did not come to the fore until the 1950s, however, and much of the major writing of the postwar period was to come from dramatists well known before 1940. Among these, the most prolific was Jean Anouilh, with such works as *Invitation to the Chateau* (1947), *Waltz of the Toreadors* (1952), *The Lark* (1953), *Becket* (1960), *Dear Antoine* (1970), and *The Pants* (1978). In these plays Anouilh continued to explore the problem of maintaining integrity in a world based upon compromises. Other prewar dramatists who made important contributions after 1945 include Marcel Achard, with *Patate* (1957) and *Eugene the Mysterious* (1964), and Armand Salacrou, with *Nights of Wrath* (1946) and *Boulevard Durand* (1960).

The most respected of the new dramatists was Henry de Montherlant (1896–1972), whose novels had won a wide following before the war. Although he had written a few minor plays, Montherlant's first produced work was *The Dead Queen* (1942), directed by Barrault at the Comédie Française. Its success led him to write *The Master of Santiago* (1948), *Port-Royal* (1954), *The Cardinal of Spain* (1960), and *The Civil War* (1965). *The Master of Santiago* is often considered Montherlant's most characteristic work because of its simple external action, complex psychology, and elevated style. The motif of sacrifice and the harsh rejection of all mediocrity runs through it. In all of Montherlant's work, the interest resides as much in the intellectual positions taken up by the characters as in their psychological traits and actions. His plays illustrate well the large role played by philosophical concerns in postwar French drama.

The enormous influence of postwar French drama, however, came from existentialist and absurdist plays. Following the war, existentialism as a philosophical outlook attracted considerable attention, especially through the essays and plays of Jean-Paul Sartre (1905–1980). A philosopher and novelist, Sartre turned to drama in 1943 with *The Flies*, and went on to write *No Exit* (1944), *Dirty Hands* (1948), *The Devil and the Good Lord* (1951), and *The Condemned of Altona* (1959). All illustrate Sartre's existentialist views. Denying the existence of God, fixed standards of conduct, and verifiable moral codes, Satre argues that each individual must choose his or her own values and live by them regardless of prevailing ideas, for to conform unquestioningly to the conventions established by others is the immoral response of a robot rather than the responsible act of a true being. Sartre's plays show characters faced with choices which require them to reassess their outlooks and to forge new personal standards. In the uncer-

tainty that followed the war, Sartre attracted a wide following, for he cast doubt upon the conformism that had made possible the Nazi atrocities. But Sartre also believed that it is necessary for people to be politically "engaged," even though the choices open to them are seldom ideal. In *Dirty Hands* he argues that to participate in political action invariably means that one's hands will get dirty, but that to refuse to become engaged merely means that others will make the choices that determine the direction of events.

The work of Albert Camus (1913–1960) was to be of equal importance. Before turning to drama, Camus had been a theatre worker in his native Algeria, a journalist, and the editor of a clandestine newspaper during the German occupation of France. His dramatic output was small: *Cross-Purposes* (1944), *Caligula* (performed 1945), *State of Siege* (1948), *The Just Assassins* (1949), and a few adaptations. His influence on the theatre came in part from his essay, "The Myth of Sisyphus" (1943), in which his discussion of the "absurd" was to supply the name for the absurdist movement. In this essay Camus argues that the human condition is absurd because of the gap between a person's hopes and the irrational universe into which he or she has been born. For Camus, the only remedy lies in each individual's search for a set of standards (admittedly without any objective basis) that will allow her or him to bring order out of this chaos. Although Camus denied being an existentialist, his conclusions were similar to those of Sartre.

Camus and Sartre differed most in their ideas about "engagement," for Camus rejected the conclusion advocated by Sartre in *Dirty Hands* and denied the validity of choosing between two immoral positions. Their difference on this point led to a prolonged and bitter debate. Between them, nevertheless, they supplied the philosophical basis for the absurdist movement which began to emerge in the early 1950s.

Although Sartre and Camus reject rationalistic views of the universe, their plays retain the traditional dramatic forms. Since they begin with the assumption that the world is irrational and then go on to create order out of chaos, their works have clear dramatic actions. On the other hand, the absurdists, while for the most part accepting Sartre's philosophical outlook, tend to concentrate upon the irrationality of human experience without suggesting any path beyond. By employing a succession of episodes unified merely by theme or mood instead of a cause-to-effect arrangement, they arrive at a structure paralleling the chaos which is their usual dramatic subject. The sense of absurdity is heightened by the juxtaposition of incongruous events producing seriocomic and ironical effects. Because they view language as the major rationalistic tool, the absurdists often demonstrate its inadequacy and subordinate it to nonverbal devices. Of the absurdists, four—Beckett, Ionesco, Genet, and Adamov—were to be most important.

Samuel Beckett (1906–   ), although not the earliest of the absurdists, was the first to win international fame, and it was his *Waiting for Godot* which in 1953 brought absurdism its first popular attention both in France and elsewhere. Irish by birth, Beckett first went to Paris in the 1920s and settled there permanently in 1938. Beckett began writing around 1930 but he did not turn to the dramatic form until he wrote *Waiting for Godot*. Since then he has written *Endgame* (1957), *Krapp's Last Tape* (1958), *Happy Days* (1961), *Play* (1963), *Come and Go* (1966), *Not I* (1973), and *That Time* (1976). In many ways, Beckett seems the characteristic dramatist of the 1950s, a decade made anxious by the threat of the cold war and of total destruction by an atomic holocaust. In fact, Beckett's characters often seem to be set down in a world that has already undergone the ravages of disaster and in which humanity's very existence is in question. Beckett is not so much concerned with man as a social and political creature as with the human condition in a metaphysical sense. His spiritual derelicts are usually isolated in time and space; they torture and console each other and themselves, raise questions which cannot be answered, and struggle on in a world that seems to be disintegrating

Figure 3.4   First production of Beckett's *Waiting for Godot*, Théâtre de Babylone, Paris, 1953. Directed by Roger Blin. Photograph by Pic.

around them. Probably more than any other writer, Beckett expressed the postwar doubts about man's capacity to understand and control his world.

Eugène Ionesco (1912–   ), a Roumanian by birth, labeled his first work, *The Bald Soprano* (1949, performed 1950), an "anti-play" to indicate a rebellion against conventional drama. The early works, which include *The Lesson* (1950) and *The Chairs* (1952), attracted little attention at first, but steadily grew in reputation after 1953, when Anouilh published an article praising *Victims of Duty*. These early plays, as well as *Amedée* (1954) and *The New Tenant* (1957), are mainly negative, for they concentrate upon the clichés of language and thought, the dominance of materialism, and the irrationality of values. Later works, such as *The Killer* (1959), *Rhinoceros* (1960), *A Stroll in the Air* (1963), *Hunger and Thirst* (1966), *Macbett* (1972), and *The Man with the Suitcases* (1975), have taken a somewhat more positive view by showing protagonists who hold out against conformity, although they cannot offer any rational basis for their actions.

Unlike Beckett, Ionesco is concerned primarily with man's social relationships, typically those of middle-class characters in family situations. Two themes run through most of his work: the deadening nature of materialistic, bourgeois society, and the loneliness and isolation of the individual. Perhaps ultimately his vision of man's condition differs little from Beckett's, but it is conceived in more domestic terms. All of his plays seek to discredit clichés, ideologies, and materialism. His characters tend to be unthinking automatons oblivious of their own mechanical behavior, just as material objects tend to proliferate and take over the space that should be oc-

Figure 3.5   Madeleine Renaud in Genet's *The Screens*, Théâtre de France (1966). Photograph by Pic.

cupied by people. Ionesco is especially antipathetic to the notion that drama should be didactic. To him truth means the absence of commitment, either ideologically or esthetically, for commitment involves a fatal step toward conformity.

Jean Genet (1910–) spent much of his life in prison, a background that figures prominently in much of his writing. His first plays, *The Maids* (presented by Jouvet in 1947) and *Deathwatch* (produced by Herrand in 1949), were at first unsuccessful, and his reputation was to be made with *The Balcony* (1956), *The Blacks* (1959), and *The Screens* (1961, not produced in France until 1966). Genet's characters rebel against organized society and suggest that deviation is essential if man is to achieve integrity. They also imply that nothing has meaning without its opposite—law and crime, religion and sin, love and hate—and that deviant behavior is as valuable as the accepted virtues. Genet, viewing all systems of value as entirely arbitrary, transforms life into a series of ceremonies and rituals which give an air of stability and importance to otherwise nonsensical behavior.

Arthur Adamov (1908–1971), born in Russia and educated in Switzerland, was attracted early to surrealism, a movement that has influenced all absurdist drama. After he turned to playwriting in 1947, Adamov's first work was produced in 1950. The early plays, for example *The Invasion* (1950), *Parody* (1952), and *All Against All* (1953), show a seriocomically cruel world of moral destructiveness and personal anxieties in which the characters are condemned to be eternal failures by their inability to communicate with each other. Time and place are usually indefinite, as in dreams. Adamov's later plays became progressively more socially oriented, especially after 1956, when he denounced his earlier work and adopted a Brechtian form. His new outlook is reflected in *Paolo Paoli* (1957), a commentary upon the materialism and hypocrisy which preceded World War I, and *Spring '71* (1960), which idealizes the men who created the Paris Commune in 1871. But with this change in mode went a decline in popularity for

Adamov's work and by the time of his death his reputation was considerably lower than that of the other three major exponents of absurdism.

Absurdism was never a conscious, clearly defined movement. The label was popularized by Martin Esslin's book *The Theatre of the Absurd* (1961). Since it was not a conscious movement, it is difficult to specify those authors who should be included within its ranks. As a label, absurdism is clearly not broad enough to encompass all of the experimental dramatists of the time, of which there were many in France. Among those who probably should not be labeled absurdists, some of the best were Jacques Audiberti (1899–1965), whose *Quoat-Quoat* (1946), *The Black Feast* (1948), *The Landlady* (1960), and *The Sentry-Box* (1965) stress the power of evil and of sex over human affairs; Georges Schéhadé (1910–), whose *Evening of Proverbs* (1954), *Tale of Vasco* (1956), and *The Journey* (1961) are often reminiscent of Giraudoux's work in their combination of fantasy precise language, and love for humanity; and Jean Tardieu (1903–), who has concentrated upon one-act "chamber" plays, such as *The Information Window* (1955) and *The ABC of Our Life* (1959), treating man's enslavement to social conventions.

Most of the *avant-garde* drama was first produced in small, out-of-the-way theatres by adventurous directors, many of them heavily influenced by Artaud and later to be among France's most respected directors. Of these, perhaps the most important was Roger Blin (1907–), a disciple of Artaud, who, after working with Dullin and Barrault, was closely associated with the absurdist movement after 1949. He is especially noted for his staging of Beckett's plays. Other important directors include André Reybaz (1922–), who introduced Audiberti, Ghelderode, and Ionesco to Parisian audiences and worked with a number of *avant-garde* theatres before becoming director of the Dramatic Center at Tourcoing in 1960; Georges Vitaly (1917–), who worked with Reybaz before founding the Théâtre La-Bruyère in 1953; Jean-Marie Serreau (1915–), a pupil of Dullin, who directed the first productions of

Adamov's plays before opening the Théâtre de Baby-lone with Blin in 1952 and going on to direct at many other theatres; and Jacques Fabbri (1925–   ), who worked with Vitaly and Reybaz before forming his own company, with which he won special renown for his staging of farces. Beginning as members of the *avant-garde*, most of these directors were later to work regularly with such established troupes as the Comédie Française and the Théâtre de France.

By the time General DeGaulle came to power in 1959, French theatre and drama had almost fully recovered from the effects of the war years. By then, they enjoyed perhaps the greatest critical esteem of any in the world. In 1959 the DeGaulle government instituted a series of policies that would affect the French theatre deeply after 1960.

German Theatre and Drama, 1940–1960

When Germany surrendered to the Allies in 1945, all theatres were closed for a time but soon they began to reopen under the surveillance of occupation forces. After 1945, the German theatre grew steadily and by the 1960s was one of the most stable in the world. Although Germany was divided after 1945, the theatre in the two areas shared many common characteristics. In both, the system of state-supported resident companies was reinstated. By the early 1960s, there were 175 professional theatres in West Germany, of which 120 were publicly owned, and in East Germany there were about 135 theatres, all state-owned. Almost every city had a dramatic company and an opera and ballet troupe of good quality. All of the subsidized troupes is a single town were typically under one manager (or Intendant), appointed by the city or state, and shared a staff of directors and designers. A *dramaturg* advised the companies on the choice of plays and other artistic matters.

Among the outstanding directors of the postwar period were Boleslaw Barlog, Fritz Kortner, Willi Schmidt, Wolfgang Langhoff, Wolfgang Heinz, and

Benno Bessen in Berlin; Harry Buchwitz in Frankfort-on-Main; Gustav Gründgens and Oscar Fritz Schuh in Hamburg; Karlheinz Stroux in Düsseldorf; Heinz Hilpert in Göttingen; Rudolf Sellner in Darmstadt and Berlin; Günther Rennert in Munich; Hans Schalla in Bochum; and Karl Kayser in Leipzig. In 1951 Erwin Piscator returned to Germany, where he directed for numerous troupes, as well as being manager of the Freie Volksbühne in West Berlin until his death in 1966. The most influential designers were Caspar Neher (1897–1962) and Teo Otto (1904–

Figure 3.6   Wieland Wagner's production of *Tannhäuser* at Bayreuth, 1954. Note the absence of three-dimensional scenery and the dependence on light and projections. This approach outraged those who favored the three-dimensionality that had prevailed at Bayreuth prior to World War II. From *Décor de Théâtre dans le Monde depuis 1935*.

1968), both attuned to Brecht's approach. They moved design in the direction of theatricalism—the frank manipulation of stage means. Although they often used realistic elements, they normally suggested place through decorative screens, projections, a few architectural details, and lighting which created mood and atmosphere.

Although more than one-hundred theatre buildings were destroyed during the war, a phenomenal rebuilding program after 1950 replaced most of them. In the new buildings, sight lines were considerably improved, boxes were eliminated, and the number of balconies reduced. The prewar emphasis upon complex stage machinery continued. For example, the Schiller Theater, opened in West Berlin in 1951, has a revolving stage, elevators, and rolling platform stages. Most of the theatres are of the conventional proscenium-arch type. A few small theatres intended as second houses are more flexible, but there has been little experimentation with spatial relationships.

In addition to permanent resident troupes, festivals were of considerable importance in postwar Germany. The most famous was still the Bayreuth Festival (revived in 1951 under the direction of Wieland Wagner until his death in 1966). After the war, Wagner's operas were performed for the first time at Bayreuth with simple scenic investiture much like that advocated by Appia, instead of the historical realism that had been used since Wagner's time. Bitterly opposed by traditionalists, the new methods won wholehearted approval from others.

Of all the German companies, two in East Berlin —the Berliner Ensemble and the Komische Oper —achieved the greatest renown. The work of the Berliner Ensemble is bound up with Brecht's late career. After he returned to Europe in 1947, Brecht's plays rapidly found their way into the repertories of most German troupes and his theory was soon known throughout the world. His fame was confirmed through the work of the Berliner Ensemble. Opened in 1949 with *Mother Courage*, the Berliner Ensemble for a time shared the Deutsches Theater with another troupe. In 1954 it was given the The-

ater-am-Schiffbauerdamm, the house in which Brecht's *Threepenny Opera* was first produced in 1928. With its appearances in Paris in 1954 and 1955, the Berliner Ensemble became internationally famous and has since been considered one of the world's finest troupes. After Brecht's death in 1956, the company continued under the direction of Helene Weigel (1900–1971), Brecht's wife, who had been its director from the beginning. Brecht's methods were also retained by the company's principal directors.

Much of the Berliner Ensemble's achievement stemmed from its long and careful rehearsals, sometimes extending over five months. When each production was ready, a *Modellbuch* containing 600–800 action photographs was made. The published *Modellbücher* have influenced many producers who have never seen the company perform. The Berliner Ensemble did much to establish the validity of Brecht's theories, while the humanitarian and social

Figure 3.7   The Berliner Ensemble's production of Brecht's *The Caucasian Chalk Circle*. Setting by Karl von Appen. From *Décor de Théâtre dans le Monde depuis 1935*.

emphases of his plays suggested an alternative to the absurdists (who tended to dramatize personal anxieties). On the other hand, since Brecht used nonrealistic devices and, like absurdists, emphasized irony and humor, the two influences have since 1960 sometimes merged.

The Komische Oper was founded in 1947 by Walter Felsenstein (1901–1979), who established the company's style, a highly selective realism. Through lengthy and rigorous rehearsals and complete control over every artistic element, Felsenstein's productions contrasted sharply with those usually seen in opera houses. The Komische Oper rapidly became one of East Germany's most popular theatres. Its appearances elsewhere have also won it a reputation only slightly below that of the Berliner Ensemble.

Figure 3.8 Walter Felsenstein's production of Mozart's *The Magic Flute* at the Komische Oper (1954). Setting by Rudolf Heinrich. Courtesy *World Theatre*.

Felsenstein's reputation as a director brought him many opportunities to direct nonmusical works, perhaps most notably at Vienna's Burgtheater. After Felsenstein's death, the company's reputation declined.

In Austria, the pattern of postwar reconstruction paralleled that in Germany. By the 1960s there were thirty-six theatres in Austria, twenty of which were located in Vienna. Four of these were state theatres, the Staatsoper and the Volksoper for opera, the Burgtheater and the Akademietheater for drama, while the Theater-in-der-Josefstadt and the Volkstheater were subsidized by the city of Vienna. The festival at Salzburg, reopened in 1946, also resumed its position as one of the finest in the world.

If Germany and Austria rebuilt one of the best systems of subsidized theatres in the world, they were less successful in developing significant new dramatists, for until the late 1950s the major German dramatist was Brecht, all of whose major works were written before 1946. Zuckmayer returned to Germany, but his *The Devil's General* (produced in 1948), depicting the inhumanity of the Nazi hierarchy, *The Cold Light* (1956), about the dilemma of an atomic physicist, and *The Pied Piper* (1975), a reworking of the fairy tale with added topical political overtones, never equaled the popularity of his prewar satire, *The Captain from Koepenick*. Wolfgang Borchert (1921–1947) won fame with one play, *The Man Outside* (1947), about a returning soldier trying to adjust to civilian life, but died before he could fulfill the promise shown by that work. Fritz Hochwalder (1911–   ) found a wide audience at home with *The Holy Experiment* (1943), *The Fugitive* (1945), and *The Public Prosecutor* (1949), all of which pose questions of individual responsibility and public guilt, but he never won a following outside of German-speaking territories.

The major drama in German during the 1950s was written by two Swiss playwrights, Frisch and Duerrenmatt, both of whom were encouraged by Kurt Hirschfeld and Oskar Walterlin of the Zurich theatre, one of the best in Europe during the Nazi regime because so many refugees settled in Switzerland. Max Frisch (1911–   ) was trained as an architect but turned to writing in 1944. His reputation rests primarily upon *The Chinese Wall* (1946), *Biedermann and the Firebugs* (1958), and *Andorra* (1961), all of which treat questions of guilt. In each play the past is reviewed and the characters construct elaborate rationalizations for their actions; none is really willing to accept responsibility. Although it is clear that Frisch longs for a world of integrity, he seems to suggest that it is unattainable because men do not learn from their mistakes. Through techniques borrowed from Wilder, Strindberg, Brecht, and others, he embodies his search and disillusionment in symbolic and nightmarish fantasy.

Friedrich Duerrenmatt (1921–   ) began writing plays in 1947. Of his many works, the most successful have been *The Visit* (1956) *The Physicists* (1962), *Play Strindberg* (1969), and *The Collaborator* (1973). Like Frisch, Duerrenmat is concerned with moral questions, which he suggests will not be solved satisfactorily because man is so readily corrupted by promises of power or wealth. Duerrenmatt is much more detached than Frisch. He emphasizes the grotesqueness of the human condition, which he expresses through a rather dark comedy. Although he is concerned with moral dilemmas, he shows the human instinct for good corrupted either by power and greed or by chance. He avoids bitterness by standing at a distance and viewing events sardonically.

Because the majority of significant postwar German drama dealt with questions of guilt related to larger political and social issues, it differed considerably in tone from the French absurdist drama, which attracted few German exponents. Of those who wrote in the absurdist vein, probably the best was Günter Grass (1927–   ), with such plays as *The Wicked Cooks* (1957), in which rival factions seek to discover the recipe of a soup, apparently symbolizing significant human experience, so that it can be reproduced according to a formula. In the 1960s Grass abandoned the absurdist for the Brechtian mode. In

Figure 3.9   Duerrenmatt's *The Physicists* at the Kammerspiele, Munich (1962). Directed by Hans Schweikart, Courtesy *World Theatre*.

The Plebeians Rehearse the Revolution (1966) Grass sets the uprising of East Berlin workers in 1953 within the framework of a rehearsal of Brecht's *Coriolanus*, a device which allowed him to comment upon the present by drawing parallels with the past.

Thus, while Germany established a strong postwar theatre, it was less successful in producing a significant new drama. Nevertheless, through the work of Brecht and other socially conscious writers, the German theatre exerted strong influence on postwar developments.

Theatre and Drama in the United States, 1940–1960

After World War II the most influential figures in the American theatre were probably the

Figure 3.10   Scene from Tennessee Williams's *A Streetcar Named Desire* with Marlon Brando, Kim Hunter, Karl Malden, and Jessica Tandy. Directed by Elia Kazan, setting by Jo Mielziner. Photo by Graphic House, Inc.

director Elia Kazan and the designer Jo Mielziner, for through their joint work on such plays as Williams's *A Streetcar Named Desire* (1947) and Miller's *Death of a Salesman* (1949) they established the productional approach that was to dominate until about 1960. Under Mielziner's influence, stage settings turned away from realism, although they retained clearly representational features. This "theatricalized realism" was essentially an extension of the new stagecraft of the 1920s. On the other hand, acting moved increasingly toward psychological truth as found in the characters' inner motivations. It was an

Figure 3.11   Jo Mielziner's settings for Arthur Miller's *Death of a Salesman* (1949). The design above shows the ▶ set as it appeared in the opening scene and for subsequent scenes that take place in the present. Below is the setting as it appeared during flashback scenes, which were identified by the projected leaf pattern. Photographs by Peter A. Juley & Son. Courtesy Mr. Mielziner.

extension of the Group Theatre's approach as taught at the Actors Studio.

Founded in 1947 by Robert Lewis, Elia Kazan, and Cheryl Crawford (although Lee Strasberg was to be the dominant figure), the Actors Studio was designed to permit selected actors to work and develop according to the Stanislavsky system. Marlon Brando (1924–   ), with his characterization of the inarticulate and uneducated Stanley Kowalski of *A Streetcar Named Desire*, came to epitomize in the popular mind the Actors Studio style. The novelty of serious acting based upon substandard speech, untidy dress, and boorish behavior captured the public imagination and began a vogue for this approach. It also, probably quite mistakenly, created an image of the Actors Studio as merely encouraging actors to explore their own psyches while ignoring the skills needed for projecting a characterization. Although much of the criticism is clearly exaggerated, Strasberg did place primary emphasis upon "inner truth" as the basis of good acting, and much of the Studio's training was determined by this goal. In 1956 the Studio began a program to assist playwrights and in 1960 it added a workshop for directors. By the 1960s, however, the influence of the Actors Studio had begun to decline as interest turned toward nonrealistic and period drama, for which the Studio's approach seemed too limited. Nevertheless, it remained a powerful force.

After the war, the theatre was seriously threatened by the rapid development of television. In 1948 there were only forty-eight stations, but by 1958 there were 512 and over fifty million television sets. The free entertainment provided by the new medium came at just the time when production costs in the theatre were rapidly increasing. Between 1944 and 1960 the price of tickets doubled, and the costs of mounting a show increased at a still faster rate. Under these circumstances, producers tended to seek vehicles with broad appeal, and to avoid both plays and production styles that might offend or confuse spectators.

The Broadway theatre continued the decline that had begun before the war. It reached the lowest point in the season of 1949–1950, when only fifty-nine new productions were mounted, but then slowly climbed to about seventy, a number which could not be greatly increased because of the relatively small number of theatres available (about thirty in the 1950s).

In the late 1940s the reduction of the American theatre to a small number of Broadway productions served to motivate several attempts to diversify the theatre. One of the most important efforts was to be the off-Broadway movement. By playing in out-of-the-way theatres or improvised auditoriums, production costs could be cut considerably, and works which would not appeal to a mass audience could be played for more restricted groups. Although its main force was to be felt during the 1950s, the off-Broadway movement can properly be traced back to the little theatres of the World War I era. It had declined markedly during the 1930s but began to revive during World War II. In 1943 the city of New York acquired the Mecca Temple on 55th Street and converted it into the City Center, where opera, musical comedy, ballet, and drama were played for limited engagements at moderate prices. Under the general direction of Jean Dalrymple (1910–   ), the City Center was to build enviable ballet and opera troupes before moving to Lincoln Center in 1966. Then in 1946–1947, Eva Le Gallienne, Margaret Webster, and Cheryl Crawford established the American Repertory Company (modeled on Miss Le Gallienne's earlier Civic Repertory Company), which performed a season of six plays before being forced to close.

The more typical off-Broadway groups, however, were begun by relatively unknown directors. The first to attract attention was New Stages, a group founded in 1947 by David Heilweil, who in 1950 also opened an arena theatre in the ballroom of the midtown Edison Hotel. But the major upturn in prestige came in 1952, when the Circle in the Square presented Williams's *Summer and Smoke*, a failure on Broadway, to high critical praise. Soon off-Broadway was viewed as a workable alternative to Broadway's commercialism. By 1955–1956, there were more than ninety off-Broadway groups, and they, rather than Broadway companies, gave the first performances in New York of works by such authors as Brecht, Ionesco, and Genet.

Of the off-Broadway groups, two—Circle in the Square and the Phoenix Theatre—were of special importance during the 1950s. The Circle in the Square was opened in 1951 by José Quintero (1924–   ) and Theodore Mann (1924–   ). In this former nightclub the actor-audience relationship was entirely flexible, although spectators nor-

mally were seated around three sides of a rectangular acting area. Here such performers as Geraldine Page, Jason Robards, Jr., George C. Scott, and Colleen Dewhurst came to prominence. After his triumph with O'Neill's *The Iceman Cometh* in 1956, Quintero was asked to direct the Broadway production of *Long Day's Journey into Night*. Its cumulative record made the Circle in the Square one of the most respected theatres of the 1950s, and it continues to play an important role.

The Phoenix Theatre was inaugurated in 1953 by

Figure 3.12   O'Neill's *Iceman Cometh* at the Circle in the Square (1956). Directed by Jose Quintero. Photograph by Jerry Dantzic.

Norris Houghton (1909–   ) and T. Edward Hambleton (1911–   ) in an out-of-the-way but fully equipped conventional theatre. It presented a diverse program of plays by such authors as Aristophanes, Shakespeare, Turgenev, Ibsen, Shaw, Pirandello, Ionesco, and Montherlant. It also attempted to use a different director for each play and frequently attracted such outstanding actors as Siobhan McKenna and Robert Ryan. Beginning in the late 1950s, the Phoenix employed a permanent acting company, which under the direction of Stuart Vaughan presented a series of plays each season. This arrangement lasted until the early 1960s, when Houghton and Hambelton formed a liaison with the Association of Producing Artists and thereafter became primarily presenters of the company's offerings.

For the most part, off-Broadway theatres in the 1950s were little concerned with experimentation in staging except in their use of arena and thrust stages. They were most interested in repertory, seeking to do a higher level of drama than that favored by Broadway. Their goals were essentially artistic.

After the war there were also a number of attempts to decentralize the theatre. One leader in this area was the American National Theatre and Academy (ANTA), which has been chartered by Congress in 1935 to stimulate the rejuvenation of the theatre outside of New York and to form an academy to train personnel. Because of lack of funds, little was accomplished, although ANTA became the principal American center for collecting and exchanging information about the theatre. After the war, the attempt to found regional theatres was given its first important impetus by Margo Jones (1913–1955), who successfully established an arena theatre in Dallas in 1947. Other pioneering groups include the Alley Theatre, founded in Houston in 1947 by Nina Vance; the Arena Stage, opened in Washington in 1949 by Edward Mangum and Zelda Fichandler; and the Actors' Workshop, begun in 1952 in San Francisco by Jules Irving and Herbert Blau. At first, most of the groups struggled along with semiprofessional

personnel while gradually building audiences. Then, in 1959, the regional theatre movement was considerably strengthened by the Ford Foundation's decision to give financial support to resident companies that had demonstrated the greatest strength. Thus, although the accomplishments of the 1950s were not great, the foundations were laid for more ambitious projects in the 1960s.

Figure 3.13 *Measure for Measure* at the American Shakespeare Festival, Stratford, Connecticut in 1973. The actors in the foreground are Lee Richardson and Christina Pickles. Directed by Michael Kahn. Courtesy American Shakespeare Festival.

Summer festivals also added diversity. At Stratford, Ontario, a Shakespearean Festival was inaugurated in 1953. Here Tyrone Guthrie used an open stage; the success of this festival and its spatial arrangements were to be influential throughout North America. An American Shakespeare Festival was instituted at Stratford, Connecticut, in 1955; thereafter it annually offered a fifteen-week season of plays. The New York Shakespeare Festival was established in 1954 by Joseph Papp, and since 1957 has played free of charge in Central Park, where the municipally owned Delacorte Theatre (seating 2,263) was inaugurated in 1962. Other Shakespearean festivals were held annually at Ashland (Oregon), San Diego, and elsewhere. Summer theatres, most of them in resort areas, also steadily increased in numbers. Additionally, by the early 1960s approximately 1,500 colleges and universities were offering courses in theatre. Thus, various groups sought to compensate for the concentration of the professional theatre in New York.

For a time after the war, the United States seemed to be rich in playwriting. Its stature increased considerably with the return of O'Neill's plays to the repertory following the success of *The Iceman Cometh* in 1956. *A Long Day's Journey into Night* (produced 1957) was one of the most impressive plays of the 1950s, and other works by O'Neill were performed to critical acclaim. Although he declined in power, Maxwell Anderson also continued to write such plays as *Joan of Lorraine* (1946), *Anne of the Thousand Days* (1948), and *The Golden Six* (1958). Clifford Odets regained some of his former strength with *The Country Girl* (1950) and *The Flowering Peach* (1954), William Saroyan returned with *The Cave Dwellers* (1957), Lillian Hellman with *The Autumn Garden* (1951) and *Toys in the Attic* (1960), S. N. Behrman with *The Cold Wind and the Warm* (1959) and *But for Whom, Charlie* (1962), and Thornton Wilder with *The Matchmaker* (1954).

The most outstanding new writers were Williams and Miller. Tennessee Williams (1911–   ) achieved his first success in 1945 with *The Glass Me-*

nagerie and rapidly consolidated it with *A Streetcar Named Desire* (1947), *The Rose Tattoo* (1951), *Cat on a Hot Tin Roof* (1954), *Orpheus Descending* (1957), and *Sweet Bird of Youth* (1959). But by the late 1950s Williams was being accused of repeating himself and thereafter both his critical stature and his output declined, although he continued to write such works as *Night of the Iguana* (1961), *The Milk Train Doesn't Stop Here Anymore* (1962), *Slapstick Tragedy* (1966), *This is [an Entertainment]* (1976), and *A Lovely Sunday for Creve Coeur* (1979).

Williams's strength lies in his ability to create interesting characters caught in critical or violent situations as they seek to recover a past or create a future more satisfying than the vulgar and materialistic present. As the dramatic action progresses, the protagonist is usually forced to abandon his illusions, often after physical or moral degradation at the hands of callous or vicious characters. Williams's sensational situations have often obscured his moral concern for the survival of love and beauty in a materialistic world. To achieve his effects, Williams has used theatrical means imaginatively, manipulating them, sometimes quite obviously, to focus attention on the inner truth of character and situation. No American playwright commanded so wide an audience as did Williams between 1945 and 1960.

Arthur Miller (1916–   ) achieved his first success with *All My Sons* (1947), an Ibsenesque play about a manufacturer of airplane engines who has put profit above the safety of wartime pilots. Miller's reputation now rests primarily upon *Death of a Salesman* (1949), *the Crucible* (1953), and *A View from the Bridge* (1955). Of his later works, which include *After the Fall* (1964), *Incident at Vichy* (1964), and *The Creation of the World and Other Business* (1973), only *The Price* (1968) achieved any real success. Through most of Miller's plays run the same ideas. His characters stray because of overly narrow (often materialistic) values and find peace in some more meaningful understanding of themselves and of their roles in society. Miller is often called a "social" dramatist, but his interests have always been moral.

Though society may encourage false values, it remains the individual's responsibility to sort out the true from the false. Miller clearly implies that it is possible to maintain one's integrity within the framework of society. Of Miller's work, *Death of a Salesman* is usually considered most significant, perhaps because it dramatizes so successfully the conflict in the American consciousness between the desire for material success and for adventure and happiness.

Few other new playwrights lived up to their initial promise. William Inge (1913–1973) gained a considerable following with such works as *Come Back, Little Sheba* (1950), *Picnic* (1953), *Bus Stop* (1955), and *The Dark at the Top of the Stairs* (1957), but his work now seems essentially a more naive version of Williams's. Other popular dramatists of the time include Robert Anderson (1917–   ) with *Tea and Sympathy* (1953) and *You Know I Can't Hear You When the Water's Running* (1966); Arthur Laurents (1918–   ), with *Home of the Brave* (1948) and *A Clearing in the Woods* (1957); and Paddy Chayefsky (1923–1981) with *The Tenth Man* (1959) and *Gideon* (1961).

Musical drama continued to be one of the most popular of forms. For the most part, successful works were adapted from well-known novels, plays, or stories. Rodgers and Hammerstein, with *Carousel* (1945), *South Pacific* (1949), and *The King and I* (1951), established the pattern which was followed by others, such as Alan Jay Lerner and Frederick Loewe with *Brigadoon* (1947) and *My Fair Lady* (1956), and Frank Loesser with *Guys and Dolls* (1950) and *Most Happy Fella* (1956). For a time it appeared that a musical drama of greater depth might develop. Gian Carlo Menotti won a considerable following on Broadway with his operas, *The Medium* (1947) and *The Consul* (1950), but his later works proved less successful. Marc Blitzstein turned Hellman's *The Little Foxes* into an opera, *Regina*, and Leonard Bernstein collaborated with Miss Hellman on *Candide* (1956), a musical play based upon Voltaire's novel, and with Arthur Laurents on *West Side Story* (1957), an adaptation of *Romeo and Juliet* to the world of New York's juvenile gangs. Despite the prestige gained by these pieces, the musical continued to be aimed for the most part at the mass audience.

By the late 1950s American drama seemed to be at a standstill, for the earlier promise had been dissipated and no new dramatists of significance had yet made their power felt. But new developments, both in theatre and drama, were in the making, and the 1960s were destined to bring renewed vigor to the American scene.

English Theatre and Drama, 1940–1960

With the coming of the war in 1939, the English theatre was soon at a virtual standstill. At the height of the German blitz, only one theatre remained open in London. The Old Vic retreated to the provinces, Donald Wolfit organized lunch-time programs, and a few others attempted to keep the theatre alive, but for the most part English theatrical life was almost completely disrupted.

Following the war, the English commercial theatre developed along lines reminiscent of the United States' Theatrical Syndicate. In 1942 Prince Littler, owner of several provincial theatres, acquired the Stoll Theatre Corporation and began to form alliances with several other theatre owners and producers. By 1947 his "The Group" controlled 75 percent of the theatres in England and owned the majority of shares of H. M. Tennant, Ltd., London's largest producing organization. "The Group" then demanded 30 to 40 percent of the gross weekly earnings of a play as a condition for leasing its theatres and reserved the right to close any play that fell below a specified weekly income.

Under these circumstances, it is not surprising that postwar English drama was innocuous. The leading dramatist was Terence Rattigan (1911–1978), who began to write plays in 1933, achieved his first popular success with *French Without Tears* (1936), and after the war turned to more serious subjects in

The Winslow Boy (1946), *The Browning Version* (1948), *Separate Tables* (1955), *Ross* (1960), and *Cause Celebre* (1977). Although Rattigan created compelling situations and interesting characters, the "drawing room" atmosphere of his plays perpetuated conservative traditions.

The commercial theatre also took poetic drama under its wing for a time during the 1950s, after E. Martin Browne had generated considerable response through his work at the Mercury Theatre. Browne's production of *A Phoenix Too Frequent* (1946) called attention to Christopher Fry and led to John Gielgud's production of *The Lady's Not for Burning* (1949), which established Fry's reputation and revived interest in poetic drama. Fry (1907–   ) went on to write *Venus Observed* (1949), *The Dark is Light Enough* (1954), *Curtmantle* (1961), *A Yard of Sun* (1970), and several adaptations. T.S. Eliot also returned to playwriting with *The Cocktail Party* (1949), which enjoyed a considerable popular success following its production at the Edinburgh Festival, and

Figure 3.14 T. S. Eliot's *The Cocktail Party* in its original production. Rex Harrison is seen at center as Harcourt-Reilly. Photo by Anthony Buckley.

he went on to write *The Confidential Clerk* (1953) and *The Elder Statesman* (1958). By 1955 interest in poetic drama was on the wane, for it too had come to seem merely an old formula dressed in poetic dialogue.

After the war, the Old Vic and the Shakespeare Festival Company were the most respected groups in England. The Old Vic returned to London in 1944, having spent the war years in the provinces. At first it had to play in the New Theatre, for its own building had been partially destroyed by bombing. At this time, the management passed from Tyrone Guthrie to Laurence Olivier, Ralph Richardson, and John Burrell, who presented a series of brilliant productions that made the Old Vic one of the most admired companies in the world. In 1946 the Old Vic also established a theatre school under the direction of Michel Saint-Denis, assisted by George Devine and Glen Byam Shaw, who utilized principles drawn primarly from Copeau. Closely allied with this school was a company—the Young Vic, under the direction of George Devine—that performed for children. After 1946 the Old Vic also had a second branch in Bristol.

Unfortunately, after 1948 the Old Vic began to decline, as Olivier and Richardson began to devote increasing amounts of time to outside commitments. In 1949 the management passed to Hugh Hunt (1911–   ), who had served as director fo the Bristol Old Vic since its formation. The return of the company to the repaired Old Vic Theatre in 1950 created considerable conflicts with the school and the Young Vic troupe, and in 1952 both of the latter were dissolved. From 1953 to 1958 the Old Vic was headed by Michael Benthall (1919–1974). The company was still good though relatively young (the leading players were John Neville, Barbara Jefford, and Paul Rogers). But the days of greatness were over, although they were recaptured briefly in 1960 with Franco Zeffirelli's brawling, lusty production of *Romeo and Juliet*. In 1963 the Old Vic was dissolved and its headquarters became the home of the National Theatre.

Figure 3.15   Franco Zeffirelli's production of *Romeo and Juliet* at the Old Vic in 1960. From *Scene Design Throughout the World Since 1950*.

As the Old Vic declined, the Stratford Festival Company gained in prestige, largely because of several reforms made by Barry Jackson, head of the theatre between 1946 and 1948. Under his management, the company became a self-contained producing organization with its own technical staff providing costumes and scenery; storage space was added and the stage was remodeled. Jackson also gained control over the entire festival so that its activities could be coordinated, and he enlivened the troupe by the addition of such vital young directors and actors as Peter Brook (1925–   ) and Paul Scofield (1922–   ). Between 1948 and 1956 the management was assumed by Anthony Quayle (1913–   ), who as joined in 1953 by Glen Byam Shaw. Such outstanding actors as Gielgud, Olivier, Redgrave, and Peggy Ashcroft appeared often, and in 1951 the number of productions given annually was reduced to permit more careful preparation. For the first time, London's critics attended the performances regularly and soon Stratford was being elevated in their reviews above the Old Vic. During this decade, novel interpretations also came to be accepted as the norm rather than as aberrations. It was out of this atmosphere that still other innovations would come in the 1960s.

After the war, repertory seasons in London were also sponsored occasionally by commercial managers. With the backing of H. M. Tennant, John Gielgud presented a notable series of plays at the Haymarket in 1944–1945, and from 1945 to 1956 the Lyric Theatre, Hammersmith, housed some outstanding revivals which were later sent on tour. Despite much fine acting, however, by 1956 the English theatre seemed merely to be looking toward the past. Many critics considered it doomed. Then, in 1956, a revolution began which soon transformed the English theatre.

The change can be attributed to two producing organizations, the English Stage Company and the Theatre Workshop, and to the dramatists with whom they worked. The English Stage Company was founded in 1956 under the direction of George Devine (1910–1966), who began his career as an actor in 1932, taught at Michel Saint-Denis' London Theatre Studio from 1936 to 1939, and directed the Young Vic Company after the war. When Devine took over the Royal Court Theatre, once the home of Granville Barker's troupe, he intended to emphasize new English plays and foreign works not yet seen in England. Failing to uncover a backlog of unproduced English dramas, Devine placed a notice in *The Stage* which induced John Osborne (1929–   ) to submit *Look Back in Anger*. The production of Osborne's play in 1956 is usually considered the turning point in postwar British theatre.

Osborne's break with the past is not to be found in his dramaturgy, for *Look Back in Anger* is straightforwardly realistic, but in his attack upon class distinctions and upon the complacency and inertia of all classes. Its protagonist, Jimmy Porter, seems to have

Figure 3.16   Osborne's *Look Back in Anger* at the Royal Court Theatre (1956). Directed by Tony Richardson. The actors are Kenneth Haigh, Alan Bates, and Mary Ure. Photograph by Houston Rogers.

Figure 3.17   John Arden's *Sergeant Musgrave's Dance* in its production at the Royal Court Theatre, London in 1965. Photo by Zoë Dominic.

no positive solution to suggest but merely denounces a long list of moral, social, and political betrayals by those who go on mouthing Edwardian platitudes. Although the play is essentially negative in tone, it caught the contemporary rebellious mood so well that Jimmy soon became a symbol of all the "angry young men." Osborne's next play, *The Entertainer* (1957), has as its protagonist a disintegrating music hall performer (originally played by Laurence Olivier). Here England's progressive decline in vigor and values is symbolized in three generations of the Rice family of entertainers. Osborne seems to have been influenced by Brecht, for he alternates realistic scenes with vaudeville routines.

Osborne's work since 1960 has been very uneven in quality. Among his successful plays have been *Luther* (1961), a psychological study of the religious reformer, and *Inadmissible Evidence* (1965), a moving evocation of the wasted life of an outwardly successful, middle-aged lawyer. But Osborne has also written a number of unsuccessful works, among

them *A Patriot for Me* (1965), *Hotel Amsterdam* (1968), *West of Suez* (1971), and *Watch It Come Down* (1976). Despite the critics' fondness for declaring that he has failed to live up to his early promise, Osborne must be considered one of the most important of postwar dramatists.

Next to Osborne, the Royal Court's most important dramatist of the early years was probably John Arden (1930–   ), author of *Live Like Pigs* (1958), *Sergeant Musgrave's Dance* (1959), *The Happy Haven* (1960), *Armstrong's Last Goodnight* (1964), and several other plays. Arden's work has been both praised highly and judged to be confused. Because he treats contemporary problems but does not seem to take sides, audiences have found it difficult to decide what he intends. But practically all of the plays pursue the same themes—the conflict between order and anarchy, between conformity and freedom, between those who wish to impose some pattern or principle and those who resist such efforts. Since 1967 Arden has written most of his plays in collaboration with his wife, Margaretta D'Arcy, who is concerned above all with conveying social messages and effecting social change. Consequently, Arden's work has become increasingly polemical, as in *Island of the Mighty* (1972), which uses the King Arthur legends to comment on English political and social goals.

Although the Royal Court made its principal contribution through its advocacy of new works, it also presented a wide range of older plays, such as *Lysistrata*, *The Country Wife*, *Major Barbara*, and *The Good Woman of Setzuan*.

The Theatre Workshop was founded in 1945 by a group of young people dissatisfied with the commercial theatre on both artistic and social grounds. Joan Littlewood (1914–   ) soon became its leader. Having no financial resources, the company toured England and the continent before settling in 1953 in a London suburb, Stratford, a working-class district. It did its important work between 1955, when it gained international recognition through an appearance at the world festival in Paris, and 1961, when Miss Littlewood resigned.

Two playwrights, Behan and Delaney, were especially associated with the Theatre Workshop. Brendan Behan's (1923–1965) first play, *The Quare Fellow*, written in 1945, was presented by the Theatre Workshop in 1956. A mixture of the comic and serious, it shows a cross section of prison life on the eve of a prisoner's execution. Similarly, *The Hostage* (1958) is built around varying attitudes toward the impending death of an I.R.A. agent and the hostage who is to be killed in reprisal. Many diversions (songs, dances, and character vignettes) enliven the play. Shelagh Delaney's (1939–   ) *A Taste of Honey* (1958) is the story of a young girl and her slatternly mother set against closely observed background. The charge that Miss Littlewood has a strong hand in reshaping the plays of both Behan and Delaney is supported in part by the failure of both to produce significant work except with the Workshop.

The Theatre Workshop is also noted for its pro-

Figure 3.18   Joan Littlewood's production of *Oh, What a Lovely War!* at the Theatre Workshop in 1963. Design by John Bury. Photo courtesy *The Report*.

duction style, perhaps best exemplified in *Oh, What a Lovely War!* (1963), a biting satire on the First World War. As the director of more than 150 of its productions, Miss Littlewood was responsible for establishing the company's approach. She drew heavily on Brechtian and music hall conventions, but also on Stanislavsky, especially "through lines" of action and improvisation. Her ultimate aim was to create a theatre to which the working classes would go with the same regularity and enthusiasm as to fun palaces or penny arcades. She sought to imbed some lasting message or significant content within a framework of techniques borrowed from popular entertainments.

Several of the troupe's successful productions were moved to commercial theatres, and this practice so weakened the company that Miss Littlewood eventually resigned. Since then she has returned occasionally to direct productions for the Workshop, but it can no longer be considered the vital force that it unquestionably was during the years between 1955 and the early 1960s.

Not all important new playwrights were attached to the English Stage Company or the Theatre Workshop. Among those who were not, one of the most important was Arnold Wesker (1932–   ), perhaps England's most socially conscious playwright of the late 1950s. His best-known works are the trilogy—*Chicken Soup with Barley* (1958), *Roots* (1959), and *I'm Talking About Jerusalem* (1960)—which trace the declining sense of purpose in the socialist movement and seek to show that workers have settled for too little and have chosen the wrong paths in seeking to remedy ills. In *The Kitchen* (1958) Wesker explores working-class conditions through the microcosm of a kitchen in a large restaurant, and in *Chips with Everything* (1962) he uses an air force camp to show that enlisted men are exploited and systematically deprived of all that is best in entertainment, art, and living conditions.

In 1962 Wesker became the leader of a working-class artistic movement, Center 42 (so named from the Trades Union Congress resolution number 42 which in 1961 called for the popularization of the arts among workers). With Center 42 Wesker intended to supply plays and music of high quality for festivals throughout the country, but after a brief burst of energy in 1962 the movement subsided, and from 1966 to 1970 it was almost wholly confined to the Roundhouse, a converted railroad shop located in north London. In 1971 Center 42 was disbanded. After 1962 Wesker wrote little, and such works as *The Four Seasons* (1966), *The Friends*, (1970), and *Love Letters on Blue Paper* (1978) had little success, perhaps because they were so unlike Wesker's early work, upon which his reputation still rests.

Another important dramatist, Peter Shaffer

Figure 3.19   Peter Shaffer's *Royal Hunt of the Sun* in its original production at the National Theatre, London, in 1964. Courtesy National Theatre, London.

(1926–   ), also began his career during the 1950s. Shaffer has written quite diverse plays, ranging through the realistic *Five Finger Exercise* (1958) to such absurdist comedies as *The Private Ear and The Public Eye* (1962) and *Black Comedy* (1965). He is most admired, however, for *The Royal Hunt of the Sun* (1964), a story about the Spanish conquest of Peru but which Shaffer has described as "an attempt to define the concept of God"; *Equus* (1973), a psychological study of a boy who has blinded several horses and of the psychiatrist who treats him; and *Amadeus* (1979), which shows the destruction of the naive and clumsy genius, Mozart, by his mediocre, urbane, and jealous rival, Salieri. In these plays Shaffer has demonstrated a masterful control of his medium, and he continues to be one of the most versatile dramatists of our time.

Of the many other dramatists, those who attracted most attention include Graham Greene (1904–   ) with plays about moral and religious questions as in

The Living Room (1953), *The Potting Shed* (1957), and *The Complaisant Lover* (1959); and Robert Bolt (1924–   ), with *The Flowering Cherry* (1957), a quasi-Chekhovian study of self-deception and failure, *A Man for All Seasons*, (1960) based on the life and martyrdom of Sir Thomas More, *Vivat, Vivat Regina* (1970), treating the story of Elizabeth I and Mary of Scotland, and *State of Revolution* (1977), concerning the Russian Revolution and its aftermath.

Much of the English theatre's accomplishment during the 1950s was made possible by a change in attitude toward subsidies. Until World War II, no direct governmental aid had ever been given the arts. Then, in 1940, the Council for the Encouragement of Music and the Arts (CEMA) was given £50,000 to assist in wartime work. In 1945 CEMA became the Arts Council, an independent organization financed by government funds, which decides how the support will be distributed. It has never had much money (in the 1960s it has only about one million dollars annually for drama), but it has used it to encourage organizations that seem capable of providing leadership. In 1948 Parliament also authorized local governments to allot a percentage of their revenues to support the arts. As a result, several municipalities began to provide subsidies for local resident companies, of which by the 1960s there were more than fifty in Great Britain, most performing a mixed repertory of classics and recent works.

Festivals—such as those at Edinburgh, Chichester, Malvern, Glyndebourne, Canterbury, and Aldeburgh—also added considerably to the vitality of the English theatre during the 1950s. Overall, the British theatre had by 1960 become one of the finest in the world.

Theatre and Drama in Italy, 1940–1960

After World War II the position of the Italian playwright remained as difficult as it had been a century earlier, for there was still a conflict between the demand for realism (which required the use of some regional dialect) and for universality (which required a more literary speech). Consequently, playwrights normally wrote with one specific region in mind. Occasionally a dramatist was able to attract a national following, but only one, Betti, achieved international stature in the postwar years. Ugo Betti (1892–1953) began writing plays in 1927, but his reputation rests primarily upon his late works, *Corruption in the Palace of Justice* (1948), *The Queen and the Rebels* (1951), and *The Burnt Flower Bed* (1953). All of Betti's plays are concerned with crises of conscience, especially among those who have gained influence through bureaucratic means. His preoccupation with guilt and power struck a responsive chord in the postwar consciousness.

Two other dramatists, Fabbri and de Flippo, won lesser international recognition. Diego Fabbri (1911–   ) has upheld the teachings of the church through dramas of traditional form. Of his plays, *Christ on Trial* (1955), showing the difficulties created by Christ's presence in the world, is probably the best known. Eduardo de Filippo (1900–   ) began writing around 1930. Although set in Naples and written in the Neapolitan dialect, his plays achieve universality because they show characters struggling to survive in the face of poverty, disease, and strained family relationships. They mingle the serious, comic, and pathetic with closely observed local detail. Among his best works are *Naples' Millionaires* (1946), *Filumena* (1955), *Saturday, Sunday, and Monday* (1959), and *The Boss* (1960). De Filippo, also a fine actor, worked for many years with his brother, Peppino de Filippo, one of Italy's most popular performers.

In production, touring companies continued to dominate, but a few men were able to establish permanent resident companies. The most important of these permanent troupes was the Piccolo Teatro, established in Milan in 1947 by Giorgio Strehler (1921–   ) and Paolo Grassi (1919–   ). It was given a rent-free theatre by the city of Milan and

Figure 3.20   Goldoni's *Servant of Two Masters* at the Piccolo Teatro, Milan. Directed by Giorgio Strehler; setting by Ezio Frigerio. From *Scene Design Throughout the World Since 1950*.

Figure 3.21   Vittorio Gassman in his own production of Alfieri's *Oreste* (1957). Setting by Gianni Polidori. Courtesy *World Theatre*.

later became the first dramatic company in Italy to receive a governmental subsidy. The Piccolo Teatro was a self-contained organization with a permanent troupe of twenty to thirty actors and a training school. Strehler directed about three-fourths of the plays but invited well-known foreign directors to stage others. He leaned heavily toward Brechtian techniques, as did his designers, Gianni Ratto until 1954 and then Luciano Damiani. Partially because of its foreign tours, the Piccolo Teatro came to be considered not only Italy's finest troupe but one of the best in the world. Permanent theatres were also established elsewhere in Italy. Perhaps the best of these were the Teatro Stabile in Genoa, founded in 1952 and headed by Luigi Squarzina, and the Teatro Stabile, founded in Turin in 1955 and headed by Gianfranco de Bosio. By the 1960s there were ten of these resident companies in Italy.

Nevertheless, most cities had to depend on touring companies. Of these, three were expecially important. Vittorio Gassman, who won an international reputation as a film star but is known in Italy as a major classical actor, from time to time assembled companies with which he presented outstanding works from the past. The Compagnia deLullo-Falk —with Giorgio deLullo as leading man and director, Rosella Falk as leading lady, and Romolo Valli and Elsa Albani as character actors— was after 1955 the best of the touring groups. Its preeminence was later challenged by the Compagnia Proclemer-Albertazzi, run by the actor-directors, Anna Proclemer and

Giorgio Albertazzi, perhaps Italy's most famous acting team. These companies toured throughout Italy.

Two Italian directors won international fame in the postwar years. Luchino Visconti (1906–1976) was one of the originators of the neorealism that gave Italian film much of its renown during the 1950s, and he brought the same stylistic quality to his stage productions. His best-known work was done in opera, especially in a series of productions starring Maria Callas. Franco Zeffirelli (1923–   ) began his career as a designer for Visconti, perhaps the greatest influence on his work. He turned to directing in 1953, at first primarily in opera, and by 1958 was being invited to direct abroad. He built a reputation for bringing classics down to earth (his productions of *Romeo and Juliet* and *Hamlet* were especially well received). In most of his productions (which he also designs), Zeffirelli has used neorealistic settings and business, an approach which has led on the one hand to accusations that he swamps the text with visual details and on the other to praise for bringing a sense of concreteness to works that all too often remain remote from audiences.

Russian Theatre and Drama, 1940–1960

During the war years the Russian theatre was devoted primarily to building morale. Since governmental supervision was considerably relaxed, many thought that the end of the war would bring still greater freedom. Instead, restrictions even more severe than those of the 1930s were imposed in 1946, and in 1948 all subsidies, except those granted to a few favored theatres, were stopped. The loss of governmental financial support was a severe blow, since 450 of Russia's 950 theatres had been destroyed during the war. By 1953 only about 250 were left.

Artistic restrictions were imposed by making Socialist Realism the only acceptable style and the Moscow Art Theatre's methods standard. Political control was strengthened in 1949 when party-appointed

Administrative Directors were placed in complete charge of each theatre. Most Western plays were removed from the repertory, and new Russian works were expected to uphold governmental policy. A large number of plays, such as Anatoly Safronov's (1911–   ) *The Muscovite Character* (1949), show the reeducation of persons who have stood in the way of party goals, while Constantin Simonov's *Alien Shadow* (1949) and Nikolai Pogodin's *The Missouri Waltz* (1950) are typical of the numerous anti-American plays. Other postwar drama, such as Vsevelod Vishnevsky's *1919—The Unforgettable Year* (1949) and A. Stein's *Prologue* (1952), glorifies Stalin's role in the development of Communism.

Following Stalin's death in 1953 many changes occurred. Although periods of freedom and restrictions alternated thereafter, in general there was a steady relaxation of the former rules, especially after Khrushchev's denunciation of Stalin in 1956. Censorship in the sense of prior judgment was no longer practiced, although many pressures were still exerted

Figure 3.22   Scene from Pogodin's *Sonnet of Petrarch* at the Mayakovsky Theatre, Moscow, 1957. From Komissarzhevsky, *Moscow Theatres* (1959).

on drama, most notably through the governing boards of theatres. Realism remained the dominant style and didacticism the dominant aim, but neither was enforced and both steadily declined in popularity. In new plays, romantic or family situations were treated more frequently, as in Pogodin's *Sonnet of Petrarch* (1957), while the theme of vindication from unjust charges, typified by Alexander Volodin's (1919–   ) *Factory Girl* (1957), became common. The conflict between generations, exemplified in Victor Rozov's (1913–   ) *The Unequal Struggle* (1960), also became a popular subject. Anti-American plays largely disappeared from the repertory, while many previously banned Russian plays became popular. The penchant for reshaping classics to bring out propagandistic themes also lessened considerably.

The changes of the 1950s meant a loss of prestige for the Moscow Art Theatre, although it continued to be at the head of its profession in terms of subsidies, salaries, and other governmental standards. Despite its official position, the Moscow Art Theatre was by 1960 looked upon by the public as something of a museum. Much the same might be said of the Maly Theatre, which retained an official position only slightly lower than that of the Moscow Art Theatre.

As these theatres declined in prestige, others rose. Some of the changes can be attributed to the abandonment in 1956 of the fixed pay scales and ranks and the prohibitions against changing companies which had hampered actors since the 1930s. Other changes can be attributed to shifts in taste. Of the older theatres, the Vakhtangov, under the direction of Reuben Simonov, became the most popular, for Vakhtangov's methods provided the most acceptable alternative to Socialist Realism. The Theatre of Satire, under Valentin Pluchek, also grew in esteem after it created a sensation in 1954 with productions of Mayakovsky's *The Bedbug* and *The Bathhouse* in a style not unlike Meyerhold's.

At the Mayakovsky Theatre (formerly the Theatre of the Revolution), Nikolai Okhlopkov returned to

Figure 3.23   Okhlopkov's production of *Hamlet* at the Mayakovsky Theatre, Moscow, 1954. Note the setting used to create the impression that Hamlet's world is a prison.

his prewar experimentation with performer-audience relationships. In the late 1950s he restaged Pogodin's *Aristocrats*, with the audience surrounding the playing area as in his productions of the 1930s. The most famous of Okhlopkov's postwar productions was probably *Hamlet* (1954), in which the setting was divided into compartments and the whole action treated as Hamlet's attempt to escape from a prison-like world. Two other prewar directors, Yuri Zavadsky at the Mossoviet Theatre and Alexei Popov at the Central Theatre of the Soviet Army, also continued to be important.

In Leningrad, the Pushkin Theatre occupied a prewar position comparable to that of the Moscow Art Theatre in Moscow and during the 1950s its prestige suffered similarly. The most admired theatre in Leningrad became the Gorky Theatre, after

1956 under the direction of Georgi Tovstogonov (1915–   ), noted for giving classics contemporary significance. Using realistic set pieces, Tovstogonov often dispensed with walls, ceilings, and similar details, and employed such cinematic techniques as moving the action forward on platforms for "close-up" effects. At the Leningrad Comedy Theatre, Nikolai Akimov (1901–1968), as both director and designer, also maintained high standards. Despite his fine work, Akimov's official position was probably reflected by the theatre in which he worked, a large room over a grocery.

By 1960, then, the Russian theatre was moving away from the restrictions and standards imposed during the Stalinist era. But the pressures to conform to party needs were still evident, and the government continued to make its presence felt when deviations became more than it wished to countenance. Nevertheless, a recovery had begun and would continue during the 1960s.

International Developments

At the end of World War II, international cooperation was sought in every aspect of life. The formation of the United Nations was followed by many other organizations designed to promote international understanding. The International Theatre Institute (ITI) was founded in 1947 under the auspices of the United Nations Educational, Scientific, and Cultural Organization (UNESCO), which provided it with a yearly subsidy. From 1950 to 1968 the ITI published *World Theatre*, a periodical designed to disseminate information. The ITI also held frequent international meetings, and since 1954 has sponsored an annual festival, the Théâtre des Nations. Other organizations have also promoted the exchange of ideas. Among these are the International Association of Theatre Technicians, the International Association of Theatre Critics, and the International Federation for Theatre Research.

International cooperation also encouraged the development of the theatre throughout the world, for newly created nations sought to display their national culture to advantage. Consequently, theatres were established in parts of the world where there formerly were few or none. In geographical scope, therefore, the theatre became more extensive after 1945 than at any time in the past.

By 1960, the theatre had rather fully recovered from the destruction of the war years. For the most part, however, it had continued along lines that had been established earlier, although there were a few notable exceptions, especially in France and England. But during the 1950s, new tensions and outlooks began to gather strength, and by 1960 the theatre was entering a period of both enormous vitality and enormous controversy.

Looking at Theatre History

In studying theatre history we need to be concerned about the "intellectual climate" of an age. Is it a period in which there is agreement on values and goals? Are there sharp divisions? If so, over what? What is being defended or attacked? What is so much taken for granted that it need not be questioned or discussed? What kinds of authority are cited to uphold beliefs or doubts: the supernatural order, scientific knowledge, cumulative human experience? In no one period is there total agreement on values and goals, but in many there is sufficient likeness to provide the cohesiveness needed for stability. In others, there is enough disagreement to produce disarray. In either case, the theatre cannot help but be affected.

In general, disarray has marked the years since 1940. The horrors of the Nazi concentration camps and the atomic bomb, the threat of world destruction that lurked behind the "cold war" of the 1950s, and the other events raised doubts not only about man's ability to act rationally but about the possibility of finding any system of belief on which to build a sane and cohesive society.

It was out of the crisis in belief that the absurdist movement emerged. The crisis is perhaps most clearly defined by Albert Camus:

> *A world that can be explained even with bad reasons is a familiar world. But, on the other hand, in a universe suddenly divested of illusions and lights, man feels an alien, a stranger. His exile is without remedy since he is deprived of the memory of a lost home or the hope of a promised land. This divorce between man and his life . . . is properly the feeling of absurdity. . . . Of whom and of what indeed can I say: "I know that!" This heart within me I can feel, and I judge that it exists. This world I can touch, and I likewise judge that it exists. There ends all my knowledge, and the rest is construction. . . .*
>
> *I said that the world is absurd, but I was too hasty. This world in itself is not reasonable, that is all that can be said. But what is absurd is the confrontation of this irrational and the wild longing for clarity whose call echoes in the human heart. . . .*
>
> *The absurd is born of this confrontation between the human need and the unreasonable silence of the world.*
>
> Albert Camus, "The Myth of Sisyphus," *The Myth of Sisyphus and Other Essays*, trans. Justin O'Brien (New York: Alfred A. Knopf, 1967), pp. 6, 19, 21, 28.

It was Martin Esslin who in 1961 first invented a label, Theatre of the Absurd, for the group of plays that seemed to stem from the position set forth by Camus:

> *The hallmark of [the Theatre of the Absurd] is its sense that certitudes and unshakable basic assumptions of former ages have been swept away, that they have been tested and found wanting, that they have been discredited as cheap and somewhat childish illusions . . .*
>
> *This sense of metaphysical anguish at the absurdity of the human condition is, broadly speaking the theme of the plays of Beckett, Adamov, Ionesco, Genet, and the other writers discussed in this book. But it is not merely the subject-matter that defines what is here called the Theatre of the Absurd. . . . [That Theatre also] strives to express its sense of the senselessness of the human condition and the inadequacy of the rational approach by the open abandonment of rational devices and discursive thought. . . . [It seeks] to achieve a unity between its basic assumptions and the form in which they are expressed.*
>
> Martin Esslin, *The Theatre of the Absurd*, revised and updated edition (Woodstock, N.Y.: The Overlook Press, 1973), pp. 4–6.

Eugène Ionesco has been not only one of the most successful but one of the most argumentative of absurdist playwrights, often taking issue with the directors of his plays and with critics. (Many of his comments are collected in *Notes and Counter Notes*.) Here are some reactions motivated by the American production of *Rhinoceros* in 1961:

> *I have read the American critics on the play and noticed that every one agreed that the play was funny. Well, it isn't. . . . The production reveals not only an absence of style . . . but above all intellectual dishonesty . . . [The play] is a fairly objective description of the growth of fanaticism, of the rebirth of a totalitarianism that grows, propagates, conquers, transforms a whole-world. . . . I really tried to say this to the American director; I clearly indicated in the few interviews I was able to give that. . . . it cannot be anything else but painful and serious.*

Some critics blame me for denouncing evil without saying what good is. . . . but it is so easy to rely on a system of throught that is more or less mechanical. . . . an unworkable solution one has found for oneself is infinitely more valuable than a ready-made ideology that stops men from thinking. . . .

One of the great critics of New York complains that, after destroying one conformism, I put nothing else in its place, leaving him and the audience in a vacuum. That is exactly what I wanted to do. A free man should pull himself out of vacuity on his own, by his own efforts and not by the efforts of other people.

Notes and Counter Notes, Writings on the Theatre, trans. Donald Watson (New York: Grove Press, 1964), pp. 207–211.

During the 1950s dissatisfactions were not expressed wholly through absurdist drama. In England, the most powerful impact was made by the "angry young men," who expressed themselves in relatively traditional dramatic forms. Although it is now usual to suggest that Osborne's *Look Back in Anger* was recognized immediately as a turning point in English drama, most reviewers voiced serious reservations about it. Here are some excerpts from one of the most negative reviews*:

We should be very frank about this. If more plays like tonight's Look Back in Anger *are produced, the "Writer's Theatre" at the Royal Court must surely sink. I look back in anger*

---

* Both reviews reprinted in *John Osborne: Look Back in Anger, A Casebook,* edited by John Russell Taylor (London: Macmillan and Company, 1968). The first review appears on p. 45 of this book, the second on pp. 51–53.

upon a night misconceived and mis-spent. . . . The principal character is self-pitying, uncouth, cheaply vulgar. . . .

J. C. Trewin in *The Birmingham Post,* 8 May 1956.

Fortunately, others were more perceptive:

If I were Mr. George Devine I should regard Look Back in Anger *as something of a test case. This is just the sort of play which the English Stage Company was created to produce. . . . If there is . . . an audience [for what Devine is trying to do] let them show their interest by filling out the performances of the play. . . .*

Of course, Look Back in Anger *is not a perfect play. But it is a most exciting one, abounding with life and vitality and the life it deals with is life as it is lived at this very moment—not a common enough subject in the English theatre. . . . Not a pleasant play, then. . . . All the same, don't miss this play. If you are young, it will speak to you. If you are middle-aged, it will tell you what the young are feeling. . . .*

T. C. Worsley in *The New Statesman.*

Between 1945 and 1960, the dominant production style in the United States was exemplified in the combined work of Elia Kazan (as director) and Jo Mielziner (as designer). Here, in his review of Tennessee Williams's *Cat on a Hot Tin Roof* (1955), Eric Bentley gives a good description of their work:

Jo Mielziner's setting consists of a square and sloping platform with one of its corners, not one of its sides, jutting towards the audience. A corner of a ceiling is above, pointing upstage. On the platform are minimum furnishings for a bed-sitting room. Around the room, steps and space suggest the out of doors. The whole stage is swathed in ever-changing light and shade. . . .

Such is the world of Elia Kazan, as we know it from his work on plays by more authors than one. The general scheme is that not only of Streetcar *but also of* Salesman: *an exterior that is also an interior—but, more important, a view of* man's *exterior that is also a view of his interior, the habitat of his body and the country of his memories and dreams. A theatre historian would probably call this world a combination cf naturalism and expressionism. . . .*

It is one of the distinctive creations of American theatre. . . . with the means of the new American theatre (school of Lee Strasberg and Harold Clurman) it does reach the cherished end of the older theatre (true grandeur of performance) at a time when the older theatre itself . . . is failing to do so. . . .

I do not think the reason for this resides in the formality itself. The effectiveness of this grandeur results . . . from the interaction between formality in the setting, lighting, and grouping and an opposite quality . . . in the individual performances. The externals of the physical production belong . . . to the old theatre, but the acting is internal, "Stanislavskyite." Within the formal setting, from the fixed positions in which they are made to stand, the actors live their roles with that vigilant, concentrated, uninterrupted nervous intensity which Mr. Kazan always manages to give. . . .

The New Republic, April 4, 1955.

4

Theatre and Drama since 1960

The 1960s saw enormous stresses develop in almost every country in the world. In The United States, these stresses were at first concerned primarily with the drive for civil rights. Spearheaded by Martin Luther King and his doctrine of passive resistance, the struggle progressed through demonstrations, sit-ins, and other forms of nonviolent protest. These techniques were so effective that they were soon taken over by other groups, especially those disenchanted by America's involvement in Vietnam. As protests gained in popularity, they moved away from nonviolence toward guerrilla tactics. Consequently, from 1968 onward violence became increasingly a part of daily life.

These patterns of protest and violence were symptomatic of deep-seated doubts about the validity of long-standing conventions and traditional values and the ability of social institutions to deal efficiently with changing needs. Individuals and groups began to elevate their own ideals above existing laws, to assert their obligation to live by their own standards, and to demand the alteration or destruction of anything contrary to their views. The result was a fragmented society lacking in strong common purposes: a tendency toward anarchy. Such conditions were most evident in the United States, but they existed almost everywhere.

The theatre could not remain aloof from the stresses of the time. It was caught in a struggle between those who wished to maintain tradition and those who championed innovation and change. This conflict was especially strong in the late 1960s and early 1970s and provoked much controversy over the nature and function of theatre. The old conception of art as detached contemplation (or as the pursuit of some superior beauty and order) was challenged by those who wished to make it reflect immediate social and political presssures and to use it as an instrument for reform. This struggle was more evident in some countries than in others. In a relatively insulated nation such as Russia the stresses were seldom intense, but elsewhere—especially the United States—they often led to frenetic experimentation. Throughout the 1960s economic prosperity gave the theatre considerable stability, for it was easy to gain financial support both for traditional and innovative work.

Thus, it was a decade in which the old and the new coexisted, sometimes in uneasy alliance, but often in radical opposition.

In the 1970s, however, a mood of hesitation and doubt began to replace the climate of defiance and challenge, and the future began to appear highly uncertain. Conservatism, both political and economic, reasserted itself. As the financial situation worsened, the exuberance of earlier years faded. The effect on the theatre is still being felt.

Theatre and Drama in Italy Since 1960

During the 1960s the Italian theatre achieved greater stability than it had previously enjoyed. In the mid-1960s there were ten resident troupes, with the best in Milan, Genoa, Turin, and Rome. But by the late 1960s, Italy, like other countries, was undergoing considerable stress, which inevitably affected the theatre. In Milan, Giorgio Strehler resigned his post at the Piccolo Teatro in 1968 when it failed to get the building he had been seeking and when it was not named a national theatre as had seemed likely. The company continued under the direction of Paolo Grassi (with Strehler as occasional guest director). In 1972 Grassi was named head of the LaScala opera company and Strehler resumed his former position at the Piccolo. At this time the two companies agreed to link their ticket offerings and to give special priority to attracting a working-class audience.

Strehler is clearly one of Italy's most distinguished directors. Under his leadership, the Piccolo Teatro ally. He has served as artistic advisor to the Salzburg Festival and has directed at the Paris Opéra, Vienna's Burgtheater, and elsewhere. In addition, he has received numerous awards and honorary degrees. He is also one of the world's most extravagant directors. Under his leadership, the Piccolo Teatro accumulated an enormous debt, and Strehler resigned his post at Salzburg after being censured for overspending. Nevertheless, he continued to be sought after because of his great talent as a director.

The stresses that began in the late 1960s caused some resident theatres to be disbanded, but there remain about eight. Most cities in Italy, however, still depend on commercial theatres dedicated to the long run and to touring. There are approximately eighty such companies in Italy.

Of all European countries, Italy appears to glorify most the virtuoso performer, even though it provides few opportunities for actors to acquire sound technical training. These conditions make for poor ensemble work and consequently, outside a few companies, the general level of acting remains poor.

Since the late 1960s, the most innovative directors in Italy have been Fo and Ronconi. Dario Fo began working in the theatre in the 1950s and soon turned to broadly farcical political satire, such as *He Had Two Pistols with Black and White Eyes*, intended to appeal to middle-class audiences. But in the late 1960s Fo came to champion a proletarian revolution and since then he has sought to attract a working-class audience with agit-prop plays satirizing capitalism, the Italian Communist party, the Italian state, the church, and other enemies of the Maoist communism he champions. Fo's productions are theatrically imaginative, often making use of oversized puppets and devices drawn from practically all forms of popular entertainment. His company performs in factories, gymnasiums, and out of doors—almost anywhere an audience can gather.

Among Fo's most popular productions are *Mistero Buffo* (1969), which combines elements from medieval farce, mime, and contemporary life, *We're All in the Same Boat—But That Man Over There, Isn't He Our Employer?* (1974), based on Italian political events between 1911 and 1923, when Mussolini came to power, and *Let's Talk About Women* (1977). Since it is so wide-ranging in its criticism, Fo's company, the Collettivo Teatrale della Commune, is now disliked by both the political right and left in Italy. Fo's company has toured widely in Europe where it has won an enviable popular and critical fol-

Figure 4.1   Luca Ronconi's production of *Orlando Furioso*, first performed at the Festival of Two Worlds, Spoleto, in 1969. Note the wheeled wagons on which the performers stand surrounded by the audience. Photograph by Pic.

lowing. A proposed tour of the United States had to be dropped when the company was denied a permit to enter the country.

Luca Ronconi came to international prominence in 1969 with his production of *Orlando Furioso*, seen first in Spoleto and later in Belgrade, Milan, Paris, New York, and elsewhere. The text was adapted by Edoardo Sanguineti from Lodovico Ariosto's sixteenth-century epic poem, an enormously long work about chivalric adventures involving mythical crea-

tures, enchanted castles, sorcerers, and other fanciful beings. Rather than performing the episodes in strict sequence, two or more progressed simultaneously in different parts of the theatrical space, since Ronconi believed that this achieved the same effect of disorder and fantasy induced by reading the poem. About fifty wheeled wagons were used in a large open space, which was also occupied by the audience, who moved about choosing what to watch.

Ronconi's subsequent productions are less well known but equally imaginative. In *XX* (1971) he divided the audience into groups and placed each in separate rooms, the walls between which were gradually removed. Each group saw a few disturbing events and heard voices and sounds elsewhere. When all the walls were gone, a *coup d'état* was announced and the audience was ordered to disperse. Ronconi declared that he had sought to show how dictatorial power can be assumed almost unnoticed until it is too late. His *Oresteia* (1972), a six-hour-long production, was highly praised for its impressive visual imagery but faulted for its acting. Ronconi has continued to build an international, though controversial, reputation through his innovative use of space and his metaphorical theatricality in such productions as *The Barber of Seville* (1974) and *Utopia* (1975), an adaptation of Aristophanes' *The Birds*. Since 1977 Ronconi has been head of the Prato Theatre Workshop, where he has continued his experiments in staging.

Italy has been less fortunate in writers than in directors. Virtually no contemporary Italian playwright has been able to win international recognition, although a number of competent dramatists have been at work since 1960. Among these are Diego Fabbri (perhaps the best known abroad), Carlo Terron, Federico Zardi, Franco Brusati, Guiseppe Patroni-Griffi, Raffaele Viviani, and Luigi Squarzina. At a conference held in the 1970s, several reasons were advanced for this lack of significant playwrights. Among these were the absence of literary advisors to companies and the lack of artistic trust that would ecourage writers to take chances.

Like many other European countries, Italy in the 1970s began to be concerned about theatre for children and youth. This concern was strengthened after 1974 by the establishment of a national festival of youth theatres.

During the past few years the extreme inflation that has plagued Italy has posed a serious threat to its theatres, many of which are now hard pressed to survive. Thus, the gains made earlier now seem to hang in the balance.

Russian Theatre and Drama Since 1960

The thaw in Russia that began after Khrushchev's denunciation of Stalin in 1956 continued after 1960, although the government from time to time applied pressures to keep the theatre within acceptable limits. One result of relaxed strictures was the presentation for the first time of many foreign plays in Russia. For example, in 1960 Brecht's works began to be introduced into the repertory, and soon plays by Miller, Osborne, Williams, and others were being produced with some frequency. On the other hand, few absurdist dramas were presented, probably because they were considered too "formalistic." Another result was revived interest in Meyerhold and Tairov. During the 1960s a complete edition of Meyerhold's writings was published, and exhibits were mounted of his and Tairov's productions. In 1974, the centenary of Meyerhold's birth was celebrated with special exhibits, performances, articles, conferences, and commemorative stamps. Thus, he was restored to official favor, although many of his methods were still considered unacceptable in a socialist state. Nevertheless, the renewed interest in Meyerhold is symptomatic of a general decline in prestige of Socialist Realism, although it continues to be the dominant mode. After 1956, Vakhtangov's methods also grew in popularity, perhaps because they were considered an acceptable compromise between the approaches of Stanislavsky and Meyerhold.

Despite all changes, the Moscow Art Theatre has continued to enjoy the greatest official prestige and its actors are still the highest paid. Although by the 1960s it had come to be viewed by many Russians as more nearly a museum than as a vital institution, its standing with the government is indicated by the new and lavish theatre built for it in 1968–1969 in honor of its seventieth anniversary.

In terms of innovation, two companies—the Contemporary and the Taganka—took the lead after 1960. The Contemporary Theatre, founded in 1957, was the first new company to be authorized in Russia since the 1930s. Under the leadership of Oleg Yefremov (1927–   ) until 1970 and then under Oleg Tabakov, the Contemporary has drawn most of its personnel and methods from the Moscow Art Theatre or its training school. The principal departures of the new company lie in its concentration on plays (such as those by Brecht, Osborne, Shatrov, and Rozov) thought to be relevant to present-day life and in its

Figure 4.2 Yefremov's production of Aksyonov's *Always on Sale* at the Contemporary Theatre, Moscow, 1966.

use of simplified settings rather than the elaborate mountings typical at the Moscow Art Theatre. The Contemporary also did much to revive the reputation of Yevgeny Schwarz (1897–1958), author of satirical fables based on fairy tales and legends, among them *The Naked King* (1933, based on "The Emperor's New Clothes"), *The Shadow* (1941), and *The Dragon* (1943), works alternately banned and permitted by Soviet authorities because of their ambiguous political overtones. By 1970 the Contemporary Theatre had achieved sufficient stature that Yefremov was appointed to head the Moscow Art Theatre in an attempt to revive that troupe's waning prestige and vigor. In 1974 the Contemporary received a new theatre (a remodeled cinema with rehearsal rooms and workshops) but retained its old quarters in order to enlarge its activities.

The Moscow Theatre of Drama and Comedy (usually called the Taganka after the suburb in which it is located) was founded in 1964 by Yuri Lyubimov (1917–   ), formerly a teacher at the Vakhtangov Theatre's training school. It now enjoys the reputation of being Russia's most experimental troupe. Many of its techniques are reminiscent of Meyerhold's. It makes liberal use of dynamic movement, dance, mime, masks, puppets, and projections, and it frequently reshapes scripts. In 1970 at the congress of the All-Union Society of Theatre Workers, it was the only theatre to be singled out for censure. The Taganka is especially popular with young audiences.

Its tendency to produce plays that lie on the edge of permissibility and its unusual production techniques have kept the Taganka at the forefront of contemporary Soviet theatre. It is indicative of the company's standing and the government's ambivalent attitude toward it that after permitting the Taganka to play in Paris in 1977 the government canceled its agreement that Lyubimov could direct abroad in 1978.

Another of Russia's controversial directors is Anatoly Efros, largely because he gives novel interpretations to scripts that sometimes call official attitudes into question. Several of his productions, though popular, have been withdrawn from the repertory (although some have later been returned). In 1979 Efros was permitted to direct Bulgakov's *Cabal of Critics* at the Guthrie Theatre in Minneapolis. The inconsistencies in the treatment of Lyubimov and Efros would seem to indicate that the Soviet government is more interested in maintaining control than in forbidding the work of these provocative artists.

Playwriting seems also to have become less doctrinaire and more free in form since 1960. Vasili Aksyonov (1932–   ) has utilized many techniques drawn from the work of Russian experiments of the 1920s in such plays as *Always on Sale* (1966), in which songs, dances, masks, and film combine to create a dim view of a conformist society, and *Your Murderer* (1977), a work reminiscent of Ionesco's *Rhinoceros*, with its protagonist who refuses to go along with the crowd. Some writers—such as Chingiz Aitmatov and Kaltai Mukhamedzhanov in *The Ascent of Mount Fuji* (1973) and G. Baklanov in *Fasten Your Seat Belts* (1975)—have treated the problem of maintaining one's integrity in the face of authoritarian demands to conform if one is to prosper. Perhaps because of the treatment accorded extreme dissident writers such as Andrei Amalrik and Aleksandr Solzhenitsyn, recent dramatists have favored diversionary or sentimental entertainment. Among the most successful of these playwrights have been Aleksandr Vampilov (1937–1972), whose *Duck Hunting* (1967) and *Last Summer in Chulimsk* (1972) are in the tradition of Russian farce; Mikhail Roschin (1933–   ), whose extremely popular *Valentin and Valentina* (1971) treats young lovers caught in a generational conflict; and Aleksei Arbuzov, perhaps the most popular and prolific of recent Russian dramatists, with such plays as *Old Fashioned Comedy* (1976, produced on Broadway in 1978 as *Do You Turn Somersaults?*), which treats awakening love between two older people.

Despite numerous changes, the Russian theatre as a whole remains rooted in Socialist Realism, al-

Figure 4.3   A setting by Nisson Chifrine for a dramatization of a novel by Sholokhov at the Theatre of the Red Army, Moscow, 1957. From *Scene Design Throughout the World Since 1950*.

though a trend toward simplified detail is especially evident in stage design. Rather than representing each place in detail, it is now common to use one fixed background representative of a play's overall mood, and to change small realistic set pieces in front of it. Among the best of recent designers have been Alexander Tychler, Nisson Chifrine, Evgeny Kovalenko, Alexander Vassiliev, Yuri Pimenov, Teimuraz Ninna, I. G. Sumbatashvili, and M. S. Saryan.

Seemingly the theatre is now as popular in Russia as anywhere in the world. Moscow's approximately thirty theatres are usually filled each night, and government statistics indicate that attendance is on the increase throughout the country. In the late 1970s there were more than 550 theatres in Russia, of which forty-seven were for children and youth (with fourteen more promised by 1982). During the summer months the major companies of Moscow and Leningrad tour the provinces, and provincial troupes

come to play in these major cities. Trains are also being used to bring live theatre to areas without resident companies. Thus, the theatre seems to be firmly entrenched in Russian life.

Theatre and Drama in Czechoslovakia Since 1960

Following World War II, most of Eastern Europe came under the domination of Russia. As a result, theatre in these countries was subjected to restrictions similar to those imposed in the USSR. Following the break with Stalinism in 1956, however, strictures were considerably relaxed and experimentation flourished, especially in Czechoslovakia and Poland.

Czechoslovakia has made its greatest international impact in the field of technology and design and above all through the work of Josef Svoboda (1920–   ). Although he began his career around 1945, Svoboda was unable to demonstrate his great versatility until the late 1950s when Socialist Realism was no longer the standard mode. Much of his work is an extension of experimentation begun with multimedia in the 1930s by E. F. Burian (1904–1959) and Miroslav Kouril (1911–   ). It is also heavily indebted to the Prague Institute of Scenography, founded in 1957 and headed by Kouril, for its staff and facilities did much of the experimentation.

The turning point in Svoboda's career came in 1958 when he began collaborating with the director Alfred Radok on two projects—Polyekran and Laterna Magika, both using a number of screens on which still and moving pictures were projected. Laterna Magika also integrated live actors into the performance. Both of these forms were shown at the Brussels World's fair in 1958 and elicited considerable praise and excitement. In 1959 Svoboda began to carry over many of the technical devices into his stage work. Since then he has experimented continuously with means to create a completely flexible

Figure 4.4   Setting by Josef Svoboda for *Their Day* by Josef Topol at the National Theatre, Prague (1959). Note the use of projections on screens of varying sizes. This was Svoboda's first attempt to apply the techniques of the Laterna Magika in theatrical production. Photograph copyrighted by Jaromir Svoboda.

stage which can change from scene to scene as the needs of the drama change. In addition to screens and projections, he has also developed platforms and steps that can move vertically, horizontally, and laterally to alter the spatial relationships and size of the acting area. He has also explored the potentials for stage use of such materials as mirrors, plastic, and various kinds of netting, and has used most of these as surfaces on which to project images (or in some instances to reflect the action as seen from above, behind, or at an angle). He has designed settings in every conceivable style and is now among the best known and most influential designers in the world, although his reputation continues to be associated especially with the development of multimedia techniques.

Svoboda's work did much to call attention to the high quality of the Czech theatre as a whole. In the 1960s there were about fifty-six companies in Czechoslovakia, but those best known abroad (aside from the Prague National Theatre) were a group of small theatres in Prague, most of which came into existence after 1962 when the government created the State Theatre Studio to assist experimental companies. Of these, three were especially outstanding. The Theatre Behind the Gate, founded in 1965 by Otomar Krejča, shared its 435-seat theatre with the Laterna Magika, for both of which Svoboda was principal designer. It was noted for its imaginative staging and thoughtful interpretation of Czech and foreign plays. The Činoherni (Actors's Club), founded in 1965 and headed by Jaroslav Vostry, performed in a theatre seating 220. Its primary emphasis was on ensemble acting (probably the best in Czechoslovakia) and a wide-ranging repertory drawn from world drama. The Theatre on the Balustrade, founded in 1958 and headed from 1962 until 1969 by Jan Grossman, seated about 200. This company was the primary home of absurdist drama in Czechoslovakia and had as its resident playwright Václav Havel (1936–   ), often considered the leading contemporary Czech dramatist. His bitingly satirical treatments of bureaucracy, *The Garden Party* (1963), *The Memorandum* (1965), and *The Conspirators* (1974) have come to be known and admired throughout the world.

The Soviet invasion of Czechoslovakia in 1968 dealt a sharp blow to the theatre. Beginning in 1969 censorship was reimposed. In that year Grossman and Havel also resigned their posts at the Balustrade, and the Činoherni was forced to change many of its policies. In 1971 Krejča was removed as director at the Gate and in 1972, reportedly because the actors remained loyal to him, the Gate was disbanded. In 1976 Krejča was permitted by authorities to leave the country for a permanent post in West Germany. The Prague Institute of Scenography was also closed. In 1977 Havel and several other writers were put on trial and Havel was sent to prison. In these and other ways the theatre has been brought increasingly into line with the government's outlook.

During the 1970s attention was drawn away from the theatres of Prague (the chief city of the Czech population) to those of Bratislava (the principal city of the Slovak population), which, though in many ways equal to those of Prague, has been little known outside of Czechoslovakia.

By 1980 Czechoslovakian drama had lost much of its earlier prestige. But there is no denying the significance of its role during the 1960s.

Theatre and Drama in Poland Since 1960

The Polish theatre followed a path not unlike that of Czechoslovakia. It too had developed a sophisticated and technically advanced theatre between the wars and it too came under Soviet domination after 1945. Poland was the first of the East European countries to ease restraints, and from 1956 until the late 1960s its government exerted little direct pressure on the theatre.

After 1956 the dominant dramatic mode was absurdism, although it took a more satirical and didactic turn than in France. The vogue was initiated with the plays of Stanislaw Ignacy Witkiewicz (1885–1939), a previously neglected surrealist writer of the interwar years, whose works such as *The Water Hen*, *The Mother*, and *The Madman and the Nun* have won increasing acceptance throughout the world as major *avant-garde* dramas. In addition to Witkiewicz's plays, Beckett's *Waiting for Godot* helped to establish the taste for absurdist drama. Soon a new school of dramatists appeared, of whom the most important were Rósewicz and Mrozek. Tadeusz Rósewicz (1921–   ), already famous as a poet, began writing plays in 1960. His *The Card Index* (1960) and *He Left Home* (1964) did much to establish the pattern that would be followed by subsequent writers, with whom the most common theme was the search for a lost order even as they rejected

the concept of absolutes. He has continued to explore this theme in such plays as *The Laocoon Group* (1974), *White Marriage* (1975), and *The Departure of Mr. Greedyguts* (1977).

Although within Poland Rósewicz is perhaps the most respected of contemporary dramatists, abroad he has been overshadowed by Slawomir Mrozek (1930–   ), whose plays depend rather heavily on caricature. For example, *The Police* (1958), one of Mrozek's numerous short plays, shows how the secret police, having been so successful that they are in danger of being abolished, order one of their own men to become an enemy agent so they may survive. Mrozek has also written a few full-length plays, of which the best known is *Tango* (1965), one of the most popular of all new plays in Europe during the late 1960s. *Tango* is a parable about the decay of values, which has become so complete that only brute force is truly effective; consequently those who are most willing to exercise power, ruthlessly and without regard for humanistic principles, become the rulers. Mrozek has continued this vein in *A Happy Event* (1971), in which he depicts left-wing anarchist youth in the form of a grown-up baby who tyrannizes his parents, blows up their house, and ends up helpless in the ruins; in *The Emigrés* (1974), a two-character play which suggests that the left-wing intellectual and the worker depend on each other to give their lives significance; and in *Slaughterhouse* (1975), which concerns an artist's loss of faith in art, his obsessive search for some new truth, and his eventual suicide.

But Poland is perhaps best known for its innovative production rather than its writing. Poland has many outstanding directors. Among the most influential have been Adam Hanuszkiewicz, whose interpretation of classics has gone quite contrary to tradition; Kazimierz Dejmek, whose respect for the text has lead him to seek within each work the style most appropriate to it; Andrzej Wajda, an eminent film director, whose stage productions have been noted for their painterly use of space; and Tadeusz Kantor, a painter who in his theatre pieces has favored im-

Figure 4.5   Scene from *The Dispute* (1978) at the Wroclaw Pantomime Theatre. Scenario, direction, and choreography by Henryk Tomaszewski. From a series of slides on the Polish Theatre. Courtesy KaiDib Films International, Glendale, California.

provisation based on plays, especially those of Witkiewicz. Henryk Tomaszewski has earned an enviable reputation both at home and abroad with his Mime Theatre using his own scripts based on literary sources. Tomaszewski seeks to find and release the hidden beauty and expressiveness of movement. His storytelling, silent works are noted not only for their great power but also for their optimistic view of human experience.

But in international reputation all of these directors have been outstripped by Jerzy Grotowski (1933–   ), director of the Polish Laboratory Theatre. Founded in Opole in 1959, Grotowski's company moved to Wroclaw (Breslau) in 1965 and was designated the Institute for Research in Acting. Until 1965 Grotowski was little known, but subsequently his reputation mushroomed. His company performed in various countries and Grotowski himself worked with many foreign troupes and lectured widely about his meth-

ods. His work was also publicized through a collection of essays by and about him, *Towards a Poor Theatre* (1968).

Ironically, Grotowski began to alter his approach just as he won international acceptance. Thus, his work can be divided in to two principal phases: before and after 1970. During the first phase, Grotowski began with the premise that the theatre has borrowed too heavily from other media, especially film and television, and thus has violated its own essence, to which he sought to return by eliminating everything not truly required by it: the actor and the audience. He called his approach "poor theatre," since it avoided all machinery and minimized all spectacle not created by the actor. His performers were not allowed to use makeup or to change costume in order to indicate a change in role or within a character; all music had to be produced by the actors themselves; he used no scenery in the traditional sense, although a few functional properties might be rearranged or used in various ways as the action demanded; he abandoned the proscenium-arch theatre in favor of a large room which could be rearranged for each production. In this way, the actor (the essential theatrical element) was thrown back on his own resources.

During this period it was the training of the actor that lay at the heart of Grotowski's concerns. In his work he drew heavily from many sources—Stanislavsky, Yoga, Meyerhold, Vakhtangov, Delsarte, Dullin, and others. His system required that the actor gain absolute control over himself physically and vocally and to an extent psychically, so that during performances he might completely transform himself as demanded by the production. Grotowski's actors had to be willing to give of themselves fully and expose themselves psychically when necessary. According to Grotowski, actors should arouse a sense of wonder because they can go so far beyond what the spectators are able to do.

In this early phase, Grotowski looked upon the theatre as something like a ritual to which spectator-witnesses are admitted. He believed that the audience

Figure 4.6   Scene from *Apocolypsis cum Figuris* at Grotowski's Polish Laboratory Theatre. This photograph was made during a performance. From a series of slides on the Polish theatre. Courtesy KaiDib Films International, Glendale, California.

is the other essential ingredient of a performance and that it must be put in a position that permits it to play its role unselfconsciously. (He argued that attempts to involve the audience directly in the action only make it self-conscious.) Therefore, for each production he decided how the audience should respond psychologically and then had the spatial arrangement designed to create the appropriate psychic distance.

In preparing a production, Grotowski searched in a script to find those patterns that he considered to have universal meaning for audiences today. Much of the script might be abandoned and the remainder rearranged. The ultimate aim was to make the actors and the audience confront themselves in something resembling a religious experience. The results were appraised variously. Some critics found Grotowski's productions among the most significant of the age, whereas others thought them incomprehensible or

pretentious. No one, however, denied the technical excellence of Grotowski's actors.

By 1970 Grotowski had come to believe that his group had reached the end of its search for technical mastery and he decided to create no new productions. He realized that while his actors had been able to eliminate the blocks that stood in their way as performers, they had not broken down the blocks between performer and audience. He then set out to eliminate "the idea of theatre," in the sense of an actor playing before an audience, and to find a way of incorporating spectators into the disarmament process. In 1973 he stated: "We came to the conclusion that we must abolish . . . payments, and that those who came to us would come to a special place where they could leave their daily lives behind. . . . We call this period of time 'Holiday,' or the day that is holy. . . . What is possible then together? A meeting, not a confrontation; a communion, where we can be totally ourselves. . . ."

Around 1970, Grotowski reorganized his company, took into it some young people with no previous professional theatrical experience, and thereafter worked to develop a "special project" with six subgroups, each headed by a member of the original company. Each subgroup was concerned with a different problem, but all were related to the main purpose: to lead participants back into the elemental connections between people and their bodies, imagination, the natural world, and each other.

The first major revelation of the new work came during the summer of 1975 when approximately 500 people from all over the world attended a "research university" organized by Grotowski at Wroclaw under the sponsorship of the Théâtres des Nations, which that year was hosted by Warsaw. The group included students, teachers, and journalists, as well as several famous directors—among them Peter Brook, Jean-Louis Barrault, Luca Ronconi, Joseph Chaikin, and André Gregory. Everyone who attended had to participate. Some of the activities involved groups going into the woods for twenty-four hours during which they were led through ritualized relivings of basic myths, archetypes, and symbols including fire, air, earth, water, eating, dancing, playing, planting, and bathing. Through this process, participants were expected to rediscover the roots of the theatre in pure ritualized experience, as well as to discover their own true being. Since 1975 Grotowski has continued to work along these lines, although with smaller groups and often with persons having no training in the theatre. The significance of this approach for the theatre has been the subject of lively debate both in Poland and elsewhere.

Since the 1960s the Polish theatre has had to weather two major political crises. The first came in 1968 when many theatrical workers objected to their nation's participation in putting down Czech liberalization. As a result, several leading critics went into exile, and Mrozek's plays were banned. By the mid-1970s, restrictions had lessened considerably. Mrozek's plays had been returned to the repertory and several new theatres were built or remodeled and prizes were established for new plays about contemporary life and for artistic innovation. During the 1970s several unsuccessful attempts were made to get companies to move outside major cities. In 1980 a second major crisis came with the widespread strikes of Polish workers who demanded greater freedom and the right to establish unions. It is too early to tell how this will affect the theatre.

Theatre and Drama in Germany Since 1960

Germany's greatest contribution in the 1960s took the form of "documentary drama" or the "theatre of fact" in which actual events, often quite recent, were used to explore the by-then characteristic concern for guilt and responsibility in public affairs and morality. The best-known writers of the form were Hochhuth, Weiss, and Kipphardt, although all wrote other types of plays as well.

Rolf Hochhuth (1931–   ) came to prominence with *The Deputy* (1963), which seeks to place much of the blame for the extermination of German Jews on Pope Pius XII's refusal to take a decisive stand against Hitler's policies. This accusation made the play controversial wherever it was performed, and in many countries it was forbidden. *The Soldiers* (1967) also aroused considerable consternation because of its suggestion that Winston Churchill conspired in the death of General Sikorski, president of the Polish government in exile, because he endangered the Anglo-Russian alliance. In the late 1960s Hochhuth seemed to tire of factual material. *The Guerrillas* (1970) is set sometime in the future and centers around a *coup d'état* in the United States, which Hochhuth suggests could come about only through someone so well placed as to be beyond suspicion. Hochhuth's first comedy, *The Midwife* (1972), has as its protagonist a woman who leads a double life (as pensioned widow and as member of the town council) in order to help the homeless, since bureaucracy has bogged down either in corruption or indifference. In *Lysistrata and NATO* (1974) Hochhuth adapted Aristophanes' basic situation to a story about an attempt to block the use of a Greek island as a NATO base. All of Hochhuth's plays are long and diffuse and must be cut severely in production. Perhaps for this reason, he has yet to win full critical acceptance. Nevertheless, he has been one of the most controversial writers, primarily because his use of recent historical figures (to whom he attributes questionable motives) has raised serious ethical questions about the limits to which a dramatist may go without becoming libelous.

Peter Weiss (1916–   ) worked as a graphic artist, filmmaker, and journalist before winning fame as a playwright. Although he began writing in the 1940s, his first play was not produced until 1962. His international reputation dates from 1964 with the production of *The Persecution and Assassination of Jean-Paul Marat as Performed by the Inmates of the Asylum of Charenton Under the Direction of the Marquis de Sade* (usually shortened to *Marat/Sade*).

Figure 4.7   Weiss's *Marat/Sade* at the Schiller Theater, Berlin (1964). Directed by Konrad Swinarski, designed by Peter Weiss. Photograph by Heinz Köster.

Set in 1808 in the asylum at Charenton where the Marquis de Sade is confined, it shows the presentation of a play written by de Sade for performance by the inmates before a fashionable audience from nearby Paris. The play that de Sade has written is Brechtian in form (making use of a presenter to introduce scenes and of songs to reflect upon the action), and the whole is intended by Weiss to provoke thought about political and social justice. The asylum serves as a metaphor for the world, and the play's ending (in which the inmates get out of hand) suggests what happens when the sensual and anar-

chistic outlook of a de Sade is given full rein. Peter Brook's production of *Marat/Sade* (seen first in London and then in New York) was to be one of the most influential of the decade, since it drew forceful attention to devices of the "theatre of cruelty," while Weiss's play provided a model on which many other playwrights were to build by imbedding social and political arguments within a context of swirling visual and aural effects.

Marat/Sade is only partially factual, but in his next play, *The Investigation* (1965), Weiss passed over completely into documentary drama. Set in a courtroom, *The Investigation* utilizes dialogue taken from the official hearings into the extermination camp at Auschwitz. Weiss's subsequent documentary plays include *The Song of the Lusitanian Bogey* (1967), about the suppression of native Africans by the Portuguese in Angola, and A *Discourse on the Previous History and Development of the Long War of Liberation in Vietnam as an Example of the Necessity for the Armed Fight of the Suppressed Against Their Suppressors as Well as the Attempt of the United States of America to Destroy the Foundations of the Revolution* (1968).

Like Hochhuth, Weiss in the late 1960s began to retreat from documentary drama, although his work continued to be based on historical sources. *Trotsky in Exile* (1970) uses material from Trotsky's life to stimulate thought about his ideas and to raise questions about our own political perspectives. *Hölderlin* (1971) is based on the life of the nineteenth-century German poet who spent much of his time locked away from the world. It shows the protagonist in flight from a world he considers deranged, and through his plight Weiss suggests that society has a tendency to destroy its visionaries.

Heinar Kipphardt (1922–   ) first won international renown with *In the Case of J. Robert Oppenheimer* (1964), all the dialogue for which is excerpted from the United States government's hearings into the loyalty of Oppenheimer after he resisted development of the hydrogen bomb. Kipphardt's primary concern, however, is with the conflict between a scientist's responsibility to his country and his duty to humanity at large—a familar issue in postwar German drama. In *Joel Brand* (1965) Kipphardt treats the attempt of the Germans during World War II to exchange one million Hungarian Jews for 10,000 Allied trucks and the failure of the attempt because the Allies could not be convinced that the offer was made in good faith. In 1973 he treated the Uruguay Tupamaros in *Who's Looking After the Guerrilla?*

The success of documentary drama in Germany seems to have stimulated playwrights in other countries to adopt the form. Consequently, many contemporary events were brought onto the stage, among them the *Pueblo* incident and various aspects of the Vietnam war. But by the early 1970s, interst in the "theatre of fact" was on the wane, above all in Germany.

Other playwrights continued the earlier concern with collective guilt. Among the most important of these writers was Martin Walser (1927–   ) in such plays as *Oak and Angora* (1962) and *The Black Swan* (1964). The latter constrasts the younger generation, who seem overly sensitive about the Nazi period, with the older generation, who lead seemingly placid lives despite their own involvement in Naziism. Most of Walser's subsequent plays, such as *The Battle of the Bedroom* (1967) and *Children's Game* (1971) have treated more private subjects. But in *The Pig Play—Scenes from the Sixteenth Century* (1975), he makes historical events reflect the political fears and lack of certainty among today's workers and intellectuals.

Tankred Dorst (1925–   ) is representative of German playwrights who have been concerned with political subjects. His early plays were in the absurdist vein. The best of these is probably *Freedom for Clemens* (1961), which shows how an imprisoned man gradually realizes that freedom is an internal state rather than external circumstances. Dorst's later plays are more straightforward. In *Toller* (1968) he uses material about the expressionist playwright to explore the relationship of the artist to political action. In *Little Man, What Now?* (1972), a review based on a novel by Hans Fallada, Dorst evokes a sense of the early 1930s with his middle-class characters who evade reality through a pursuit of popular culture idols of the time even as the political situation disintegrates. Subsequently, Dorst announced his intention to write a series of plays about the German middle class from the 1920s to the present. Among these is *On Chimborazo* (1975), set on a hill near the border with East Germany where the characters reminisce and come to understand themselves as they wait to light a signal fire to friends on the other side of the border.

By the mid-1960s the new German playwrights seem to have tired of the preoccupation with guilt. Nevertheless, most still were concerned with the shortcomings of contemporary society. These plays have often been seen as continuations of the folk-play tradition because of their choice of characters from everyday life, their use of dialects and colloquial speech (as opposed to the high German which has long been standard on the German stage), and their concern for neo-naturalistic situations. These plays also owe much to the influence of Odon von Horvath (1901–1938), whose plays such as *Tales of the Vienna Woods* (1930) and *Kasimir and Karoline* (1931), depicting the terror and repression that lies beneath the familiar and banal, had been banned in Germany since the 1930s but were revived in the 1960s to great acclaim.

One of the most successful writers in this vein is Martin Sperr (1944–   ), noted especially for a trilogy of plays that treat successively peasant life, small town life, and city life: *Hunting Scenes from Lower Bavaria* (1966), *Tales of Landshut* (1967), and *Munich Freedom* (1971). All depict man as selfish, corruptible, and cruel. Following an illness of several years, Sperr returned to the theatre in 1977 with *Spitzeder*, a street-ballad entertainment about an actual nineteenth-century trickster. Other writers in this tradition include Franz Xaver Kroetz (1946–   ), who in such plays as *Dear Fritz* (1970) and *Sterntaler* (1977) is concerned with the outsider trying to cope with the spiritual numbness created by contemporary society; Thomas Bernhard (1931–   ), whose works include *Party for Boris* (1970), *The Celebrities* (1976), and *Before Retiring* (1979), all of which are concerned with depravity, death, and decay; and Wolfgang Bauer (1941–   ), whose *Magic Afternoon* (1968), *Change* (1969), and other plays center around the drop-outs of society who pass their time in sexual games and gratuitous violence.

The most admired of recent playwrights is Peter Handke (1942–   ), who has been concerned above all with language and its relationship to reality and behavior. He began his playwriting career in 1966 with *Offending the Audience*, in which four un-named and undifferentiated speakers make a series of statements to the audience about the clichés concerning theatregoing and the nature of theatrical illusion. Ultimately he argues that a theatrical performance is not a reflection of reality but is the reality of that moment. Probably Handke's best known work is *Kaspar* (1968), in which a young man who has been brought up in total isolation (and therefore without speech) is gradually reduced to conformity through language; at the end he is indistinguishable from a host of almost identical figures. In these and other plays, such as *My Foot My Tutor* (1969), *The Ride Across Lake Constance* (1971), and *The Unreasonable Are Dying Out* (1974), Handke has been preoccupied with the way human beings are brutalized and dehumanized by conventions that reduce everything to conformity and are punished when they try to break out of mechanistic patterns.

Today the German theatre seems to have recovered from the lack of dramatic talent that marked the immediate postwar period. Other writers that deserve attention include Peter Hacks, Leopold Ahlsen, Jochen Zeim, Hartmut Lange, Hans Gunter Michelsen, Karl Wittlinger, Rainer Werner Fassbinder, Siegfried Lenz, Helmut Baierl, Heiner Müller, and Botho Strauss. In addition, many playwrights who had begun their careers earlier— among them Frisch, Duerrenmatt, and Grass— continued to be productive.

During the 1960s the popularity of Brecht grew steadily and by the 1970s his plays had surpassed

Figure 4.8   Peter Handke's *Kaspar* as presented by the Chelsea Theatre Center in 1973. Directed by Carl Weber; video by Video Free America. The actors are Guy Boyd, Christopher Lloyd, Randal Chicoine, Robert Einenkel, and Veronica Castang. Photograph by Amnon Nomis. Courtesy Chelsea Theatre Center.

even those of Shakespeare in numbers of annual performances in Germany. Brecht's company, however, has had to deal with a number of problems. By the time of Helene Weigel's death in 1971, the Berliner Ensemble was considered by many to have become a museum. When Ruth Berghaus was named director, she attempted to revitalize the company through highly experimental productions of such plays as Wedekind's *Spring's Awakening* and Strindberg's *Miss Julie*. Her efforts met with considerable opposition, being damned by many critics as "self-indulgent formalism." In 1977 she was replaced by Manfred Wekwerth, who had worked closely with Brecht. Under Wekwerth, the company has regained much of its former vitality.

The Festival Theatre at Bayreuth also underwent significant changes during the 1970s. In 1973 the Wagner family relinquished much of its control over the festival and archival materials when the Richard Wagner Foundation was formed. This foundation will maintain, but not run, the festival, and a member of the Wagner family is to direct future festivals "if no better qualified applicants come forward." In 1976 the one-hundreth anniversary of the festival was celebrated with great fanfare and controversy, especially because of the innovative staging of the Ring cycle by the French director, Patrice Chereau. As the festival entered its second centrury, its future seemed reasonably secure.

During the 1960s the basic organizational patterns of the German theatre remained unchanged. Virtually every town of any size had one or more subsidized theatres which performed a cross section of world drama. Not until the late 1960s was this arrangement seriously challenged. Perhaps the greatest source of unhappiness was the almost unlimited decision-making power of the state-appointed theatre managers (*Intendanten*). The dissatisfaction came to a head in 1969 when in several cities actors disrupted performances with demands for a greater voice in the theatre's affairs. This crisis was met in various ways. Cologne appointed a triumvirate of directors, each with his own group of performers, working under a single supervisor; Wuppertal turned to a six-man directorate under a supervisor; Frankfurt and Kiel attempted a participatory directorate, in which every member of the company was involved; and in West Berlin a commune was established (the most widely publicized solution). Nevertheless, most companies continued under the old system, al-

though a large proportion are now headed by new or young directors who are more sensitive to the problems than were their predecessors. In 1972 more than twenty companies received new Intendants.

Because Germany has so many theatres, it is difficult for any one of them to gain dominance. Perhaps the best of the theatres in West Germany are those of Hamburg, Munich, and Berlin. The last has become especially well known, in large part because of the highly innovative work of Peter Stein, currently Germany's most influential director.

As elsewhere in the late 1960s in Germany there was much argument over the extent to which the repertory should be made relevant to the immediate social and political scene. It was often charged that the typical season seemed more concerned with preserving the past than reflecting the present. But the attempt of some directors to politicalize the repertory led to factionalism and dissension. To take care of the demand for relevance, most companies began to place increased stress on experimental theatres where innovation in techniques and subject matter could be more easily accommodated than in the large houses. In the 1970s, however, the repertory became more conservative, and light comedy began to be a major element, though it was often interpreted as a commentary on bourgeois values.

Dissension in the late 1960s also led to a decline in attendance, and some theatres began to experience financial difficulties. In the early 1970s doubts were voiced that West Germany really needed all of the approximately 200 subsidized stages then in existence. It was suggested that some should be abandoned. More typical, however, was the exploration of schemes for cooperation among companies by exchanging productions, lending sets and costumes, and combining publicity campaigns.

In the 1970s, the theatres of West Germany and Austria encountered still other problems as inflation increased. The security provided by these companies can in times of financial stress become a source of difficulty. For example, at Vienna's Burgtheater (which celebrated its two-hundredth anniversary in

1976) actors with ten years' service are guaranteed employment until the age of sixty when they retire on pension. In 1976 this company had 145 actors of which 103 were tenured.

The problems of the subsidized theatres stimulated the growth of private companies, so that by the mid-1970s there were about eighty-five, many of them touring widely. Subsidized theatres began to book touring productions into their houses as a way of saving money, but this created considerable controversy over indirect subsidization of private companies—no small concern since only an average of about 20 percent of the costs of state-subsidized theatres is covered by box-office receipts. East German theatres have faced fewer problems, since the state maintains almost complete control over wages and other economic factors in its approximately fifty-five state companies (playing in about eighty theatre buildings and twenty-five auxiliary spaces), most of which perform both drama and opera.

The stresses of the late 1960s also led to the formation of free theatres, cooperatives (which linked a number of small companies), and lunch-time theatres. They seem also to have stimulated interests in children's theatre as a means of reaching and building future audiences. Formerly, most theatres had performed one children's play each year (usually at Christmas and most often based on a fairy tale). During the 1970s, some companies were formed to play exclusively for children and youth. Of these, the best known is the Grips Theatre in West Berlin. Like several other troupes, Grips has abandoned fairy tales for material related directly to the children's own lives. This approach is usually referred to as "emancipatory theatre," since it seeks to free its audience from false conceptions and traditional repressions. A number of theatres also cater exclusively to adolescents. Such theatres are not numerous but they are growing in popularity. In 1976 the Alliance for Children's and Young People's Theatre was formed to help the companies deal with common problems and concerns. An annual festival of children's theatres was also established.

As elsewhere, in Germany the theatre in 1980 was beset with problems, but it remained one of the most fully decentralized and best supported in the world.

Theatre and Drama in France Since 1960

After General DeGaulle came to power in 1959 his minister of culture, André Malraux, retained many of the previous government's policies but also made a number of reforms. He continued to subsidize promising new dramatists and companies and sought to extend decentralization. In addition to founding several new "dramatic centers," the Gaullist regime also promoted municipal cultural centers (*maisons de la culture*) and supplied 50 percent of the funds necessary to finance them. The first of the cultural centers was opened in 1962; there are now more than twenty. In addition to theatrical performances, these centers include facilities for films, music, dance, the visual arts, and public lecturers. Some of these centers are located in the suburbs of Paris, for it became clear that the residents of those areas were too far removed from the center of the city to benefit adequately from its resources.

Malraux also reorganized the state theatres. He removed the Odéon from the control of the Comédie Française, renamed it the Théâtre de France, and installed Barrault's company in it. Similarly, the Théâtre National Populaire (TNP) was elevated to a rank equal to that of the other state theatres. Jean Vilar continued to head the TNP until 1963, when he was succeeded by George Wilson, a long-time member of the company.

Among the new directors who came to the fore in the early 1960s, the most important were Planchon, Bourseiller, and Béjart. Roger Planchon (1931–   ) after 1957 was head of the Théâtre de la Cité in Villeurbanne, an industrial suburb of Lyons, where he was very successful in attracting the working-class audience he sought. In his productions, Planchon borrowed many techniques from film (since he con-

Figure 4.9   Planchon's production of *Dead Souls*, adapted by Adamov (1960). Théâtre de la Cité, Villeurbanne. Setting by René Allio. Photograph by Pic.

sidered this medium most familiar to his unsophisticated theatregoers) and from Brecht. He made liberal use of projections (captions, commentaries, and pictures) and often utilized turntables to show the action from different angles, as in the cinema. He presented plays by Molière, Marivaux, Shakespeare, Kleist, Marlowe, Racine, Brecht and other major writers, but he usually gave them working-class interpretations. Consequently, his productions were often controversial. But their liveliness, richness, clarity, and novelty won Planchon one of the largest followings in France.

Antoine Bourseiller (1930–   ) came to prominence in 1960 when he won the prize offered annually for the best production by a young company. He then became head of the Studio des Champs-Elysées and staged a number of critically praised productions for other companies, including Barrault's,

before being appointed director of the dramatic center in Aix-en-Province in 1966. Since then he has directed numerous productions for theatres throughout France.

Bourseiller declared his desire to shock audiences into reassessing their preconceptions and became noted for novel interpretations of standard works. His approach is perhaps best typified in a controversial production of Molière's *Don Juan* (presented by the Comédie Française in 1967), in which the actors (dressed in varying shades of blue leather) performed in a setting (made of copper and brass) that gave the effect of an echo chamber. Bourseiller attempted to relate the action to recent events (even to concentration camps) and at the end, rather than being taken away to Hell, Dom Juan was consumed by what appeared to be a giant sun.

Maurice Béjart (1937–   ) is noted primarily for his work with the Twentieth Century Ballet Company, which since 1959 has been based in Brussels. He is not so much concerned with traditional dance forms as with using dance to bridge the gulf between men of all nations. His work is often denounced by purists because it mingles so many diverse elements, but if his dance vocabulary is limited, his use of it has aroused intense emotional response. Béjart has not confined his work to dance, having directed operas for several companies (including the Paris Opéra) and plays, perhaps most notably for Barrault's Théâtre de France. His contributions to the French theatre during the 1960s came primarily through his attempts to break down the barriers between the arts and to fuse them in a total sensory experience.

In the late 1960s the wave of dissatisfaction which swept the world brought a number of changes in the French theatre. In May 1968 an uprising of workers and students virtually paralyzed the country and prompted DeGaulle to retire. At this time Barrault resigned as head of the Théâtre de France and, since the troupe was under contract to him, the Odéon was left without a company.

Upon leaving the Théâtre de France, Barrault conceived and directed *Rabelais* (1968), a three-hour

Figure 4.10   Maurice Béjart's production of Berlioz's *The Damnation of Faust* at the Paris Opéra (1964). Photograph by Pic.

adaptation of material drawn from Rabelais' writings and intended as timely commentary on repression and revolution. Drawing liberally on practically all recent trends in staging, the production was originally presented in a sports arena in Paris before being seen in London, New York, and elsewhere. In 1970 Barrault attempted to duplicate this success with a project based on Jarry's life and writings, *Jarry sur la Butte*, but the results were disappointing. In 1971 Barrault became director of the Théâtre des Nations, an international festival which until 1976 was always held in Paris. (It is now held in a different country each year. In addition to productions from various countries, the festival features workshops, lectures, and discussions designed to provoke thought and to encourage understanding and innovation.) Barrault also continued his own company, which since 1974 has been housed in the 900-seat Théâtre d'Orsay,

constructed inside a former railway station. In addition to his own productions there, he has served as host to other companies, especially foreign, each season.

Under President DeGaulle's successors, the French government continued the policy of decentralization. In the early 1970s it reorganized the national theatres and for the first time designated companies outside Paris as national theatres. These include the Théâtre National de Strasbourg (a former dramatic center); the Théâtre de l'Est Parisien (in a suburb of Paris); and Planchon's troupe in Villeurbanne, now called the Théâtre National Populaire, under the direction of Planchon and Patrice Chereau. (The Parisian troupe that had held the title Théâtre National Populaire was retained but renamed the Théâtre National du Palais de Chaillot.) Planchon has sought to justify his company's status as a national theatre by performing for a month at a time in several of France's larger towns, while giving a full season of plays in his home theatre. Planchon continued his leftist interpretation of scripts and often evolved his own scenarios, as in *Gilles de Rais* (1976), which, though set in the past, drew parallels with social conditions of our times.

In Paris, the Odéon remained virtually unused, except for visiting companies, until 1970 when it was assigned to the Comédie Française. That company has used the Odéon primarily as a home for new and *avant-garde* works and has sought thereby to broaden its appeal. In 1975 the rules governing the Comédie Française were revised: the number of *sociétaires* was increased from thirty to forty; the length of contracts was reduced from twenty to ten years; the percentage of the profits going to the company was increased and for the first time the *pensionnaires* were included among the beneficiaries; and greater freedom to perform elsewhere was granted the actors. The Comédie's principal theatre was extensively remodeled in preparation for the celebration of that company's three-hundredth anniversary in 1980.

Governmental attempts to assist the theatre did not meet universal approval. Dissatisfaction was often expressed about the way subsidies were distributed, and a major crisis developed in 1974 when the Minister for Cultural Affairs announced a reshuffling of directors among several state theatres and dramatic centers. As a result of the controversy, the government articulated a number of policies and goals: greater mobility among directors with contracts running from three to no more than ten years; increased aid for new plays and their production; help for young companies by associating them with dramatic centers; increased funds for cultural activities, and the creation of an office to encourage the diffusion of culture. While most of these goals were applauded, they did not silence complaints, especially about the arbitrary assignment of directors and subsidies.

The unrest of the late 1960s also provoked dissatisfactions with traditional organizational patterns. One result was the establishment of several theatres in the suburbs of Paris as the potential for audiences there began to be recognized. Within cities, other groups began to give performances in cafés, artists' centers, and other nontheatrical environments.

One of the most interesting and innovative of these groups is the Grand Magic Circus, headed by Jerome Savary, who began his career in 1967 as a director but soon grew dissatisfied with conventional theatre. It was while working in New York with the La Mama company that he conceived the Grand Magic Circus. He began to attract wide favorable attention in 1970 with *Zartan*, "the story of Tarzan's deprived brother," described by Savary as the "marvelous story of colonialism from the Middle Ages to the present." Savary then conceived *The Last Days of Solitude of Robinson Crusoe* (1972) as the story of a modern Everyman freed from loneliness, passivity, and speechlessness, and went on to produce a number of similar works, among them *Adventures in Love* (1976) and *1001 Nights* (1978). Although Savary's productions are thinly veiled commentaries on the contemporary world, he does not consider these messages primary. Rather, for him the function of the theatre is to be a "life show"—a pretext for

people to come together in a joyous celebration. He has stated his dislike of Grotowski and the Living Theatre (both of which he labeled "cerebral") and has sought to appeal to all types of audiences in a very direct manner. His company has played on beaches, in hospitals, in parks—almost anywhere except in traditional theatres. He has won a considerable following with his productions that have the zest of children's theatre, circus, and carnivals created by extensive exchanges between audience and performers, improvisations, acrobatic feats, satirical thrusts, and stunning effects of all sorts.

Festivals also continued to grow in number. The most important, nevertheless, remained that at Avignon, which in 1976 celebrated its thirtieth anniversary. During the 1970s Avignon became a major showcase for provincial theatres, new plays, and experimental productions. During some seasons, there were as many as sixty performances a day.

Of the directors who have come to prominence since 1965 two of the most important have been Mnouchkine and Garcia. Ariane Mnouchkine (1940–   ) has worked with the Théâtre du Soleil, a commune composed of about forty members. Until it was torn down in 1968, the Cirque d'Hiver was the company's home and there it created a considerable stir with productions of Wesker's *The Kitchen* and Shakespeare's *A Midsummer Night's Dream*. The group is probably best known for *1789—The Revolution Must Stop Only with the Perfection of Happiness—Saint Just*, originally presented in Milan in 1970 and then moved to an abandoned cartridge factory just outside Paris. This production dealt with the early years of the French Revolution and argued that the Revolution was frustrated by those who became more concerned about property than justice. Staged on platforms surrounding a standing audience (which was treated as the mob), it was highly praised and extremely successful. It was followed by *1793* (1972), a much less effective treatment of later phases of the Revolution; *The Age of Gold* (1975), which as the title suggests deals with various aspects of materialism; and Molière's *Don Juan* (1978).

Figure 4.11 Arrabal's *The Automobile Grave-yard* as directed by Victor Garcia at the Théâtre des Arts, Paris, in 1967. Photo by Bernand.

Victor Garcia (1934–   ) came to Paris from his native Argentina in the early 1960s and has since worked with companies throughout the world. He made his first deep impression in 1966 with a production of Arrabal's *The Automobile Graveyard*, which ran for two years. Since then he has directed in Spain (where for Nuria Espert he has staged Genet's *The Maids* and Lorca's *Yerma*), England (where for the National Theatre he directed Arrabal's *The Architect and the Emperor of Assyria*), Brazil (where he gutted a theatre in order to create a spirally arranged setting and seating for Genet's *The Balcony*), and elsewhere.

Though the theatrical scene in France remained lively after 1960, few new playwrights of importance appeared. Older writers, such as Anouilh, Montherlant, Ionesco, Beckett, Adamov, and Sartre, continued to write, but few won international fame. Those who did include René de Obaldia (1918–   ), who

in such works as *The Agricultural Cosmonaut* (1965), *In the End the Bang* (1968), and *The Baby Sitter* (1971), treats the inanities and concealed lies of life, which he brings to the surface and treats as wholly logical; Romain Weingarten (1926–   ), in whose best-known play, *Summer* (1966), childhood experience is counterpointed with the quarrels of two lovers and the comments of two cats on humanity and life; Françoise Sagan (1935–   ), whose *Castle in Sweden* (1960, *The Vanishing Horse* (1966), *Piano on the Lawn* (1971), and *It's a Fine Day and Night* (1978) are characterized by penetrating psychological insight, bittersweet lyricism, and elegant diction; and Marguerite Duras (1914–   ), who after a notable career in films and as a novelist turned to dramas of minute internal dissection, usually of female characters, in such plays as *Entire Days in the Trees* (1965), *A Place without Doors* (1969), and *The Eden-Cinema* (1978).

But the best known of all French playwrights since 1960 has been Fernando Arrabal (1932–   ), who was born in Spain, moved to Paris in 1955, and has written all of his plays in French. His early plays emphasize a childish, thoughtless cruelty couched in a form similar to that used by the absurdists. For example, in *Fando and Lis* (1958) the two childlike protagonists seek to reach the town of Tar but always arrive back at the same place. Fando both loves and resents the paralyzed Lis because she is wholly dependent upon him, but he is also very proud of her beauty, so much so that he leaves her exposed for strangers to view. As a result of exposure, Lis becomes ill and when she falls and breaks his drum, Fando beats her so cruelly that she dies. Fando then misses Lis but fails to comprehend his part in her death.

Around 1962 Arrabal became interested in what he called *théâtre panique*, "a ceremony—partly sacrilegious, partly sacred, erotic and mystic, a putting to death and exaltation of life, part Don Quixote and part Alice in Wonderland." Among his later works are *Solemn Communion* (1966), *The Architect and the Emperor of Assyria* (1967), *And They Handcuffed the Flowers* (1970), *Young Barbarians Today* (1975), and *King of Sodom* (1979). Of these, the second is perhaps most characteristic. It includes only two characters, who enact a series of ritualized human situations: master and slave, judge and criminal, mother and child, male and female, sadist and masochist, and so on. Eventually one decides that he must be punished and asks the other to kill and eat him. When this is done, they seem somehow to merge. But now a new figure appears, apparently beginning the whole cycle over again. Through such plays, Arrabal not only challenges all values, he ferrets out all the hidden corners of the human psyche.

After 1970 Jean-Claude Grumbert (1940–) was among the most admired of young writers. His *Dreyfus* (1974) is set in a Jewish ghetto in a Polish town around 1930 where amateurs, while rehearsing a play about the Dreyfus affair, explore the phenomenon of anti-Semitism. It won the critics award as the best play of the 1974– 1975 season. *On the Way Back from the Paris Exposition* (1975) treats the French working-class movement at the turn of the twentieth century. In the late 1970s André Benedetto came to the fore with such plays as *The Jacobin Drapers* (1976) and *St. Do-Nothing, or the Right to Be Lazy* (1978). The popularity of Grumberg and Benedetto suggests that a renewed concern for socially conscious drama is emerging in France.

Despite this considerable number of competent writers, however, the overall impression is that France has declined in dramatic vigor since the 1950s, when its plays were perhaps the most admired in the world.

English Theatre and Drama Since 1960

After 1960 three companies were especially important in English theatrical life: the Royal Shakespeare Company, the National Theatre, and the English Stage Company. In 1961 the Stratford Memorial Theatre was given a new charter and a new title,

The Royal Shakespeare Company (RSC). Its new status owed most to Peter Hall (1930–), who after beginning his directing career in 1955, had worked at Stratford since 1957 and had been named head of its company in 1960. Upon assuming the new post, Hall at once set out to overcome one of the troupe's principal problems: the inability to hold a company together and build an ensemble because the season at Stratford lasted only about six months each year. To remedy this situation, Hall took a lease on the Aldwych Theatre in London and transformed the organization into a year-round operation. Since then the company has divided its efforts between Stratford and London. Hall also broadened the repertory to include plays other than those by Shakespeare so that actors would have diversified experience.

By 1962 the RSC's activities had been so enlarged that Peter Brook and Michel Saint-Denis were added to the management. The RSC also began an experimental program, and in 1963– 1964 Peter Brook, in collaboration with Charles Marowitz, produced a series of programs under the overall title, "Theatre of Cruelty." Out of this season came Brook's production of Weiss's *Marat/Sade*, one of the most influential productions of the decade and the one that did most to draw attention to Artaud's theories. By the mid-1960s the RSC was London's major *avant-garde* troupe, noted both for its innovative techniques and for its wide-ranging repertory, with plays by Hochhuth, Pinter, and numerous continental and British dramatists of the past and present. The Aldwych also became the home of the World Theatre Season, an arrangement under which each spring major companies throughout the world came to London for limited engagements.

Throughout the 1970s the RSC was plagued by inflation. In contrast with the subsidized theatres of Germany, in which only about 20 percent of costs were covered by box-office receipts, the RSC had to support approximately 80 percent of its expenditures through ticket sales, which became increasingly difficult despite the fact that it consistently played to full houses. Nevertheless, it continued its extremely ambitious program, producing well over one hundred plays in a five-year period. Not only did it renew the past through outstanding productions of plays by Gorky, Gillette, Boucicault, and others (including Shakespeare), but it continued its experimentation through work at The Other Place and Studio Theatre in Stratford and at the Roundhouse, The Warehouse, and elsewhere in London.

In 1968, Hall, Brook, and Saint-Denis resigned their posts as directors of the RSC and were succeeded by Trevor Nunn (1940–   ), assisted by an

advisory board. After that time most of the directing has been done by Nunn, Clifford Williams, Terry Hands, and John Barton assisted by younger directors and supplemented by others brought in from time to time.

Of the directors associated with the RSC, Peter Brook (1925–   ) has been the most influential. He began directing while still in his teens and first worked at Stratford in 1946. During the 1950s he built an enviable reputation with productions starring such actors as Olivier, Paul Scofield, and the Lunts, and with plays by such authors as Shakespeare, Fry, Anouilh, Eliot, Duerrenmatt, and Genet. But he is now best known for a series of productions after 1960, including *King Lear* (1962), *Marat/Sade* (1964), *The Tempest* (1968), and *A Midsummer Night's Dream* (1970). As a director, Brook has not been so much an innovator as an eclectic who has transformed borrowings from many sources into his own vital expression. For example, for *A Midsummer Night's Dream* he borrowed from Meyerhold, *commedia dell-arte*, circus, and radical theatre groups of the 1960s, but the results were uniquely his own. For this production Brook sought to divest the play of its romantic aura of fairies and haunted woodlands and to make it more immediately relevant to our time. He interpreted the script as an exploration of love, and consequently he used the same pair of actors as Theseus and Hippolyta and Oberon and Titania, and treated the enchanted scenes as lessons on love for the betrothed royal couple. The stage was enclosed on three sides by white, unadorned walls broken only by two nearly invisible

Figure 4.12   Peter Brook's production of Shakespeare's *A Midsummer Night's Dream* with the Royal Shakespeare Company in 1970. Alan Howard as Oberon and Jon Kane as Puck on trapezes; Sara Kestelman as Titania and David Waller as Bottom. Design by Sally Jacobs. Photograph by permission of the Royal Shakespeare Company

doors at the rear. The forest was suggested by loosely coiled metal springs attached to fishing rods. The flying was accomplished with trapezes lowered and raised to varying heights within the setting. Most of the performers wore a kind of coverall but there was a sprinkling of *commedia dell'arte* and circus costumes. Despite all these distinctive features, the text was given its full poetic value. It is such novel and imaginative approaches that have made Brook one of the most effective and respected directors of the age.

In 1971 Brook assumed direction of the International Center for Theatre Research, based in Paris and including participants from all over the world. In the summer of 1971 the group gave its first performance, *Orghast*, in Iran at the Persepolis Festival. It received a mixed reception, in part because the play used an invented language. The company then worked on Handke's *Kaspar* and a twelfth-century Persian poem, "Conference of the Birds." In 1972 it traveled and played in Africa; in 1973 it appeared in America where it worked with El Teatro Campesino and the National Theatre of the Deaf. In 1974–1975 it prepared Shakespeare's *Timon of Athens* and *The Ik* (a play based on a book about an African tribe whose hunting grounds are turned into a national park) and subsequently performed them in Paris, London, New York, and elsewhere. Through this work Brook has sought to discover acting and directing devices and techniques that can transcend the barriers created by differences in language and culture.

Beginning in the 1960s the RSC had a powerful rival in the National Theatre. England was one of the last European countries to establish a national theatre, though it had long contemplated such a move. Parliamentary approval for the company was given in the late 1940s but it was not implemented until 1963, when the Old Vic company was dissolved and its building assigned to the new troupe. Laurence Olivier was named director and Kenneth Tynan literary advisor. The National Theatre rapidly built a reputation for excellence through its extremely eclectic choice of plays and production

Figure 4.13   View of auditorium and stage of the Olivier Theatre in the National Theatre, London. Photograph by Reg Wilson. Courtesy National Theatre and Mr. Wilson.

styles. It sought to assemble for each production the team best suited to that script. Consequently, it utilized numerous English and foreign directors (among them Brook, George Devine, Jonathan Miller, Franco Zeffirelli, Ingmar Bergman, and Victor Garcia) and designers (among them Motley, Sean Kenny, Josef Svoboda, and René Allio). It also from time to time staged seasons of experimental plays, and in 1972 began to tour throughout England with productions able to play almost anywhere.

In 1970 the National Theatre added the Young Vic troupe, designed to appeal primarily to children and youth. It soon became something of a focus for the growing interest in theatre for the young and served as host for a National Festival of Theatre for Young People. Its significance was recognized in 1975 when it was separated from the National Theatre to become an independent organization.

In 1973 Peter Hall replaced Laurence Olivier as director of the National Theatre. (Olivier's great service to the theatre was recognized in 1970 when he became the first actor in English history to be raised to the nobility.) In 1976 the company began its move from the Old Vic (which became the home of the Prospect Theatre Company) to its new building, designed by Denys Lasdun and built at a cost of some $32 million. One of the most advanced theatre plants anywhere, it includes three performance spaces: the 890-seat Lyttleton proscenium theatre; the 1,160-seat Olivier open-stage theatre with a revolving stage 40 feet in diameter divided into two parts that can be lowered to workshops 45 feet below; and the 400-seat Cottesloe laboratory theatre. There are more than one hundred dressing rooms, several stage-sized rehearsal rooms, and numerous workshops. These impressive facilities have proven a mixed blessing, how-

Figure 4.14   The National Theatre's production of Strindberg's *The Dance of Death* (1967). The actors are Geraldine McEwan, Robert Stephens, and Laurence Olivier. Photograph by Zoë Dominic.

ever, as about one third of the National Theatre's subsidy has been consumed by costs of heating, lighting, and maintenance. By 1979, the company had accumulated a £300,000 debt.

The English Stage Company (more commonly called the Royal Court after the theatre in which it is housed), founded by George Devine in 1956, continued after 1960 to be one of the principal champions of new playwrights. Of the writers launched during the 1960s perhaps the most important were Edward Bond, Joe Orton, and David Storey. In 1969 the company enlarged its program when it opened the Theatre Upstairs, devoted entirely to short runs of new plays. (The parent company continued to produce a mixed repertory of new and established works.) Although the management has changed rather often since Devine retired in 1965, the company's basic goals have remained rather constant. Thus, a large share of the credit for England's strength in playwriting must go to the Royal Court, even if by the mid-1970s this role was being threatened by inflation, which forced the company to reduce its program, and by the many fringe companies devoted to new plays.

Outside of London the number of resident companies increased after 1960 to more than fifty. Perhaps the best of these were at Bristol, Birmingham, Manchester, Nottingham, Coventry, and Glasgow, all subsidized by local governments. Nevertheless, the English theatre remained within relatively conservative limits until 1968, when the censorship that had been in effect since 1737 was abolished. A number of plays previously forbidden were produced immediately, among them *Hair* (banned because of nudity and obscenity), Osborne's *A Patriot for Me* (forbidden because of homosexual scenes), Hochhuth's *The Soldiers* (banned because it was considered offensive to Churchill's memory), and Edward Bond's plays (forbidden because they were considered immoral).

More important perhaps, the change in law gave impetus to small groups (comparable to American off-off-Broadway companies) which up to that time had made little impact. After 1968 these "fringe" groups increased rapidly in number. They performed at universities, in pubs, playgrounds, meeting halls, or almost anywhere an audience could be assembled, and at lunchtime or late at night, as well as at more traditional hours. Their great flexibility (in approach, place, and time of performing, subjects, and desired audiences) did much to bring variety to the English theatre. Of the fringe groups, the one with the most extensive program has been Interaction, a commune founded by Ed Berman in 1968. It has operated a mobile theatre (the Fun Art Bus), a street theatre (Dogg's Troupe), two *avant-garde* companies (the Ambiance and The Other Company) which play at the Almost Free Theatre, a theatre for the elderly, and the British-American Repertory Company. Through such varied activities Berman hopes to make the arts a vital part of an urban community and to bridge the gap between classes and nations. Other important fringe groups include the People Show, the Pip Simmons Theatre, the Freehold, the Portable Theatre, and Triple Action. Such companies have contributed enormously to the vitality of the English theatre, especially through their appeal to audiences that had previously ignored the theatre. Most were also highly critical of British social and political institutions.

Additional diversity was offered by the Edinburgh Festival, which has steadily increased in number of offerings and in popularity. By 1980 some 300 fringe groups from Britain and elsewhere were participating in the festival and offering almost 150 premieres.

Part of the appeal of the English theatre during the 1960s lay in its relatively cheap admission prices, which permitted audiences to attend the theatre as easily as movies. During the 1970s, however, this advantage began to fade. A "value added" (or sales) tax imposed in 1972 increased ticket prices by some 10 percent, and thereafter other increases in production costs, combined with rapid inflation, served to drive ticket prices ever higher. Subsidized theatres made frequent appeals for supplementary grants to avoid serious deficits. Regional arts associations were also

formed throughout Britain to deal with financial crises, encourage cooperative ventures, and promote the arts in their areas. By the late 1970s private corporations were beginning to assist some organizations by underwriting productions.

Despite its problems, the English theatre continued to be among the best in the world. Much of its strength could be attributed to its excellent playwrights. Among these, the one with the greatest critical reputation was Harold Pinter (1930–   ), who, after beginning his career as an actor, turned to playwriting in 1957 with *The Room*. Since then he has written regularly for the theatre, television, and films. His stage works include *The Dumb Waiter* (1957), *The Birthday Party* (1958), *The Caretaker* (1960), *The Homecoming* (1965), *Old Times* (1970), *No Man's Land* (1975), *Betrayal* (1978), and *The Hothouse* (1980). Although there is much variety among them, almost all of Pinter's plays have in common a few characteristics: everyday situations that gradually take on an air of mystery or menace; unexplained, unrevealed, or ambiguous motivations or background information; and authentic, seemingly natural though carefully wrought dialogue. With Pinter silence is an integral part of language, and he treats all speech as one type of stratagem whereby characters seek to cover their psychological nakedness. Thus, an "unspoken subtext" is often as important as the dialogue. In Pinter's plays everything may at first seem amusing or pleasantly ambiguous, but gradually the tone changes to anxiety, pathos, or fear as the characters confront some predicament and seek to defend themselves against some unknown, often undefined danger from outside or within the room in which the action occurs. As a dramatist, Pinter falls somewhere between Beckett and Chekhov. Like Beckett, he isolates characters and lets them wrestle with their anxieties in an unverifiable universe; like Chekhov, he creates a realistic texture of background and dialogue in which surface act and speech are merely evasions or disguises of deeper conflicts and uncertainties.

Probably the most controversial contemporary

Figure 4.15   Pinter's *The Homecoming* as directed by Peter Hall for the Royal Shakespeare Company in 1965. Seen here are Michael Craig as Teddy, Terence Rigby (seated) as Joey, and Ian Holm as Lenny. Courtesy Royal Shakespeare Company.

English playwright is Edward Bond (1935–   ), who achieved overnight notoriety in 1965 with a private performance at the Royal Court of *Saved*, in which a baby is stoned to death in its carriage by its father and his roustabout friends. Even more shocking perhaps was *Early Morning* (1968), a surrealistic farce about Victorian life in which Florence Nightingale and Queen Victoria are involved in a lesbian relationship and virtually all the characters indulge in cannibalism. Bond's first play to receive a public performance, *Narrow Road to the Deep North* (1968), is set in Japan and avoids the more shocking features of the earlier works, although it too emphasizes the callousness of mankind. *Lear* (1971) uses many of the characters and situations from Shakespeare's play but alters them to make a despairing statement about human brutality and inhumanity. Selfishness, callousness, and violence continued as preoccupations in Bond's later works: *Bingo* (1973), *The Fool* (1975), *The Bundle* (1977), and *The Woman* (1978). Bond has been denounced by many critics as sensational, decadent, and overly preoccupied with violence, but ultimately his plays are based on moral (even self-righteous) concerns about a world in which the lack of love and compassion has bred a callousness that accepts the horrible as normal.

Joe Orton (1933–1967) also won a reputation for sensationalism, but was less philosophically inclined than Bond. In *Entertaining Mr. Sloane* (1964) he shows a brother and sister encouraging a young murderer to rid them of their senile father and when he has done so, thinking he will then be able to blackmail them, they turn the tables and agree to divide him sexually between them six months at a time. This amoral tale is given its distinctive tone in part because it is set within the framework of conventional drawing-room drama with its decorous speech and manners. Similarly, *Loot* (1966) parodies the conventions of the detective thriller through a story of murder, robbery, and chicanery in which the criminals and police eventually agree to share the loot; and *What the Butler Saw* (produced 1969) treats a series of complex family and sexual relationships through the conventions of bedroom farce. More than any other English playwright, Orton has achieved commercial success with subjects almost wholly amoral.

Among the most successful of recent dramatists has been David Storey (1933–   ), who began his career as a novelist and turned to playwriting in 1967 with *The Restoration of Arnold Middleton*. Since then he has written *In Celebration* (1969), *The Contractor* (1970), *Home* (1970), *The Changing Room* (1971), *The Farm* (1973), *Life Class* (1974), and

Figure 4.16   David Storey's *The Contractor* as performed at the Royal Court Theatre, London, in 1970. Directed by Lindsay Anderson. Photo by Tom Murray.

Mother's Day (1976). Stylistically, Storey's plays bear a distant resemblance to those of Pinter and Chekhov in their surface realism and their absence of clear-cut meaning, but they lack the sense of menace found in Pinter's works. Storey is concerned above all with various kinds of alienation: class from class, person from person, man from himself, the reality from the ideal, and so on. These various forms of alienation are perhaps most fully developed in *Home*, set in an asylum where the four main characters, through seemingly random dialogue, point up the ironic implications about alienation contained in the play's title (which may mean country, dwelling, or sense of belonging). Storey also often gives focus to his concerns through detailed physical activity. In *The Contractor* a group of working men put up a tent for a wedding in the first act and take it down during the last act; during this process a cross section of attitudes and relationships are demonstrated by the workmen and their employers. Similarly, in *The*

Changing Room, members of a semiprofessional rugby team (all of whom have other jobs during the week) change into their uniforms in the first act and back to their street clothes in the final act; class, social distinctions, and purposelessness are similarly divested and reassumed after a short period of community achieved by a harsh ritual. Probably no writer today has so precisely recreated the detail of real-life situations or has used them to imply so much about modern man and social conventions as has Storey.

Other prominent dramatists include Stoppard and Nichols. Tom Stoppard (1937–   ) came to prominence in 1967 with *Rosencrantz and Guildenstern Are Dead*, a play reminiscent of Beckett's works, for Stoppard makes protagonists of two attendant lords from *Hamlet*, and though they sense that important events are going on around them they are killed without understanding anything about the life of which they have been a part. Stoppard has continued this highly theatrical and brilliant exploration of the nature of reality in such plays as *The Real Inspector Hound* (1968), *Jumpers* (1972), *Travesties* (1974), *Dirty Linen* (1976), and *Night and Day* (1979).

Peter Nichols (1929–   ) achieved his first stage success with *A Day in the Death of Joe Egg* (1967), which deals with the attempts of a schoolteacher and his wife to cope with their spastic child, whom they view as a joke played on them by life but who ultimately serves as a catalyst to bring to the surface their suppressed anxieties and frustrations. This mixture of humor, compassion, and astringent observation is continued in *The National Health* (1969), a play about elderly patients who drag out their lives in a hospital ward against a background of television programs which romanticize medical practice. Song and dance and music hall devices are prominent elements in Nichols's later plays, *Forget-Me-Not Lane* (1971), *Privates on Parade* (1977), and *Born in the Gardens* (1979).

During the 1970s Alan Ayckbourn (1939–   ) became England's most popular playwright with a series of farces treating marital and extramarital difficulties. The most successful were *How the Other*

Figure 4.17   Tom Stoppard's *Rosencrantz and Guildenstern Are Dead* as performed at the National Theatre, London, in 1967. Photograph by Anthony Crickmay.

Half Loves (1969), *Absurd Person Singular* (1972), *The Norman Conquests* (1973), *Bedroom Farce* (1975), and *Joking Apart* (1978).

Several major new playwrights of the 1970s were linked by a shared dislike for contemporary society, especially the economic manipulation and exploitation of the lower by the upper classes. They sought to capture working-class speech patterns and to depict sexual frustration and violence as consequences of socioeconomic and political frustration. Most began by working with fringe groups, but upon gaining public recognition had their plays presented by established procedures. Among the best of these writers were Trevor Griffiths (1935–   ) with *Occupations* (1970), *The Party* (1972), and *Comedians* (1974); Howard Brenton (1942–   ), with *Christie in Love* (1969), *Weapons of Happiness* (1976), and *Sore Throats* (1979); Howard Barker (1946–   ), with *Cheek* (1970), *Stripwell* (1975), and *That Good Between Us* (1977); David Hare (1947–   ), with *Slag*

(1969), *Teeth 'n' Smiles* (1975), and *Plenty* (1978); and Stephen Poliakoff (1952–   ), with *City Sugar* (1976), *Strawberry Fields* (1977), and *American Days* (1979). This group of writers led one critic to declare that by the late 1970s the dominant style in English theatre was Socialist Realism.

Other fine dramatists since 1960 include Christopher Hampton, Peter Terson, David Mercer, Charles Wood, David Rudkin, Heathcote Williams, E. A. Whitehead, David Halliwell, Snoo Wilson, and Brian Clark. They are evidence of the strength of English dramatic writing, which, despite the problems faced by England during the 1970s, placed the British theatre among the best to be found anywhere.

Theatre in the United States Since 1960

After 1960 production costs continued to soar with the result that on Broadway ticket prices became ever higher. The need to attract large audiences led New York's producers to restrict their offerings primarily to musicals, comedies, and plays that had proven popular elsewhere. Broadway gradually gave up the out-of-town tryout and increasingly imported productions from the United States' resident theatres or from London. Thus, it lost its significance as a presenter of new plays while remaining the primary center of the United States' commercial theatre. Its economic woes continued into the early 1970s, giving rise to the perennial prediction that the theatre was dying, but from 1974–1975 onward each successive season set new records for the highest box-office receipts.

During the 1960s the musical remained the most popular form on Broadway. Large-cast, multiple-set productions with large choruses, lavish (and frequently athletic) dance sequences, tuneful songs, and easily-understood plots continued. Among the most popular musicals of the 1960s were Jule Styne's *Funny Girl* (1964), Jerry Bock's *Fiddler on the Roof*

Figure 4.18   Angela Lansbury and Len Cariou in a scene from Stephen Sondheim's *Sweeney Todd* (1979). Directed by Harold Prince. Photograph by Martha Swope.

Figure 4.19   Scene from *A Chorus Line* (1975) as directed by Michael Bennett. Photograph by Martha Swope.

(1964), Jerry Herman's *Hello, Dolly!* (1964) and *Mame* (1966), John Kander's *Cabaret* (1966) and *Zorba* (1968), and Cy Coleman's *Sweet Charity* (1966). After 1968 the musical underwent several changes under the influence of rock music and concern for alternative life-styles. The crucial production was *Hair* (1968) by Galt McDermot, Gerome Ragni, and James Rado, with its barely discernible story, single setting, "street-people" clothing, dependence on lighting and electronic means, liberal use of obscenity, and introduction of nudity on the Broadway stage. Thereafter, numerous musicals employed similar means, among the most successful being Stephen Schwartz's *Pippin* (1972) and *Godspell* (1974). Several productions also capitalized on the popular music and attitudes of past eras, as in *Grease* (1972) and the black musicals *Bubbling Brown*

Sugar (1976) and *Ain't Misbehavin'* (1978). Although the older form of musical continued in such works as John Kander's *Chicago* (1975) and Charles Strouse's *Annie* (1977), the 1970s was primarily a time of experimentation with musical form. Most influential in this period were Harold Prince, producer and director, and Stephen Sondheim (1930–   ), composer and lyricist. Sondheim's *Company* (1970) had no chorus and used the principal performers in song-and-dance sequences; *Pacific Overtures* (1976) drew on conventions of the Japanese theatre; and *Sweeny Todd* (1979) approached opera in its use of music throughout. Furthermore, all of Sondheim's works offered ironic views of human behavior and social values and they avoided the happy endings of earlier musicals. Michael Bennett's *A Chorus Line* (1975) also contributed to change with its use of the chorus as principal character and its presentational style. Despite all changes, the musical retained (and seems likely to continue) its popularity with Broadway audiences.

The most successful playwright on the Broadway stage after 1960 was Neil Simon (1927–   ), who after a somewhat tentative beginning with *Come Blow Your Horn* (1961) turned out a string of hits, among them *Barefoot in the Park* (1963), *The Odd Couple* (1965), *The Last of the Red Hot Lovers* (1970), *The Sunshine Boys* (1972), *California Suite* (1976), and *Chapter Two* (1979), all combining zany humor, eccentric characters, and hints of pain and desperation beneath the comic surface.

The most prestigious American playwright of the 1960s was Edward Albee (1928–   ), whose first four plays, all short, were produced off-Broadway in 1960–1961. These early works, especially *The Sandbox* (1959) and *The American Dream* (1960), were thought to ally Albee with the absurdists; but with *Who's Afraid of Virginia Woolf?* (1962), his first full-length play and first Broadway success, Albee, through his exploration of tortured psychological relationships, demonstrated an affinity to Williams and Strindberg. In *Who's Afraid of Virginia Wolf?*, the facades of the characters are gradually stripped away during the course of an all-night drinking bout to show people creating hells for each other through inability to accept weaknesses. Most of Albee's subsequent work has been concerned with values. *Tiny Alice* (1964), a puzzling parable, seems to suggest that man reconciles himself to his lot by constructing unverifiable systems to explain why he has been martyred by life; *A Delicate Balance* (1966) shows several characters seeking to escape anxieties and how the protagonist comes to recognize that friendship is more important than self-protectiveness; *Box* and *Quotations from Chairman Mao Tse-tung* (1968) appear to point up the dangers of triviality, boredom, conflicts among ideologies and between rich and poor, which, if not corrected, may reduce the world to something like an empty box; *All Over* (1971) seems to argue that if we do not develop inner strengths (which must include self-knowledge, compassion, and the will to act on conviction), it will soon be all over with mankind, since external authoritarian guides are dying out; *Seascape* (1974) suggests that human beings have lost their vitality and that the future belongs to other creatures (here shown as two amphibians who crawl out of the water onto the beach) as they discover love and consideration; and *The Lady from Dubuque* (1979) which returns to the themes of attempted isolation and the inability of human beings to escape the inevitable.

In these complex plays, Albee has become increasingly abstract until in his latest works the relationship between story and meaning is often purely conjectural. Consequently, in recent years critics have tended to downgrade Albee's importance. Nevertheless, during the 1960s he was almost universally considered the American dramatist of greatest stature.

In the early 1960s Arthur Kopit (1938–   ) was often ranked with Albee. He first came to prominence in 1960 with *Oh, Dad, Poor Dad, Mama's Hung You in the Closet and I'm Feeling So Sad*, a parodistic work reminiscent of Tennessee Williams's

Figure 4.20   Edward Albee's *A Delicate Balance* as presented by the Royal Shakespeare Company in 1967. Courtesy Royal Shakespeare Company.

more bizarre creations but treated through absurdist techniques. In it, Mme Rosepettle, whose household includes piranhas, Venus's-flytraps, and the stuffed body of her dead husband, tries to protect her son from life's harsh realities only to have him break free from her domination. Kopit had little further success until 1968 with *Indians*, in which he used Buffalo Bill's Wild West Show as a framework for suggesting how the Indians' betrayal has been transformed into entertainment, thus permitting us to ignore the reality. It is a variation on the by-now familiar theme of the American dream gone awry. *Wings* (1978) has as its central character a woman who, having suffered a severe stroke, battles to regain the power of speech and all that it symbolizes.

An oft-expressed need has been for a permanent resident company in New York like those found in major European cities. In the 1960s an effort was made to remedy this lack with the Lincoln Center for the Performing Arts (with facilities for opera, ballet, concerts, and plays). In anticipation of the Center's completion, a repertory company was formed in 1963 under the direction of Elia Kazan and Robert Whitehead. Expectations were high, since at that time Kazan was considered the United States' finest director and since he was promised new plays by Arthur Miller (*After the Fall* and *Incident at Vichy*) and S. N. Behrman (*But for Whom, Charlie*). The results were so disappointing that after one season Kazan and Whitehead resigned. They were replaced by Herbert Blau and Jules Irving, who had been outstandingly successful at the Actors' Workshop in San Francisco. In 1965 the company moved into its newly completed home (the Vivian Beaumont Theatre, designed by Eero Saarinen and Jo Mielziner) at Lincoln Center. But Blau and Irving soon ran into difficulties and in 1967 Blau resigned. Thereafter Irving continued slowly to build a company, but eventually the artistic and financial problems became so great that in 1973 Irving resigned. Joseph Papp was then named director of the theatre, which he ran in conjunction with his numerous other activities at the Public Theatre, but in 1978 he found it impossible to

continue. The theatre remained unused for some time, but in 1980 Richmond Crinkley began still another attempt to establish a successful company at Lincoln Center.

For a time New York also had a second repertory company, the Association of Producing Artists (APA). Founded in 1960 by Ellis Rabb, the APA formed a liaison in 1964 with the Phoenix Theatre, which thereafter served as its producer. The APA won high critical praise but because of financial difficulties had to be disbanded in 1970. Its repertory was impressive, ranging through works by Shaw, Chekhov, Pirandello, Shakespeare, Ionesco, and others. The company was sometimes accused of being too conservative because it only produced already proven works, but for a time it provided the most impressive cross section of drama to be seen in the United States.

During the 1960s the New York theatre continued to be enlivened by off-Broadway. Of the many off-Broadway groups, the most influential was to be the Living Theatre, founded in 1946 by Judith Malina (1926–   ) and Julian Beck (1925–   ). Originally they were interested in poetic drama and nonrealistic production techniques and during the 1950s also came under the influence of both Artaud and Brecht. The turning point in their work came in 1959 with their production of Jack Gelber's *The Connection*, a drama that pretends that the audience is being allowed to watch the making of a documentary film about real dope addicts. The overall effect was that of a naturalistic slice of life. The production won a number of awards in New York and in Paris at the Théâtres des Nations. Another important production was Kenneth Brown's *The Brig* (1963), which recreates the repetitive and senseless routine of a day in a Marine prison camp.

In 1963 the company lost its theatre because of failure to pay taxes and in 1964 it went abroad. Thereafter it toured throughout Europe and became increasingly committed to anarchy and revolution. Although it preformed Genet's *The Maids* and a version of *Antigone*, its major productions after 1964 were works of its own creation: *Mysteries and Smaller Pieces*, *Frankenstein*, and *Paradise Now*, all advocating total freedom from restraints. Its best-known production was probably *Paradise Now* (1968), in part because it coincided with and mirrored a period of great unrest in Europe and America. The action of the piece was divided into eight parts designed to increase the audience's political perceptions and to move ever nearer the present; at the end the audience is urged to move into the streets to continue the revolution. All barriers between actors and spectators were eliminated and both roamed the stage and auditorium indiscriminately. The performers were intensely aggressive, confronting spectators, and seeking to overcome, through insults and obscenities, all opposition. The overall effect was that of an inflammatory political meeting.

When the Living Theatre returned to the United States in 1968 it received enormous publicity and aroused intense controversy. After returning to Europe, it split into three groups in 1970. The Becks took their contingent to Brazil, where they were jailed for several months before returning to the United States in 1971. At that time they announced plans for a new work, *The Legacy of Cain*, to be performed in the streets over a period of several weeks. These plans were never realized.

No group was better known or more influential in the late 1960s than the Living Theatre. For a time the disaffected almost everywhere echoed its attitudes and practices: denigration of any text that could not be transformed into an argument for anarchy and social change; downgrading language in favor of Artaudian techniques; athleticism in performance; insistence on confronting and overriding audiences; evangelical tone; and freewheeling lifestyle. As social conditions changed in the 1970s, however, the Living Theatre's influence waned rapidly. Hoping to regain its prestige, in 1976 the company once more returned to Europe. Since then it has performed in Germany, England, and elsewhere, but it has failed to attract the following it once commanded.

Figure 4.21   Scene from the film *Paradise Now: The Living Theatre In Amerika* by Marty Topp; produced by Universal Mutant, Ira Cohen, producer; courtesy of Mark Hall Amitin.

By the time the Living Theatre left the United States in 1964 the off-Broadway theatre was beginning to undergo many of the same economic pressures felt on Broadway, and consequently it began to be less adventurous than in earlier years. By the mid-1970s it cost about $75,000 to produce even a simple play off-Broadway and it was increasingly difficult to recover the initial investment. In 1975, while selling out nightly, *Chorus Line* lost $18,000 each week before it was moved to Broadway. Thus, off-Broadway lost most of its former appeal.

As it declined, it was replaced by off-off-Broadway. It is usual to date off-off-Broadway from 1958 when Joe Cino began to use his Café Cino as an art center. By 1961 plays were a regular part of his offerings and others had begun to take up the idea. Soon plays were being presented wherever space could be found. Most of the participants were unpaid and budgets were infinitesimal, but nevertheless by 1965 some 400 plays by more than 200 playwrights had been seen off-off-Broadway.

The most influential of the off-off-Broadway producers of the 1960s was Ellen Stewart, who began to present plays in a basement room in 1961. After running into trouble with fire inspectors, she created the LaMama Experimental Theatre Club (ostensibly a private organization and therefore exempt from many regulations governing public performances). During the season of 1969–1970 LaMama alone produced more plays than were seen on Broadway that year. In 1969 the LaMama organization acquired its own building with two theatres and in 1974 quadrupled its space through the acquisition of an annex.

Beginning in 1964, Miss Stewart also took productions abroad, where her freewheeling experiments attracted such favorable attention that she was invited to found branches in several countries. Thus the LaMama organization came to be known throughout the world. Miss Stewart considered LaMama to be a playwright's theatre intended to nourish talent. Her encouragement of innovation meant that many LaMama plays were amateurish, but it also meant that many talented writers were given a hearing that might otherwise have been denied. Nevertheless, LaMama illustrates well the perils of off-off-Broadway in the 1960s — the determined pursuit of novelty and the lack of standards by which to judge it.

LaMama's dedication to experimentation also required new directorial approaches, the results of which were manifested most clearly in the work of Tom O'Horgan, who worked for LaMama before winning renown around 1968 with productions of *Hair*, *Futz*, and *Tom Paine*. O'Horgan tended to place primary emphasis on frantic physical activity, pulsating light effects, electronic sound, and gimmickry of various sorts. His productions were colorful, unabashedly frenetic, and joyful. But his tendency to subordinate script to directorial embellishments led to a break with LaMama. For a time O'Horgan suffered a decline in reputation and then made a forceful though temporary comeback in 1971

with *Lenny* and *Jesus Christ Superstar*. Although controversial, many of O'Horgan's techniques were important because so many plays of the time were verbally inarticulate and required the "physicalization" he used so liberally.

During the 1970s the LaMama organization was much less influential perhaps because it became more interested in developing resident ensemble companies than in playwrights. Some LaMama companies presented plays of particular interest to ethnic groups (Puerto Rican, black, and native American). The best known of all these ensembles was headed by Andrei Serban, who worked with Greek mythic material, invented language, and ritualized action to create productions of enormous emotional impact in *Medea*, *The Trojan Women*, and *Electra* (all first performed in 1974). Beginning in 1977, Serban worked with other companies and adapted his techniques to productions of such plays as *The Cherry Orchard* and *Agememnon* at Lincoln Center and *The Ghost Sonata* at the Yale Repertory Theatre.

Other important off-off-Broadway groups of the 1960s included the Judson Poets' Theatre (founded in 1961 by Al Carmines and especially important for promoting small-scale musicals, most of them written by Carmines); the American Place Theatre (founded in 1964 by Wynn Handman to rejuvenate the American theatre by encouraging outstanding authors to write plays, and now housed in one of the mid-Manhattan skyscrapers which, owing to tax incentives, have included theatres); and Theatre Genesis (established in 1964 by Ralph Cook and housed in St. Mark's in the Bowery).

In the 1970s off-off-Broadway was subjected to many of the same stresses that earlier had afflicted off-Broadway. In 1975 Actors Equity, in an attempt to improve the economic position of its members, sought to end showcase productions, a major element in off-off-Broadway. Under the showcase arrangement, a company may present a play for a limited number of performances without paying any of those involved. This permitted many plays and actors to be seen that could not have been financed under union restrictions. The Equity proposal was roundly rejected by its members. Thus, the showcase arrangement survived and off-off-Broadway continued to be the most lively part of New York's theatre.

In 1980 there were about 150 off-off-Broadway groups of one sort or another, and among them they produced an average of fifty plays each week. Many companies were linked through the Off-Off-Broadway Alliance, formed in 1972 to assist members with common problems. The companies were so numerous that only a few can be named here. Some of the best were the Chelsea Theatre Center (which between 1965 and 1980 was headed by Robert Kalfin who presented an outstanding series of foreign plays); the Manhattan Theatre Club, which since 1970 has sought to assist new playwrights through readings and productions in its three theatres; and the Circle Repertory Theatre Company, which presents plays in rotation.

Of all the off-off-Broadway groups, the New York Shakespeare Festival Public Theatre is now the most important. It is the creation of Joseph Papp (1912–   ), who began work in 1954 with the New York Shakespeare Festival, which since 1957 has given performances free of charge in Central Park, where the municipally owned Delacorte Theatre was inaugurated in 1962 to accommodate it. In 1964 Papp began to take some of his productions into New York's neighborhoods, since one of his goals was to reach unsophisticated audiences and prove to them that theatre could be both entertaining and relevant. In 1967 Papp acquired the Astor Library and converted it into the Public Theatre with five auditoriums. It opened with *Hair* (which after its initial run was restaged on Broadway by O'Horgan to become one of the greatest hits of the decade). Since then Papp has run an increasingly complex program and has supplied Broadway with several hits, among them *Two Gentlemen of Verona* and *Much Ado About Nothing*, the Pulitzer Prize-winning plays *No Place to Be Somebody* (by Charles Gordone) and *That Championship Season* (by Jason Miller), and the musical *Chorus Line*. Furthermore, Papp's productions have garnered a large number of the awards given annually for excellence in the theatre. Nevertheless, Papp has been dogged by financial problems and on several occasions has been threatened with closure. These problems were eased after 1971 when the city of New York purchased the Public Theatre and leased it back to Papp for one dollar per year. From 1973 to 1978, Papp also ran the company at Lincoln Center.

Many devices and attitudes in the off-off-Broadway theatre were closely related to developments in "happenings," which revived many of the techniques of the futurists, dadaists, and surrealists. The key figure in this movement was Allan Kaprow (1927–   ), a painter and art historian, who in the 1950s became interested in "environments" (that is, the extension of the concept of art to include the entire setting in which it is seen or in which it occurs) and, believing that all those who attend an exhibit become a part of the total context, he gradually began to give the spectators things to do. In 1959 he published an outline for an artistic event that he labeled a "happening" because he considered the term to be neutral. Later that year he gave the first public showing of such an event—*18 Happenings in 6 Parts*. The gallery was divided into three compartments and various things went on simultaneously in each while images were projected on a variety of surfaces, and music and sound effects provided a background. All those who attended became a part of the event as they carried out instructions passed out to them when they entered.

Many persons other than Kaprow were interested in happenings, and the term eventually came to be used as a designation for any event in which improvisation and chance plays a large role. Though happenings were not always theatrical, many of their characteristics were carried over into theatrical practice and goals during the 1960s. First, as "institutionalized art" came under attack, there were many attempts to transcend the confines of the theatre, museum, or concert hall and to put art into more readily accessible and familiar surroundings. There were also attempts to enlarge the audience by removing art from the atmosphere of fixed places and fixed attitudes which had made it the preserve of the privileged classes. Second, emphasis was shifted from observation to participation—from the product to the process—as event and spectator were brought into closer relationship. Sometimes the audience and the performers were the same. Third, emphasis shifted to awareness and away from the artist's intention. Fourth, simultaneity and multiple focus tended to replace orderly sequence and cause-to-effect arrangement. Usually there was no pretense that everyone could see and hear the same things at the same time. Fifth, since happenings were essentially nonverbal, they promoted the retreat from the conceptual into the perceptual. Thus, they tended to be multimedia events appealing to the total sensory apparatus.

Many of these ideas were synthesized in *environmental theatre*, a term popularized by Richard Schechner, then editor of *The Drama Review*. In 1968 Schechner published six "axioms" designed to clarify environmental theatre. First, he declares that events may be placed on a continuum with "Pure/Art" at one end and "Impure/Life" at the other and extending from traditional theatre at one pole through environmental theatre to happenings and ending with public events and demonstrations at the other pole. Thus, he locates environmental theatre somewhere between traditional theatre and happenings. Second, in environmental theatre "all the space is used for performance; all the space is used for the audience." Spectators are both "scene-makers" and "scene-watchers," for, as in a street scene from daily life, those who watch are part of the total picture, even when they consider themselves to be mere spectators. Third, "the event can take place either in a totally transformed space or in a 'found' space." In other words, space may be converted into an "environment" or a place may be accepted as it is and the production adapted to it. Fourth, "focus is flexible and variable." Fifth, "all production elements speak their own language" rather than being mere

supports for words. Sixth, "a text need be neither the starting point nor the goal of a production. There may be no text at all." The key concept here is an extension of Kaprow's idea of environments, so that the site of a performance is made an integral part of the whole, encompassing both actors and spectators so that they may interact as an entity. Such an attempt almost automatically means abandoning traditional theatre architecture in favor of places already suitable as environments or that may easily be converted. Furthermore, focus almost automatically becomes multiple or variable. Schechner considers the Polish Laboratory Theatre, the Living Theatre, the Open Theatre, and several other groups to be environmental.

In 1968 Schechner formed his own company, the Performance Group, to carry out some of his ideas. Their theatre is a converted garage with towers and platforms scattered about it (the arrangement changes somewhat from one production to another) all of which may be used by both actors and spectators. Their first production was *Dionysus in 69*, a reworking of Euripides' *The Bacchae* into a series of rituals, most of them relating to the flesh and sex or to freedom and repression. Overall, the production became a plea for greater freedom coupled with a warning against blindly throwing off restraints. Subsequently the group presented *Makbeth* (based on Shakespeare's play), *Commune* (1970), a company-created work about the American past and present, and Sam Shepard's *The Tooth of Crime* (1973), a play about rivalries in the pop music world treated in terms of gangsterism. Its greatest success was won with the production in 1975 of Brecht's *Mother Courage*. In recent years, Schechner has become increasingly interested in ritual and shamanism and has sought to inject these elements into production.

One of the groups cited by Schechner as a major example of environmental theatre—the Open Theatre—attracted a large following during the 1960s. Founded in 1963 by Peter Feldman and Joseph Chaikin, the Open Theatre was more nearly a workshop than a producing organization, and showed its work

Figure 4.22   *Commune* as presented by the Performance Group in 1970. Photograph by Elizabeth LeCompte.

publicly only at irregular intervals. It was concerned especially with exploiting those aspects of the theatre that distinguish it from films and television—the sense of direct human contact and its constantly changing components. It drew heavily on "role playing" and "games" theories of human behavior, especially as they relate to "transformation" (that is, the idea that reality constantly shifts as we take on and

discard roles in relation to the changing context). The Open Theatre utilized many techniques reminiscent of Grotowski's "poor theatre": the actors wore rehearsal clothes which remained unchanged throughout a performance; they used no makeup and few properties; scenery was almost nonexistent and lighting minimal; actors performed in a large open space; and they moved freely out of one role into another in a series of transformations.

The relationship between the Open Theatre and its playwrights was close. Typically, the writer supplied an outline, scenes, situations or motifs; working from this base, the actors explored the possibilities through improvisations, metaphorical associations, and other techniques; the playwright then selected those results that seemed most effective. Some of these experiments came to nothing, but others yielded outstanding results, especially in collaboration with Terry and Van Itallie. Megan Terry (1932–   ) is probably best known for *Viet Rock* (1966), a play about the horrors of war in Vietnam. She also used transformational techniques in works not written for the Open Theatre, most notably in *Approaching Simone* (1970), which traces the life of the French philosopher and mystic Simone Weil. Perhaps Jean-Claude Van Itallie's (1936–   ) best work is *The Serpent* (1969), which mingles material from the Bible with recent events, such as the assassinations of John F. Kennedy and Martin Luther King, and suggests that the serpent is that impulse within man that makes him break the limits set on him, whereas God is an idea invented by man to set limits on himself.

In 1970 the Open Theatre was reconstituted as a collective and thereafter performed primarily for university and prison audiences. It was dissolved in 1974. Chaikin has since worked on a production of *Electra*, and with Van Itallie he created *A Fable* (1975), concerning a journey in search of the "golden times." Megan Terry founded her own company, the Omaha Magic Theatre, which she seeks to root in the community. Other former members of Chaikin's group established the Medicine Show Theatre Ensemble. Thus, though the Open Theatre has been dissolved, its influence has continued.

Similarly, although "happenings" as a term fell out of favor during the 1960s, the kind of activity it was created to describe continued and came to be called "art-performance." Under the latter designation it has been seen in museums and other places associated with the visual arts but also in theatrical contexts. Some of the most innovative work done in the theatre since 1970 has derived from this interest. Three visually oriented groups have been especially important: the Mabou Mines, the Ontological-Hysteric Theatre, and the Byrd Hoffman Foundation.

The Mabou Mines, a collective founded in 1969, is directed by Lee Breuer, who also has developed most of the company's scripts, many of them inspired by literary works. Among these are *Shaped Like an Egg* (based on Colette's fiction), *Mercier and Camier* (based on a novel by Samuel Beckett), and *A Prelude to Death in Venice* (inspired by Thomas Mann's novel). The company's early work, such as *Red Horse Animation*, relied primarily on highly evocative visual images and athletic movement, but more recent productions, such as *Shaggy Dog Animation* and *B-Beaver Animation*, have shifted much of the emphasis to dialogue. Nevertheless, the company's reputation is based on its creation of images that set up a multiplicity of associations and meanings.

The Ontological-Hysteric Theatre was founded in 1968 by Richard Foreman, author and director of all its productions. Foreman uses a proscenium-arch stage on which he arranges very precisely organized pictures and actions designed to make the spectator concentrate not only on the "art that is made" but also on the fact that "art is being made." His actors are amateurs and the dialogue and commentary are recordings. The visual images and their juxtaposition, the comments made and the questions asked by recorded voices combine to create thought and response quite different from those of traditional theatre. Foreman seeks to create "a theatre not of emotions, not of ideas, but a representation of the efforts, effects, strategies, and inventions of whatever it is in us, and through us, that does 'thinking.'"

The Byrd Hoffman Foundation was created in 1969 by Robert Wilson, an artist whose theatrical pieces owe much to his work with autistic children. His performers range in age from four to ninety years and come from all professions. His productions, among them *Deafman Glance*, *A Letter to Queen Victoria*, *Einstein on the Beach*, and *Death, Destruction and Detroit*, are usually very long (typically five to twelve hours, although one lasted for seven uninterrupted days) and are composed of slow-moving sequences of images that shift almost imperceptibly (it often takes a performer an hour to complete a single gesture). Abstract, the pieces are intended to induce contemplation rather than to tell a story. Through such means, Wilson seeks to alter perceptual awareness and place the members of the audience in touch with their own inner consciousness and obsessive fantasies.

During the 1960s the off-Broadway and off-off-Broadway theatres produced plays by a vast number of young dramatists, most of whom did not subsequently fulfill their early promise. Among the best of those who did were Shepard, Wilson, and Rabe. Sam Shepard (1943–   ) has been one of the most prolific of recent writers, as well as one of the most imaginative. Most of his plays are elaborate theatrical metaphors, as in *Angel City* (1976), in which a film company seeking to stave off economic disaster by concocting an elaborate disaster film serves as a metaphor for society seeking to defuse the fear of its own impending disaster through a preoccupation with disaster. Shepard draws on many ingredients of contemporary popular culture—cinema, rock music, science fiction, cartoons, sports, and the jargon of disc jockeys. In some respects, his techniques resemble those of Strindberg's late plays, as in *Mad Dog Blues* (1971), in which film stars and folk heroes materialize and take part in the action. Also, as in Strindberg's plays, characters may display radically different behavioral patterns from one scene to another. Such techniques have often confused audiences about Shepard's concerns. Some of his more recent plays, such as *Curse of the Starving Class* (1976) and *Buried Child* (1978), have concentrated on family situations and have used more conventional techniques, but all of his works have dealt with the decay and violence at the heart of American society. Lanford Wilson (1937–   ), resident dramatist at the Circle Repertory Theatre in New York, has been concerned with misfits, as in *The Rimers of Eldritch* (1967), in which the gossip of small-town characters is used to unfold the action, and *Hot L Balti-*

Figure 4.24   David Rabe's *Streamers*. Directed by Mike Nichols. Photograph by Martha Swope.

Figure 4.23   Scene from Lanford Wilson's *Fifth of July* (1980). In the foreground are Christopher Reeve and Swoozie Kurtz. Directed by Marshall Mason. Photograph by Martha Swope.

more (1973), in which a wide assortment of misfits await the demolition of the delapidated urban hotel in which they live. Wilson's best-known plays typically divide attention among numerous characters whose combined stories or points of view make up the action, but his most praised play, *Talley's Folly* (1979), concentrates on two characters who, though outwardly mismatched, find in each other what they most desire. In all his plays Wilson provides a sympathetic picture of eccentric or deviant characters seeking to find their way in a conformist world. David Rabe (1940–   ) wrote his best-known plays out of dislike for the Vietnam war. *The Basic Training of Pavlo Hummel* (1971) shows the gradual dehumanization of a naive and patriotic young soldier, while *Sticks and Bones* (1971) concerns a veteran blinded in Vietnam and the effect upon his family of his return home. Both plays use nonrealistic devices to depict the horror of war and the American penchant for accepting all that happens as normal. *Streamers* (1976), which takes place just as the Vietnam war is beginning, derives much of its power from the veteran soldiers who in recalling the Korean conflict make us recognize the price exacted by all wars. *The Boom Boom Room*, on the surface quite unlike the other plays in having as its protagonist a female go-go dancer, resembles them in its concern with the destruction of human beings when they are treated as objects and when their need for love is unfulfilled and is met with selfishness and violence.

Among the numerous other playwrights associated with off-Broadway and off-off-Broadway, some of the best were Rochelle Owens with *Futz* (1961) and *Beclch* (1969); Paul Foster with *Balls* (1964) and *Tom Paine* (1968); Terrence McNally with *Sweet Eros* (1968) and *Next* (1969); Ronald Ribman with *Ceremony of Innocence* (1968) and *The Poison Tree* (1976); Israel Horowitz with *The Indian Wants the Bronx* (1968) and *The Primary English Class* (1976); and Robert Patrick with *Kennedy's Children* (1973) and *My Cup Runneth Over* (1978).

These playwrights were collectively important, for together they did much to shift American drama toward experimentation with form and toward disaffection from the values of the past. Many abandoned the cause-to-effect arrangement of incidents leading from exposition to complication, crisis, and resolution, in favor of organizational patterns more nearly musical—that is, the introduction of a theme followed by variations on it. Characteristically, these works were episodic and loosely organized; most downgraded language in favor of nonverbal sound, song, music, and metaphorical spectacle, the whole usually intended to convey some perception about popular attitudes, political or social conditions or lifestyle. The plays also did much to lessen earlier strictures on acceptable subject matter, behavior, and language in the theatre. Perhaps the most notable changes came with the introduction of nudity

and obscenity, both of which made their first great impact in 1968 with the appearance of *Hair* on Broadway. In 1969 *Che!* brought explicit sexual acts on stage and later that year *Oh, Calcutta* included a large number of scenes performed entirely in the nude. By the early 1970s, although the limits of permissibility were still somewhat vague, almost any sexual theme or obscenity had become potential material for stage use.

A number of theatres grew out of the political and social unrest of the 1960s, when they were usually referred to as "radical theatres." Of these, the most sophisticated artistically was the Bread and Puppet Theatre, founded in 1961 by Peter Schumann and based in New York until 1970 when it moved to Vermont. Using puppets of varying sizes, live actors, and stories based on myths, the Bible, and well-known tales, it sought to promote love, charity, and humility and to denounce the evils of materialism and deception. Other important radical theatres were the San Francisco Mime Troupe (founded in 1959 by R. G. Davis to perform silent plays, radicalized in 1966, after which it rejected Davis and presented agit-prop spoken plays about current issues performed in a broad caricature style); El Teatro Campesino (founded in 1965 by Luis Valdez to dramatize the plight of grape pickers in California and later used to encourage pride in Mexican-American culture); and the Free Southern Theatre (founded in 1963–1964 by Gilbert Moses and John O'Neal as an extension of the civil rights movement). During the 1960s a number of people also became interested in "guerrilla" theatre—seizing on a gathering or occasion and presenting unscheduled, brief, pithy, attention-getting skits as means of arousing interest in some issue. As the mood of the country changed in the 1970s, guerrilla theatre declined rapidly and the radical theatres tended to lose their appeal.

One of the most encouraging developments after 1960 was the emergence of a strong black theatre movement. It differed from its forerunners in accepting the integrity of the black experience and in its unwillingness to compromise because of white sensibili-

Figure 4.25   Scene from *The Domestic Resurrection Circus* as performed by the Bread and Puppet Theatre in Vermont, 1974. Courtesy Craig Hamilton.

ties. It began in 1963 with the Free Southern Theatre and received additional impetus in 1964 when LeRoi Jones and others founded the Black Arts Repertoire Theatre School in New York, although this organization soon came to an end because the radical tone of some productions brought a cessation of government funding which had partially supported it. Other organizations soon sprang up throughout the country. By the late 1960s there were more than forty groups, three of them of special importance. The Negro Ensemble Company (NEC), founded in New York in 1968 and directed by Douglas Turner Ward, Robert Hooks, and Gerald S. Krone, produced a wide range of plays meaningful to blacks though not necessarily written by blacks. The quality of its work was generally high, but it was often accused of insufficient dedication to the black cause, a charge which it has in recent years tried to disprove. Nevertheless, it is the only one of the three groups that still survives as a significant force in the theatre. The New Lafayette Theatre, founded in 1967 by Robert Macbeth, served as something of a cultural center for

Harlem. After 1969 it received several grants intended to encourage plays about black life. It also served as a clearing house for black groups throughout the country through an information service and through *Black Theatre Magazine*. Unfortunately, dissension within the company brought its dissolution in 1973. Neither of these groups was sufficiently separatist to suit LeRoi Jones (later called Imamu Amiri Baraka), who, totally alienated from whites, headed the Spirit House in Newark, dedicated to a wholly black culture. These three groups inspired a great many others, although some were not able to survive. But in 1980 there were numerous black theatre companies in the United States, most of them linked through the Black Theatre Alliance.

The upsurge in black theatrical activity brought a corresponding increase in opportunities for black actors and directors. Furthermore, the number of black dramatists increased markedly. Some representative writers are Hansberry, Jones, Bullins, Ward, Elder, and Walker.

Lorraine Hansberry (1930– 1965) won recognition with A *Raisin in the Sun* (1959), a compassionate drama about a hardworking black family in Chicago whose dreams are shattered but whose values mature in the process. Before her untimely death, Miss Hansberry completed only one more play, *The Sign in Sidney Brustein's Window* (1964), concerning a naive idealist who is too busy to recognize the problems within his own family. Some of Miss Hansberry's uncompleted works have also been assembled by her husband, Robert Nemiroff.

LeRoi Jones (Imamu Amiri Baraka, 1934–   ) is one of the most important black writers both for the quality of his work and because his career illustrates the movement of many black writers away from interest in integration to a desire for separatism. His early plays, such as *The Toilet* (1964) and *Dutchman* (1964), treat black-white relationships—often sympathetically, sometimes bitterly, but with considerable understanding and compassion. After the mid-1960s Jones became increasingly anti-white, an attitude reflected in such plays as *Home on the Range*

and *The Death of Malcolm X*. One of the most powerful of his later plays is *Slave Ship* (1969), which traces the black experience from African days to the present and seeks to build solidarity among blacks and a total rejection of white society.

The most prolific of black writers has been Ed Bullins (1935–   ), formerly resident playwright at the New Lafayette Theatre and editor of *Black Theatre Magazine*, and from 1971 till 1973 associate director of the New Lafayette. After leaving the New Lafayette, he headed a workshop for playwrights at Papp's Public Theatre. His work is varied in subject and tone, but it is unified by a concern for and pride in blackness. One of his ongoing projects is a lengthy cycle of plays about black life in the industrial North and West, of which *In the Wine Time* and *In New England Winter* have been shown with considerable success. One of Bullins's prime targets is the black pseudointellectual, as in *The Electronic Nigger* (1968) and *Clara's Old Man* (1965), although the latter play is more deeply concerned with how life has forced a woman to assume responsibilities abdicated by others. Other plays by Bullins include *The Pig Pen* (1970), *The Taking of Miss Janie* (1975), and *Daddy* (1977).

The Negro Ensemble Company achieved considerable success with the plays of Ward, Elder, and Walker. Douglas Turner Ward, the NEC's artistic director, through such works as *Day of Absence* (1967) and *The Reckoning* (1969), has used broad caricature to show blacks outwitting whites and to suggest that they have been forced into deception in order to survive. Lonne Elder III, director of the NEC's playwriting program, is noted for one play, *Ceremonies in Dark Old Men* (1969), a compassionate play about life in Harlem and the ceremonies men enact in order to escape their unpleasant situation. One of the NEC's greatest successes was won with Joseph A. Walker's *The River Niger* (1972), which, using three generations of a black family in Harlem, seeks to trace the black man's odyssey. Ultimately it is a debate drama about racial obligations and roots and an argument for the importance of ac-

Figure 4.26   Scene from Joseph A. Walker's *The River Niger*, as produced by the Negro Ensemble Company, 1972. Photograph by Bert Andrews.

tion. Its high point is a poem, "The River Niger," written by the sixty-year-old, near-alcoholic father, which metaphorically depicts the African stream reaching all the way into Harlem.

Other black playwrights who should be mentioned include Charles Gordone, Ntozake Shange, Richard Wesley, Ben Caldwell, Ron Milner, Ossie Davis, Adrienne Kennedy, Melvin van Peebles, Ted Shine, Philip Hayes Dean, Vinette Carroll, and Leslie Lee. By the mid-1970s the emphasis in black playwriting shifted away from defining the black experience through negative comparisons with whites and toward viewing blacks in relation to other blacks. Perhaps most encouraging, it appeared that black theatre and drama might for the first time in American history be able to sustain themselves on a continuing basis.

In addition to blacks, other ethnic groups, especially Puerto Rican, Mexican-American, and native American, became increasingly concerned with theatre during the 1970s. Many of these theatres sought to promote social action and to establish a close relationship with the communities they serve. Still other theatres were established to express the concerns and serve the needs of women, homosexuals, and other minority groups.

The 1960s saw the greatest expansion of the American theatre outside of New York since the nineteenth century. The first important impetus came in 1959 when the Ford Foundation made sizeable grants to a number of small companies that had managed to gain footholds in cities scattered throughout the country. This financial boost permitted such groups as the Alley Theatre in Houston, the Arena Stage in Washington, and the Actors' Workshop in San Francisco to become fully professional and relatively stable. The movement toward resident companies was further strengthened when Tyrone Guthrie announced his intention of founding a theatre in Minneapolis. When his theatre was opened in 1963 the favorable publicity motivated other cities to seek similar companies. By 1966 the regional theatres had so burgeoned (to about thirty-five) that for the first time in the twentieth century more actors were employed outside of than in New York. These troupes resembled European subsidized theatres in presenting a repertory of classics and recent successes and in relying little on new plays.

A step toward acknowledging the government's responsibility to support the arts was taken in 1965 when federal legislation established the National Endowment for the Arts as an agency to make grants of appropriated funds to groups or projects with considerable potential for growth and audience appeal. Thereafter federal appropriations for the arts steadily increased until 1980, although they were still woefully small in proportion to the country's population. The federal government also encouraged each state to establish an arts council, and consequently most states have an official body charged with assisting

Figure 4.27   Interior of the Tyrone Guthrie Theatre, Minneapolis. Note the thrust stage and steeply banked seating. Sir Tyrone Guthrie's 1963 production of Chekhov's *The Three Sisters*, The Guthrie Theatre, Minneapolis/St. Paul.

and encouraging the arts. Many of these groups provide at least some subsidy to theatres. In addition, regional councils have linked member states in an effort to coordinate plans for assisting the arts, and within states numerous communities have formed arts councils to deal with local concerns and needs. Despite these advances, few theatre groups had any

assurance of continuing financial assistance (as do European companies) and consequently they seldom could make long-range plans. Consequently, resident theatres have come and gone with some regularity.

The kind of theatrical activity associated with off-off-Broadway theatre spread to the rest of the coun-

Figure 4.28   Phyllis Frelich and John Rubinstein in a scene from Mark Medoff's *Children of a Lesser God* at the Taper Forum. Used by permission of the Center Theatre Group/Mark Taper Forum. Photograph by Jay Thompson.

Figure 4.29   Scene from Adrian Mitchell's *Hoagy, Bix and Wolfgang Beethoven Bunkhaus* at the Indiana Repertory Theatre. Courtesy Indiana Repertory Theatre.

try during the 1970s. Many of these companies were small and made little impact beyond their immediate area, but they were indicative of a widespread desire to bring live theatre to all parts of the nation. In 1980 there were approximately 165 nonprofit professional theatres in the United States.

Nonprofit theatres (especially the larger resident companies) have become increasingly attractive to playwrights, since pressures there are considerably fewer than on Broadway. Resident groups usually are not concerned with long runs, nor do they expect to succeed or fail on the basis of a single production. Thus, they can afford to take more chances. Several resident companies—among them the Arena Stage in Washington, the Long Wharf Theatre in New Haven, the Dallas Theatre Center, the Mark Taper Forum in Los Angeles, and the Actors' Theatre of Louisville—have been especially helpful to writers.

During the 1960s universities also increased their involvement with the theatre and a number of them established resident companies. The University Resident Theatre Association now includes about forty member groups ranging from those that are fully professional to those composed entirely of students.

In 1980 the American theatre seemed suspended between optimism and doubt. On the one hand, it was enjoying the largest income of its history and was distributed more widely geographically than at any time since 1875. On the other hand, inflation was a source of anxiety and an inducement to caution. Nostalgia for a simpler time may account for the great number of revivals on Broadway which provided some of its greatest hits in the late 1970s—*Evenings at Seven*, *Oklahoma!*, *Peter Pan*, and *The King and I*.

Most of the extremes of the 1960s disappeared as many innovations of that time were assimilated into common practice. A new generation of playwrights also demonstrated a renewed interest in language and in nondidactic, apolitical storytelling. Among the most prominent of these writers were David Mamet with *American Buffalo*, *A Life in the Theatre*, and *Lone Canoe*; Michael Cristofer with *Shadow Box* and *The Lady and the Clarinet*; Preston Jones with

The Last Meeting of the Knights of the White Magnolia and *The Oldest Living Graduate*; Bernard Pomerance with *The Elephant Man*; and Thomas Babe with *A Prayer for My Daughter*.

Another source of anxiety was the potential competition from improved electronic equipment and mass media: video cassettes; home box-office and a network of cable television companies that was seeking to produce plays with the intention of transmitting them into the home; and holographic projections with all the three-dimensionality of the live human being.

Postscript

What the future will bring for the theatre can only be a matter for speculation, for accurate prediction would require the ability to foresee the course of world events. Western theatre has always reflected changing views about man and his world. Thus, as conceptions about psychology, morality, sociology, and politics have altered, so too has the theatre. Many recent innovations that now seem important will in the future no doubt fade into oblivion because they were false starts, whereas others, perhaps unnoted in this book, will in retrospect be recognized as forerunners of major changes. History is constantly being rewritten because it is from present perspectives that we view the past, and as our values and interests change, so too does our estimate of the past. It is future conceptions of man—what sort of creature he is, what kinds of appeals must be made to his senses, what kinds of personal, moral, social, and political ideals he is capable of sustaining—that will determine the direction to be taken by theatre and drama. And that is history yet to be lived and recorded.

Looking at Theatre History

For the most part, history has been written from what is called the "consensus" point of view; that is, historians in each era have more or less consciously sought to agree on the significant issues and events and to focus on them. This does not mean there has always been unanimity among historians or that ideas about the appropriate focus have not changed from one generation to another, but it does mean that once a view or approach is accepted, it tends to become the norm for its age. For theatre history this point can best be illustrated in relation to the American situation, where the "melting pot" theory of culture has led to an almost total preoccupation with tracing the mainstream of the English-language stage. While that aspect of American theatre unquestionably is important, even primary, the "consensus" attitude has discouraged interest in the multicultural richness of the nation's theatrical history. As a result, most of us know little (or even care) about the theatrical traditions of native Americans (the Indians), Mexican-Americans, Chinese-Americans, or the various foreign-language, religious, and other groups that have contributed to the totality of our theatrical heritage. Since 1960 the consensus approach to history has come under strong attack, and increasingly there has been an attempt to broaden the scope of historical inquiry. These beginnings have yet to be fully implemented in theatre history. Until they are, the richness of our past will not be fully revealed to us.

Challenge to "consensus theatre" was also a hallmark of the 1960s. No group was more crucial in this role than the Living Theatre. Its challenge reached a climax in *Paradise Now* (1968), described by the company as "a vertical ascent toward Permanent Revolution." The production's most notorious feature, direct confrontation with audiences, was little understood, for in actuality the audience was cast as obstacles to successful revolution. Here is a passage from the printed version of the work:

> *The Confrontations are an attempt to define and thereby understand the characteristics of the stumbling block at each [phase], and of the form of action that can overcome it. Thus at the beginning the stumbling block is The Culture which is overcome by Aesthetic Assault; and at the end the stumbling block is Stasis which is overcome by Impetus. The Confrontations are guides to the relationship between the actor and the public at each stage of the trip. The Resistance to the Revolutionary Change is treated as the obstacle. The energy form designed is an appropriate strategy for the actor to use to transform the obstacle.*

> Paradise Now, *Collective Creation of the Living Theatre*, Written down by Judith Malina and Julian Beck (New York: Vintage Books, 1971), pp. 11–12.

One major goal since 1960 has been to discover what is truly essential to "theatre." The search is probably best summed up in Grotowski's conception of "the poor theatre":

> *By gradually eliminating whatever proved superfluous, we found that theatre can exist without make-up, without autonomic costume and scenography, without a separate performance area (stage), without lighting and sound effects, etc. It cannot exist without the actor-spectator relationship of perceptual, direct, "live" communion. . . . when rigorously tested in practice it undermines most of our usual ideas about theatre. It challenges the notion of theatre as a synthesis of disparate creative disciplines. . . . This "synthetic theatre" is the contemporary the-*

atre, *which we readily call the "Rich Theatre" —rich in flaws.*

> Jerzy Grotowski, *Towards a Poor Theatre* (New York: Simon and Schuster, 1968), p. 19.

Simultaneously, all the technological means of the space age were being adapted to theatrical purposes, barriers between the arts were being broken down, and multimedia events of all sorts were flourishing. Josef Svoboda is probably the best known of those who sought to extend the theatre's range of expression through technological devices. Here are some excerpts from his statements about the production of Luigi Nonno's opera *Intoleranza* (produced in Boston in 1965):

> *Instead of film I used television techniques in such a way as to project a TV image onto many screens placed on the stage. . . . We were able to transmit parallel actions that were performed in adjoining studios, in fact in studios as far as three miles from the stage. All these studios were joined with each other by audio and visual monitors, so that the actors could see the conductor in relation to themselves, the actors in the studio could see what was being played on the stage, and . . . the actors on the stage see what was played in the studios. In this way, the conductor was absolute master of the rhythm of the performance. . . .*

> Jarka Burian, *The Scenography of Josef Svoboda* (Middletown, Conn.: Wesleyan University Press, 1971), p. 103.

By the 1970s the ferment of the 1960s had faded. Here are some of Margaret Croyden's comments on what went wrong:

> *As in the case of movements composed of all kinds of personalities, and especially where*

personality was itself supposed to be an artistic vehicle, some individuals lost sight of their original aim of building an authentic new theatre and got caught up in all sorts of fads and ego trips. . . . untried techniques were grafted onto undigested philosophies, the gestalt therapy theories mixed with R. D. Laing, confrontation politics with Artaud, consciousness expansion with Yoga, spontaneity with disciplined exercise, guruism with collective living, freakism with simplicity.

A serious problem . . . was the experimentalists' reliance on self-expression as a predominant aesthetic—the old romantic tenet. Self-expression became the answer to all arguments and served to hide a dearth of shallow ideas and unworkable theatrics. . . . it cultivated an intense and limited subjectivism and bred . . . a new anti-intellectualism. . . .

> Margaret Croyden, *Lunatics, Lovers and Poets: The Contemporary Experimental Theatre* (New York: McGraw-Hill Book Co., 1974), p. 289.

Of the dominant mood in the mid-1970s, Hilton Kramer wrote:

The idea of the avant-garde, which commanded such immense prestige in the 60s, no longer inspires the same automatic assent. . . .

The appetite for outrage and innovation, for shock and squalor, for assaults on the audience and on the medium, has clearly diminished, where it has not completely disappeared. The taste now is for clarity and coherence, for the beautiful and the recognizable, for narrative, melody, pathos, glamour, romance, and the instantly comprehensible. . . . for art that is a pleasure rather than a moral contest.

Does this mean that the innovations of the 60s have disappeared without trace? Not at all, but where they survive . . . they have been . . . co-opted by the establishment, and put to eminently more benign use.

> "A Yearning for 'Normalcy'—The Current Backlash in the Arts," *The New York Times*, May 23, 1976, Section 2, pp. 1, 25.

In 1979 Russell Vandenbroucke, Literary Manager of the Mark Taper Forum, visited several nonprofit professional theatres in the United States. Among his reactions were these:

The conclusions to be drawn from my trip are discouraging: no city or theatre monopolizes bad work; instead of being the norm, professional competency is often extraordinary; . . . regional theatres as a whole have survived infancy and puberty, but have yet to prove their potency and fertility. . . .

He goes on to suggest a need to jar the theatre out of its current stasis:

If one persists in taking art seriously, one is forced either to leave the theatre or become some kind of aesthetic terrorist. Any vital activity, any reaction to move the theatre off dead centre, would be welcome.

> "The American Regional Theatre: Twenty Plays and a Polemic," *Theatre Quarterly*, 10 (Spring 1980), p. 60.

One of the ways of studying contemporary theatre history is by reading magazines and newspapers that report on current productions, experiments and theories. This is especially crucial for keeping up with the contemporary theatre, since it usually takes a year or more for a book to get into print. Some of the publications that are helpful in keeping abreast of current happenings in the theatre are listed at the end of this book's bibliography.

Perhaps even more important in the study of contemporary theatre history is regular attendance at theatrical performances, for what one sees on the stage tonight is a part of tomorrow's history. Few historical accounts of an event can ever be as vivid as personal participation in it.

Bibliography

This bibliography lists books that are either the most authoritative or the most representative of major points of view. Except in rare cases, the works are in English.

Introduction

Appleton, William W. *Madame Vestris and the London Stage*. New York, 1974.

Arvin, Neil E. *Eugène Scribe and the French Theatre, 1815–60*. Cambridge, Mass., 1924.

Brockett, Oscar G. *History of the Theatre*. 4th ed. Boston, 1981.

Carlson, Marvin. *Goethe and the Weimar Theatre*. Ithaca, N.Y., 1978.

———. *The French Stage in the Nineteenth Century*. Metuchen, N.J., 1972.

———. *The German Stage in the Nineteenth Century*. Metuchen, N.J., 1972.

Felheim, Marvin. *The Theatre of Augustin Daly: An Account of the Late Nineteenth Century Stage*. Cambridge, Mass., 1956.

Hopkins, Albert A. *Magic: Stage Illusions and Scientific Diversions*. New York, 1897.

Moynet, Jean-Pierre. *French Theatrical Practice in the Nineteenth Century (L'Envers du Théâtre)*. Translated and augmented by Allan S. Jackson and M. Glen Wilson. Binghamton, N.Y., 1976.

Odell, George C. D. *Shakespeare from Betterton to Irving*. 2 vols. New York, 1920.

Rees, Terence. *Theatre Lighting in the Age of Gas*. London, 1978.

Rowell, George. *The Victorian Theatre, 1792–1914*. 2d ed. London, 1979.

Vardac A. N. *Stage to Screen: Theatrical Method from Garrick to Griffith*. Cambridge, Mass., 1949.

Watson, Ernest B. *Sheridan to Robertson: A Study of the 19th Century London Stage*. Cambridge, Mass., 1926.

Weinberg, Bernard. *French Realism: The Critical Reaction, 1830–1870*. Chicago, 1937.

Chapter 1: The Beginnings of the Modern Theatre, 1875–1915

Antoine, André. *Memories of the Théâtre Libre*. Translated by Marvin Carlson. Coral Gables, Fla., 1964.

Appia, Adolphe. *The Work of Living Art* and *Man is the Measure of All Things*. Coral Cables, Fla., 1960.

Bablet, Denis. *Edward Gordon Craig*. New York, 1967.

————. *Esthétique Générale du Décor de Théâtre de 1870 à 1914*. Paris, 1965.

Bentley, Eric. *The Playwright as Thinker: A Study of Drama in Modern Times*. New York, 1946.

Block, Haskell. *Mallarmé and the Symbolist Drama*. Detroit, 1963.

Bogard, Travis, et al. *Revels History of Drama in English*. Vol. 8: American Drama. New York, 1977.

Bourgeois, Maurice. *J. M. Synge and the Irish Theatre*. New York, 1965.

Braun, Edward. *Meyerhold on Theatre*. New York, 1969.

Brockett, Oscar G., and Findlay, Robert R. *Century of Innovation: A History of European and American Theatre and Drama Since 1870*. Englewood Cliffs, N.J., 1973.

Brustein, Robert. *The Theatre of Revolt*. New York, 1964.

Byrne, Dawson. *The Story of Ireland's National Theatre: The Abbey*. Dublin, 1929.

Carter, Huntly. *The Theatre of Max Reinhardt*. New York, 1914.

Carter, Lawson A. *Zola and the Theatre*. New Haven, Conn., 1963.

Chiari, Joseph. *Symbolism from Poe to Mallarmé*. 2d ed. New York, 1970.

Cole, Toby, ed. *Playwrights on Playwriting. The Meaning and Making of Modern Dance from Ibsen to Ionesco*. New York, 1961.

Cole, Toby, and Chinoy, Helen K., eds. *Directors on Directing*. Indianapolis. 1963.

Cornell, Kenneth. *The Symbolist Movement*. New Haven, Conn., 1951.

Craig, Edward Gordon. *On the Art of the Theatre*. 2d ed. Boston, 1924.

Dahlstrom, C. E. W. L. *Strindberg's Dramatic Expressionism*. Vol. 7 of University of Michigan Publications, Language and Literature. Ann Arbor, 1930.

Fuchs, Georg. *Revolution in the Theatre*. Translated by C. C. Kuhn. Ithaca, N.Y., 1959.

Fuerst, Walter R., and Hume, Samuel J. *Twentieth Century Stage Decoration*. 2 vols. London, 1928.

Garten, H. F. *Modern German Drama*. New York, 1959.

Gassner, John. *Form and Idea in the Modern Theatre*. New York, 1956.

————. *The Theatre in Our Times: A Survey of the Men, Materials and Movements in the Modern Theatre*. New York, 1954.

Glasstone, Victor. *Victorian and Edwardian Theatres*. Cambridge, Mass., 1975.

Goldberg, Rosalee. *Performance: Live Art 1909 to the Present*. New York, 1979.

Gorchakov, Nikolai A. *The Theatre in Soviet Russia*. Trans. Edgar Lehman. New York, 1957.

Gorelik, Mordecai. *New Theatres for Old*. New York, 1940.

Grube, Max. *The Story of the Meiningen*. Translated by Ann Marie Koller. Coral Gables, Fla., 1963.

Hunt, Hugh, et al. *The Revels History of Drama in English*. Vol. 7: 1880 to the Present Day. New York, 1979.

Jasper, Gertrude. *Adventure in the Theatre: Lugné-Poë and the Théâtre de l'Oeuvre to 1899*. New Brunswick, N.J., 1947.

Kochno, Boris, *Diaghilev and the Ballets Russes*. New York, 1970.

Koht, Halvdan. *The Life of Ibsen*. 2 vols. New York, 1931.

Lamm, Martin. *August Strindberg*. New York, 1971.

Lehmann, Andrew G. *The Symbolist Aesthetic in France, 1885–1895*. Oxford, 1950.

Lumley, Frederick. *Trends in Twentieth Century Drama: A Survey Since Ibsen and Shaw*. 2d ed. London, 1960.

MacCarthy, Desmond. *The Court Theatre, 1904–07*. London, 1907.

Marker, Lise-Lone. *David Belasco: Naturalism in the American Theatre*. Princeton, N.J., 1975.

Matlaw, Myron. *Modern World Drama: An Encyclopedia*. New York, 1972.

Miller, Anna Irene. *The Independent Theatre in Europe, 1887 to the Present*. New York, 1931.

Moderwell, Hiram. *The Theatre of Today*. New York, 1914.

Newmark, Maxim. *Otto Brahm: The Man and the Critic*. New York, 1938.

Rischbieter, Henning. *Art and the Stage in the Twentieth Century*. Greenwich, Conn., 1968.

Roose-Evans, James. *Experimental Theatre: From Stanislavsky to Today*. New rev. ed. London, 1973.

Sayler, Oliver M., ed. *Max Reinhardt and His Theatre*. New York, 1926.

Schorske, Carl E. *Fin-de-Siècle Vienna: Politics and Culture*. New York, 1980.

Segel, Harold B. *Twentieth-Century Russian Drama*. New York, 1979.

Shattuck, Roger. *The Banquet Years: The Arts in France, 1885–1918*. New York, 1961.

Slonim, Marc. *Russian Theatre from the Empire to the Soviets*. Cleveland, 1961.

Speaight, Robert. *William Poel and the Elizabethan Revival*. London, 1954.

Stanislavski, Konstantin. *An Actor Prepares*. Translated by Elizabeth R. Hapgood. New York, 1936.

————. *Building a Character*. Translated by E. R. Hapgood. New York, 1949.

————. *Creating a Role*. Translated by E. R. Hapgood. New York, 1961.

————. *My Life in Art*. Translated by J. J. Robbins. Boston, 1924.

Stein, Jack M. *Richard Wagner and the Synthesis of the Arts*. Detroit, 1960.

Tairov, Alexander. *Notes of a Director*. Translated by William Kuhlke. Coral Gables, Fla., 1969.

Trewin, J. C., and Kemp, T. C. *The Shakespeare Festival: A History of the Shakespeare Memorial Theatre*. London, 1953.

Valency, Maurice. *The Flower and the Castle: An Introduction to Modern Drama*. New York, 1963.

Volbach, Walther. *Adolphe Appia, Prophet of the Modern Theatre*. Middletown, Conn., 1968.

Wagner, Richard. *Opera and Drama*. Translated by Edwin Evans. London, 1913.

Waxman, S. M. *Antoine and the Théâtre Libre*. Cambridge, Mass., 1926.

Wellek, René. *A History of Modern Criticism, 1750–1950*. Vols. 3 and 4. New York, 1965.

Williams, Raymond, *Drama from Ibsen to Eliot*. London, 1952.

Chapter 2: The Theatre in Europe and the United States between the Wars

Artaud, Antonin. *The Theatre and Its Double*. Translated by Mary C. Richards. New York, 1958.

Balakian, Anna E. *Surrealism*. New York, 1959.

Bentley, Eric. See under chapter 1.

Bishop, G. W. *Barry Jackson and the London Theatre*. London, 1933.

Bogard, Travis, et al. See under chapter 1.

Braun, Edward. See under chapter 1.

Brecht, Bertolt. *Brecht on Theatre*. Translated by John Willett. New York, 1964.

Breton, André. *What Is Surrealism?* London, 1936.

Brockett, Oscar G., and Findlay, Robert R. See under chapter 1.

Brustein, Robert. See under chapter 1.

Cheney, Sheldon. *The New Movement in the Theatre*. New York, 1914.

Clurman, Harold. *The Fervent Years: The Story of the Group Theatre in the Thirties*. New York, 1957.

Cole, Toby. See under chapter 1.

Davis, Hallie Flanagan. *Arena*. New York, 1940.

Donoghue, Denis. *The Third Voice: Modern British and American Verse Drama*. Princeton, N.J., 1959.

Downer, Alan S. *Fifty Years of American Drama, 1900–1950*. Chicago, 1951.

Esslin, Martin. *Antonin Artaud*. New York, 1977.

————. *Brecht: The Man and His Work*. Garden City, N.Y., 1960.

Fowlie, Wallace. *Age of Surrealism*. Bloomington, Ind., 1960.

Garten, H. F. See under chapter 1.

Gielgud, John. *Early Stages*. New York, 1939.

Goldberg, Rosalee. See under chapter 1.

Gorchakov, Nikolai. See under chapter 1.

———. *The Vakhtangov School of Stage Art*. Moscow, n.d.

Gorelik, Mordecai. See under chapter 1.

Greene, Naomi. *Antonin Artaud: Poet Without Words*. New York, 1970.

Gropius, Walter, ed. *The Theatre of the Bauhaus*. Middletown, Conn., 1961.

Guthrie, Tyrone. *A Life in the Theatre*. London, 1960.

Hogan, Robert G. *After the Irish Renaissance*. Minneapolis, 1967.

Hoover, Marjorie L. *Meyerhold: The Art of Conscious Theatre*. Amherst, Mass., 1974.

Houghton, Norris. *Moscow Rehearsals: An Account of Methods of Production in the Soviet Theatre*. New York, 1936.

Hunt, Hugh, et al. See under chapter 1.

Innes, C. D. *Erwin Piscator's Political Theatre*. New York, 1972.

Issacs, Edith J. R. *The Negro in the American Theatre*. New York, 1947.

Kirby, Michael. *Futurist Performance*. New York, 1971.

Knapp, Bettina. *Louis Jouvet, Man of the Theatre*. New York, 1958.

Knowles, Dorothy. *French Drama of the Interwar Years, 1918–39*. New York, 1967.

Krutch, Joseph W. *The American Drama Since 1918*. Rev. ed. New York, 1957.

Ley-Piscator, Maria. *The Piscator Experiment*. New York, 1967.

Lumley, Frederick. See under chapter 1.

MacClintock, Lander. *The Age of Pirandello*. Bloomington, Ind., 1951.

Macgowan, Kenneth, and Jones, Robert E. *Continental Stagecraft*. New York, 1922.

Mackay, Constance D. *The Little Theatre in the United States*. New York, 1917.

Marshall, Norman. *The Other Theatre*. London, 1947.

Matlaw, Myron, See under chapter 1.

Moderwell, Hiram K. *The Theatre of Today*. New York, 1925.

Moussinac, Leon. *The New Movement in the Theatre: A Survey of Recent Developments in Europe and America*. London, 1931.

O'Connor, John, and Brown, Lorraine, eds. *Free, Adult, Uncensored: The Living History of the Federal Theatre Project*. Washington, D.C., 1978.

Piscator, Erwin. *The Political Theatre: A History, 1914–1929*. Translated by Hugh Rorison. New York, 1978.

Quinn, Arthur H. *A History of the American Drama from the Civil War to the Present Day*. 2d ed. New York, 1949.

Richter, Hans. *Dada: Art and Anti-Art*. New York, 1966.

Rischbeiter, Henning. See under chapter 1.

Roose-Evans, James. See under chapter 1.

Saint-Denis, Michel. *The Rediscovery of Style*. New York, 1960.

Samuel, Richard, and Thomas, R. H. *Expressionism in German Life, Literature and the Theatre, 1910–1924*. Cambridge, 1939.

Segel, Harold B. See under chapter 1.

Simonov, Reuben. *Stanislavsky's Protegé. Eugene Vaktangov*. Translated by Miriam Goldina. New York, 1969.

Slonim, Marc. See under chapter 1.

Sokel, Walter H. *The Writer in Extremis: Expressionism in Twentieth Century German Literature*. Stanford, Calif., 1959.

Stanislavski, Konstantin. See under chapter 1.

Symons, James. *Meyerhold's Theatre of the Grotesque: The Post-Revolutionary Productions, 1920–1932*. Coral Gables, Fla., 1971.

Tairov, Alexander. See under chapter 1.

Theatre Arts. 32 vols. Detroit and New York, 1916–1948.

Trewin, J. C., and Kemp, T. C. See under chapter 1.

Wellek, René. See under chapter 1.

Wengler, Hans. *Bauhaus*. Cambridge, Mass., 1969.

Willett, John. *Expressionism*. New York, 1970.

———. *The Theatre of Bertolt Brecht*. New York, 1959.

———. *The Theatre of Erwin Piscator*. New York, 1979.

Williams, E. Harcourt. *Old Vic Saga*. London, 1949.

Williams, Raymond. See under chapter 1.

Chapter 3: Theatre and Drama, 1940–1960

Allsop, Kenneth. *The Angry Decade: A Survey of the Cultural Revolt of the 1950s*. London, 1958.

Barrault, Jean-Louis, *The Theatre of Jean-Louis Barrault*. Translated by J. Chiari. New York, 1961.

Bentley, Eric. *In Search of Theatre*. New York, 1953.

Bogard, Travis, et al. See under chapter 1.

Bordman, Gerald. *American Musical Theatre*. New York, 1978.

Bowers, Faubion. *Broadway, USSR: Theatre, Ballet and Entertainment in Russia Today*. New York, 1959.

Brecht, Bertolt. See under chapter 2.

Brockett, Oscar G., and Findlay, Robert R. See under chapter 1.

Browne, Terry. *Playwrights' Theatre: The English Stage Company at the Royal Court*. London, 1975.

Brustein, Robert. See under chapter 1.

Chiari, Joseph. *The Contemporary French Theatre: The Flight from Naturalism*. London, 1958.

Cole, Toby. See under chapter 1.

Donoghue, Denis. See under chapter 2.

Elsom, John. *Post-War British Theatre*. Boston, 1979.

Esslin, Martin. See under chapter 2.

———. *The Theatre of the Absurd*. Rev. ed. New York, 1969.

Fowlie, Wallace. *Dionysus in Paris: A Guide to Contemporary French Theatre*. New York, 1960.

Freeman, E. *The Theatre of Albert Camus*. London, 1973.

Garten, H. F. See under chapter 1.

Gassner, John. *Directions in Modern Theatre and Drama*. New York, 1965.

———. *Theatre at the Crossroads: Plays and Playwrights of the Mid-Century American Stage*. New York, 1960.

Goldberg, Rosalee. See under chapter 1.

Gorchakov, Nikolai, See under chapter 1.

Grossvogel, David I. *The Self-Conscious Stage in Modern French Drama*. New York, 1958.

Guicharnaud, Jacques. *Modern French Theatre from Giraudoux to Beckett*. New Haven, Conn., 1961.

Hainaux, René, ed., *Stage Design Throughout the World Since 1935*. New York, 1956.

———. *Stage Design Throughout the World Since 1950*. New York, 1964.

Houghton, Norris. *Return Engagement: A Postscript to "Moscow Rehearsals."* New York, 1962.

Hunt, Hugh, et al. See under chapter 1.

Kienzle, Siegfried. *Modern World Theatre: A Guide to Productions in Europe and the United States Since 1945*. Translated by A. and F. Henderson. New York, 1970.

Krutch, Joseph W. See under chapter 2.

Lee, Vera. *Quest for a Public: French Popular Theatre Today*. Cambridge, Mass., 1970.

Lumley, Frederick. See under chapter 1.

Matlaw, Myron. See under chapter 1.

Popkin, Henry. *The New British Drama*. New York, 1964.

Price, Julia. *The Off-Broadway Theatre*. New York, 1962.

Rischbeiter, Henning. See under chapter 1.

Roose-Evans, James. See under chapter 1.

Saint-Denis, Michel. See under chapter 2.

Segel, Harold B. See under chapter 1.

Slonim, Marc. See under chapter 1.

Strasberg, Lee. *Strasberg at the Actors Studio*. New York, 1965.

Styan, J. L. *The Dark Comedy: The Development of Modern Comic Tragedy*. Cambridge, 1962.

Taylor, John R. *Anger and After: A Guide to the New British Drama*. London, 1962.

Trewin, J. C., and Kemp, T. C. See under chapter 1.

Weales, Gerald. *American Drama since World War II*. New York, 1962.

Wellwarth, George E. *The Theatre of Protest and Paradox: Development in the Avant-Garde Drama*. New York, 1964.

Willett, John. See under chapter 2.

Chapter 4: Theatre and Drama Since 1960

Abramson, Doris E. *Negro Playwrights in the American Theatre*. New York, 1969.

Addenbrooke, David. *The Royal Shakespeare Company: The Peter Hall Years*. London, 1974.

Ansorge, Peter. *Disrupting the Spectacle: Five Years of Experimental and Fringe Theatre in Britain*. London, 1975.

Biner, Pierre. *The Living Theatre*. 2d ed. New York, 1972.

Brecht, Stefan. *The Theatre of Visions: Robert Wilson*. Frankfurt am Main, 1978.

Bogard, Travis, et al. See under chapter 1.

Bordman, Gerald. See under chapter 3.

Brockett, Oscar G. *Perspectives on Contemporary Theatre*. Baton Rouge, La., 1971.

————, and Findlay, Robert R. See under chapter 1.

Brook, Peter. *The Empty Space*. New York, 1968.

Browne, Terry. See under chapter 3.

Brustein, Robert. *Revolution as Theatre: Notes on the New Radical Style*. New York, 1971.

Burdick, Elizabeth B., et al., eds. *Contemporary Stage Design, USA*. Middletown, Conn., 1974.

Burian, Jarka. *The Scenography of Joseph Svoboda*. Middletown, Conn., 1971.

Clark, Brian. *Group Theatre*. New York, 1971.

Cohn, Ruby. *Just Play: Beckett's Theatre*. Princeton, N.J., 1979.

Cook, Judith. *The National Theatre*. London, 1976.

Croyden, Margaret. *Lunatics, Lovers and Poets: The Contemporary Experimental Theatre*. New York, 1974.

Davy, Kate, ed. *Richard Foreman: Plays and Manifestoes*. New York, 1978.

Engel, Lehman. *The American Musical Theatre*. Rev. ed. New York, 1975.

Esslin, Martin. See under chapter 3.

————. *The Peopled Wound: The Work of Harold Pinter*. New York, 1970.

Filler, Withold. *Contemporary Polish Theatre*. Warsaw, 1977.

Goldberg, Rosalee. See under chapter 1.

Grodzicki, August. *Polish Theatre Today*. Warsaw, 1978.

Grotowski, Jerzy. *Towards a Poor Theatre*. New York, 1968.

Hainaux, René. *Stage Design Throughout the World*. New York, 1972.

————. *Stage Design Throughout the World, 1970–1975*. New York, 1976.

Hayman, Ronald. *British Theatre Since 1955: A Reassessment*. New York, 1979.

————. *Theatre and Anti-Theatre: New Movements Since Beckett*. New York, 1979.

Hill, Errol, ed. *The Theatre of Black Americans*. 2 vols. Englewood Cliffs, N.J., 1980.

Hinchliffe, Arnold. *British Theatre, 1950–1970*. Totowa, N.J., 1975.

Hunt, Hugh, et al. See under chapter 1.

Kerensky, Oleg. *The New British Drama: Fourteen Playwrights Since Osborne and Pinter*. New York, 1979.

Kienzle, Siegfried. See under chapter 3.

Kirby, Michael. *Happenings*. New York, 1966.

Kostelanetz, Richard. *The Theatre of Mixed Means*. New York, 1968.

Lesnick, Henry, ed. *Guerrilla Street Theatre*. New York, 1973.

Little, Stuart. *Enter Joseph Papp: In Search of a New American Theatre*. New York, 1974.

Marowitz, Charles, and Trussler, Simon. *Theatre at Work: Playwrights and Productions in the Modern British Theatre*. New York, 1968.

Matlaw, Myron. See under chapter 1.

Mitchell, Loften. *Black Drama*. New York, 1967.

Neff, Renfreu. *The Living Theatre USA*. Indianapolis, 1970.

Novick, Julius. *Beyond Broadway*. New York, 1968.

O'Connor, Garry. *French Theatre Today*. London. 1975.

Orenstein, Gloria. *The Theatre of the Marvelous: Surrealism and the Contemporary Stage*. New York, 1976.

Pasolli, Robert. *A Book on the Open Theatre*. New York, 1970.

Patterson, Michael. *German Theatre Today*. London, 1976.

Rischbeiter, Henning. See under chapter 1.

Roose-Evans, James. See under chapter 1.

Sainer, Arthur. *The Radical Theatre Notebook*. New York, 1975.

Schechner, Richard. *Environmental Theatre*. New York, 1973.

————. *Public Domain: Essays on the Theatre*. Indianapolis, 1969.

Schevill, James. *Breakout! In Search of New Theatrical Environments*. Chicago, 1972.

Segel, Harold B. See under chapter 1.

Taylor, John Russell. *The Angry Theatre*. London, 1969.

————. *Second Wave: British Dramatists for the Seventies*. New York, 1971.

Taylor, Karen M. *People's Street Theatre in Amerika*. New York, 1973.

Temkine, Raymond. *Grotowski*. New York, 1972.

Transky, Paul I. *Czech Drama Since World War II*. White Plains, N.Y., 1978.

Trewin, J. C. *Peter Brook*. London, 1971.

Valency, Maurice. *The End of the World: An Introduction to Contemporary Drama*. New York, 1980.

Vinson, James, ed. *Contemporary Dramatists*. 2d ed. New York, 1977.

Weales, Gerald. *Jumping Off Place: American Drama in the 1960s*. New York, 1969.

Ziegler, Joseph. *Regional Theatre: The Revolutionary Stage*. Minneapolis, 1973.

Information about recent developments must still be sought primarily in periodicals and newspapers. Some of the most helpful on the contemporary theatre are:

Arts Reporting Service
British Theatrelog
Bühnentechnische Rundschau
Comparative Drama
International Theatrelog
Modern Drama
Modern International Drama
The New York Times
Performing Arts Journal
Performing Arts Review
Plays and Players

The Drama Review (TDR)
Theatre Crafts
Theater der Zeit
Theatre Design and Technology
Theater Heute
Theatre in Poland
Theatre Journal (formerly *Educational Theatre Journal*)
Theatre Quarterly
Travail Théâtral
Variety
The Village Voice

Index